The Spirit of NLP

The Process, Meaning and Criteria for Mastering NLP

Revised Edition

L. Michael Hall, Ph.D.

Crown House Publishing
www.crownhouse.co.uk

First published by

Crown House Publishing Ltd
Crown Buildings, Bancyfelin, Carmarthen, Wales, SA33 5ND, UK
www.crownhouse.co.uk

and

Crown House Publishing Ltd
P.O. Box 2223, Williston, VT 05495-2223, USA
www.CHPUS.com

First published 1996
Revised Edition 2000; reprinted 2001 (twice), 2003

British Library Cataloguing-in-Publication Data
A catalogue entry for this book is available
from the British Library.

ISBN 1899836047

LCCN 2003111153

Printed and bound in the UK by
The Cromwell Press Ltd.
Trowbridge, Wiltshire

Dedications

To Richard Bandler, a central genius of NLP from whom I learned the NLP Model, who along with John Grinder, exemplified the spirit of NLP in their original modeling of excellence.

Contents

List of figures

Acknowledgments

Richard Bandler	Don Wolfe	Eric Robbie
Chris Hall	Max Steinback	Wyatt Woodsmall
Bob Klaus	Tad James	Will McDonald

Chapter One on propulsion systems (compulsion, fetishes, etc.) comes primarily from Richard Bandler (who else!) as does Chapters Two and Three on *Trance* with contributions from Don Wolfe.

In Chapter Four regarding linguistics and the Meta-Model, I used primarily the presentation of Eric Robbie, with the piece about Belief Change from Richard Bandler and the piece on Linguistic Markers from Chris Hall.

From Chris Hall, along with Dr. Max Steinbach, I took most of the materials in Chapter Five about the 'Sleight of Mouth' patterns.

As far as I remember, credit goes to Wyatt Woodsmall for Chapter Six on Synesthesia, although Eric Robbie claims it as his. From Wyatt I put together Chapter Seven regarding Submodalities although I wrote most of it from the presentations of Eric Robbie.

The materials on Strategies came from several different presentations: Tad James addressed the subjects of Elicitation and Structure, Bob Klaus addressed the Strategy of Excellence, Wyatt Woodsmall presented the NLP pie of E.B. (External Behavior), I.S. (Internal State), and I.P. (Internal Processing), and both Bandler and Robbie presented the section on Modeling and Momentarily Becoming Someone Else.

Over the years, I have focused on states of consciousness and so derived Chapter Nine from Richard Bandler, Tad James, and Wyatt Woodsmall. The collection of information about Meta-Programs came in part from Chris Hall, Eric Robbie, Wyatt Woodsmall, Bob Klaus, and myself.

Regarding the Kinesthetic Time Line, credit for this goes to Will McDonald, who has passed from this life. To the best of my ability I have sought to give credit for the material to the trainer as my memory and notes have indicated.

Foreword

Introducing The Spirit of NLP

The Meaning, Process, and Criteria for Mastering NLP

"NLP is an attitude, backed by a methodology that leaves behind a trail of techniques."
—*Richard Bandler*

What truly is the very spirit of NLP? What distinguishes a Practitioner of this art of modeling excellence from a Master Practitioner? Wherein lie the distinctive meanings and criteria involved in mastering the NLP model? What process enables us to master it?

I wrote the following, based first upon my own Master Practitioner Training and Trainer's Training with Richard Bandler. To this I have also added (or contaminated, as the case may be) my own experiences and readings over the years with regard to the field of NLP, first as a psychotherapist and then as a trainer. I have done so in order to answer these initial questions.

Years have now passed since my original training with Richard Bandler, and yet my initial appreciation of Richard, who began this field with what I have here designated as *The Spirit of NLP*, has grown. I speak now of that playful, curious, outrageous, and passionate attitude that both he and John Grinder brought to, and learned from, the original three 'therapeutic wizards' (Fritz Perls, Virginia Satir, and Milton Erickson).

As I got to know Richard through the trainings and then worked with him to edit and produce various materials, I became aware of his role as the creative genius behind NLP. Many do not seem to see this or recognize his genius. Perhaps they are disconcerted or offended by the rough exterior that he presents. And he certainly can offend when he wants to! Yet beneath it, especially when he and John began their journey, he has a spirit of passion in 'going for it' and a curiosity for all things possible. This very spirit functions, foundationally, to endow NLP today with a quality of the dramatic and the dynamic.

The NLP paradigm, as a communication and behavioral model, arose in part when the men and women who later became the co-founders and developers of NLP began to translate Bandler. Even John Grinder became involved for this very reason. Apparently he found in the young brash kid at the university someone who had an incredible natural ability to imitate the voice, tonality, and patterns of Perls and Satir after listening to them on audiotape. John wanted to learn that genius. And Richard also wanted to learn *how* he did it. So, with Richard's gift and Johns genius for pulling something apart linguistically, NLP was born.

Bandler and Grinder originally set out to model Virginia Satir, Fritz Perls, and Milton Erickson. And yet as they did, they became aware of Richard's genius in unconsciously imitating the experts with astonishing ease and speed. Even surprising himself with his ability at modeling of Perls and Satir, he and John set out to pull apart the component pieces in terms of neurology and language in order to understand how this magic worked and how they could enable others to access the same excellence.

Richard Bandler's spirit, then, with his wild and wonderful ideas, his gruff style, and his unpredictable curiosity lies at the heart of this revolutionary technology for human resourcefulness. In this perspective, NLP reflects and represents his genius of modeling.

I first realized this by reading all of the 'classic' seminar books edited by Steve and Connirae Andreas. From those works, I decided to begin my own NLP training with Richard Bandler. Later, in 1989, during a Master Practitioner training in San Diego, I took extensive notes. I later published these with the approval of NLP Products and Promotions for the participants.

In 1990, Richard asked me to create another set of notes, this time for his Trainers' Training. After that adventure, Richard asked me to transcribe his work with *Applied Neuro Dynamics*, given during a London Seminar, as well as a training in hypnosis. I transcribed and edited the materials that later became the basis for the book, *Time for A Change*. Simultaneously, Richard was wanting to revive the Society of NLP. So I worked with him with regard to producing a directory that would describe the Society, present articles of contemporary and cutting-edge aspects of NLP, and make a complete listing of all the members. In spite of four months' work on that project however, it never saw the light of day.

In the years since, I have not only continued to use and develop NLP as part of my psychotherapeutic practice as a cognitive psychologist, but I have conducted numerous NLP Practitioner and Master Practitioner trainings. More recently, I researched and published articles (in *Anchor Point* and *NLP World*) regarding the historical roots of NLP in the works of Alfred Korzybski and Gregory Bateson. I also wrote a series on *The Almost Inventors of NLP*. For my doctorate in cognitive psychology, I created an integration of NLP with several other models (i.e. Reality Therapy, Adlerian, Frankl's Logotherapy, Ellis' REBT, etc). (See *Languaging*, 1996).

The Spirit of NLP currently extends and expands the notes that I originally made. I have reformatted the text to focus primarily on conveying *the spirit* of NLP. At the same time, I think that it does offer, to a large degree, a tribute to the genius, attitude, and passion of Richard Bandler as one of the co-founders of this domain.

I believe that identifying that spirit, specifying its components and discovering its strategy, offers a significant contribution to the ongoing development of NLP. Wouldn't you like to have the strategy that Richard used (along with John) in coming up with NLP in the first place?

Of course, the NLP model itself says that we all inevitably keep manifesting our states and strategies in our ongoing communications anyway. Does it not make sense then that Richard Bandler would continue to construct, design, and present his trainings of NLP in a way that would manifest at least some of his original 'spirit' or strategy which made this field possible? I believe so.

Having started with these understandings and assumptions, I have constructed the text as you now find it. You will find in these pages most of the essential academic and informational data within the NLP Master Practitioner training. And you will find more. You will find within, behind, and beyond the words of the text, the spirit of NLP.

Why This Approach?

(1) *To highlight the heart of NLP as modeling.*
If NLP primarily functions as 'a model, not a theory' then its strength lies in focusing much more on the *model and modeling* part rather than mere theory and theorizing about it. As 'the structure of subjectivity' (*NLP: Volume I*, 1980), the heart of this domain lies in modeling what works. It does not lie in theorizing and/or attaching to NLP various psychological and philosophical systems. Yet in recent years many have attempted to do precisely that.

(2) *To emphasize the importance of a congruent attitude.*
Many people know the model of NLP. They know how to speak the jargon, language, ideas, etc., of NLP while simultaneously lacking *the spirit* of NLP. Over the years I have sadly met numerous people with Practitioner and even Master Practitioner training, who yet lack a ferocious 'Going For It!' spirit.

In character and personality, they do not come across as having excitement, curiosity, nor high level state management skills over their own moods, passions, or commitments. They know NLP. They can even 'do NLP' with clients and customers. Yet they seem unable to reframe themselves to keep themselves resourceful when tough times come their way. And this lack of congruity (a major concept and concern in this model) undermines the public's understanding and appreciation of NLP.

(3) *To highlight the place of NLP in Cognitive Science.*
In my experience, it seems that numerous not-so-sane people have taken the NLP model and run with it in such a way as to give NLP, and the NLP community, a bad reputation. One all too common misunderstanding about NLP confuses NLP with the New Age movement. Others dismiss it by claiming that "NLP is manipulative mind-control," or "NLP is mysticism."

For anyone who knows the NLP model, such assertions only indicate the speaker's ignorance. Yet those who don't know better might actually come to believe such statements about NLP.

To the extent that it presents (or assumes) a philosophy and a psychology, we would locate NLP in the Constructivist school and in the school of the Cognitive sciences, especially Cognitive Psychology. Gilliland, et al. (1989) placed the NLP model under *Cognitive Psychology* in their tenth chapter (pp. 249ff). This makes eminent sense. After all, NLP arose from such renown cognitivists as George Miller, Noam Chomsky, Karl Pribram, *et al.* What would we expect, after all, from a model that emerged from such fields as Linguistics, General Semantics, Information Processing, the neurosciences, Gestalt therapy, Family Systems, Bateson's research group in Palo Alto, etc?

If any paradigm of human nature, behavior and experience does not represent a religious or mystic viewpoint, we must definitely include NLP in that category. As a model of mind, emotion, behavior, etc, NLP claims no psycho-theology and provides very little explanations and theory. This emphasis, in fact, stands out boldly in some of those original seminars of Bandler and Grinder and can still be seen in the early books edited by the Andreases such as *Frogs Into Princes*. The NLP model strictly utilizes the scientific model, and the TOTE model in particular, to establish its way of tracking consciousness (see Dilts, *NLP, Volume I,* 1980).

Becoming a Master NLP-er

Learning To Live With Passion
One of the primary lessons that I learned from my trainings with Richard Bandler concerns his belief about what it takes to master this field. For him, to master NLP, you have to let it completely permeate your thinking and feeling. You have to let it become so integrated in your everyday states that you live and function in a high level Meta-State. In this book I designate this state as *the spirit* of NLP. Richard has his own names for it: 'Going for it!', 'Developing your own ferocious resolve!' And in his memorable words, looking out on the world with eyes of passion while sizzling inside and thinking; "Your ass is mine!"

Does such language sound offensive? I know many people take offense at it. Yet nothing in that last statement warrants your taking offense. I call it a 'classic Bandlerism'. Richard exults in that kind of language and terminology. He uses it to interrupt states, to get people to stop being so polite, and to get them to loosen up, and to become much more ferocious. Dancing around other people's approval, conforming to what everybody else thinks and feels, fearing to own your own unique differences—such thoughts, feelings and responses are antipathetic to the spirit of NLP.

To truly master NLP, you need to develop and install a propulsion system inside yourself. A *propulsion system,* in fact, recalls the first words I used in describing the master training notes that I created out of my experience with Richard. A propulsion system, in this sense, refers to a strong and driving compulsion to growing, learning, becoming, mastering, etc, and a similar aversion away from stagnation, hesitation, indecision, fear, mediocrity, self-satisfaction, ego-trips, etc.

This personal propulsion system demonstrates the same kind of energy that I see in Tony Robbins' work. Robbins's books, *Unlimited Power* (1989) and *Awaken the Giant Within* (1990), present one of the best records of much of the basic NLP practitioner material. But it has more than just that. Those works present the Master Practitioner attitude of passion. I love the way Tony ends all his audiotapes with "Live with passion!" And if anything serves as the Master Practitioner mantra, that certainly sounds like it! *Live the passion.*

The first source of the following material arose from a Master Practitioner Training with Richard Bandler. I trust that, as I have expanded upon the notes, they will continue to manifest the spirit, language, and thinking of NLP as it came from that source. I have also been greatly influenced by Robert Dilts and his books (*NLP, Volume I; Roots of NLP; Applications of NLP*, etc.). Much also comes from my own ongoing experiences and trainings with hundreds of people as I have introduced them to….

The Passion of NLP

For just a moment, step back and go meta from these passionate statements: 'Going for it!' 'Access your ferocious resolve' 'Live with passion!' 'Your ass is mine!' etc. What do you notice about these statements? What do they all presuppose in terms of states of consciousness, beliefs, values, etc?

Do they not presuppose a very powerful and high-level state of feeling resourceful and empowered? Do not these statements describe someone at their best and ready to tackle the challenges of life with some real gusto? Certainly, these phrases do not describe the state of the timid, the hesitating, the fearful, the victimized, the bored, the uncommitted, or the non-resilient, do they?

In such statements we have encoded the central attitude and one of the chief legacies of NLP. NLP not only refers to a psychology of human functioning, behavior, and experience, it also speaks of a psychology of human enrichment, empowerment, and vitality. As a model of excellence, when we fully release it, the NLP Model will make the 'humanistic self-actualizing movement' look pale in comparison. Perhaps this explains why Tony Robbins has gone so far with the NLP model. The very title of his books speaks about this kind of super-resourcefulness: *Unlimited Power, Awakening the Giant Within*. These are not mild phrases. The small-minded could not handle such intensity or expansiveness.

Because NLP models human excellence, it presents no mild paradigm. Doesn't it then make sense that it should not create or generate mild people? On the contrary, it should generate some wild and woolly people! It should generate people with such a passion for life who have so much 'Go for it!' and execute their visions and values with such a 'ferocious resolve' that these become the people who truly change the world. Such people ultimately turn things around in politics, education, religion, economics, parenting, athletics, therapy, etc. They become the high achievers.

What powerful legacy did I receive as a result of my trainings with Richard Bandler? I would certainly say it did *not* consist of the academic facts or information within the NLP model. As valuable as I found these, another legacy stood out even more (a legacy I hope that you will receive in the pages to come). What legacy do I speak of? The legacy of a ferocious spirit, about how to live with more vigor, life, and energy. The legacy of developing a never-say-die spirit as you move through the world. Or to use another

Bandlerism, "Now open your eyes and look out on the world and say inside your mind, 'A piece of cake!' "

NLP as a Model of 'Raw and Ferocious Vitality'

Gauge yourself. In terms of experiencing such *raw vitality* in your spirit, how ready do you feel? Would you want the people around you to become so empowered with a sense of their value, their dignity, their resourcefulness, their uniqueness, etc? This would mean the complete end of 'controlling' people by old techniques of manipulation. But then, neither would you have to worry about them turning destructive. After all, who are the people who go wild, burn down cities, and riot in the streets? Not empowered men and women with bold visions in their minds and resourceful skills in their repertoire. It is the disempowered who do such things.

We have nothing to fear from empowered people. Empowered people spend their time and energy dreaming their dreams and making their visions of new potentials come true. So when you awaken the giant within you and discover the unlimited power the Creator (or the Universe) has put within you, you will not become a Hitler. You will probably become more of an Einstein, an Edison, a Spielberg, or a Mother Teresa.

Part of my heritage lies in the Judeo-Christian background. Once upon a time I even graduated from a seminary. Actually that background prepared me for the power and vitality of the NLP model. And from time to time you will see that I have integrated a smidgen of that viewpoint with NLP. Many of the philosophical assumptions in both disciplines correlate highly . To the extent that NLP manifests a cognitive orientation for enabling people to become more empowered, we have a strong frame of agreement. Biblical passages assert the same, "As a man thinks in his heart, so he is." Personal empowerment, "For God has not given us the spirit of fear, but of power, love, and a sound mind" (*II Timothy 1:7*). This does away with the 'belief' propagated by Lord Acton,"Power corrupts, and absolute power corrupts absolutely."

People who feel full and empowered typically do not misuse or corrupt their powers or the powers they can develop with a model such as NLP. With empowerment of our person, our inner self, comes a greater sense of transcendence (or spirituality), and this more typically leads to a more ethical perspective, not less; to a more long-term perspective, not short; and to a more extensive view about the dignity and humanity of people from all groups and cultures, not more prejudice.

When people become and feel disempowered and unresourceful, when they do not feel full or that their lives have meaning, direction, or resources, then they focus solely on trying to satisfy their ego needs. When such people then have some external 'power' entrusted to them—then the likelihood of misusing or abusing such powers increases.

This core of raw vitality in NLP has produced some delightful, surprising, and powerful technology within the NLP domain. And as far as I can tell, this raw vitality of the NLP spirit has gotten Richard into lots of trouble. For example, many still don't know how to take him. They don't know what to make of his strong language, his four-letter words, his use of aversion techniques to create the 'push' of the propulsion system, his confrontational style, his stories of his drug-use days, etc. I also have to admit to having felt pretty shocked by all of this when I first met him. I couldn't believe that someone like him could have put together the NLP model!

Of course, this kind of a response doesn't shake Richard at all. In fact, I think he enjoys it. He has said that sometimes people will read *The Structure of Magic, Volume I* and then, from that writing, make a mental picture of him as the author. Then later when they meet him, they tell him that he has changed!

Yet Richard's pattern of sorting for differences, feeling fully comfortable in expressing his differentness, looking for patterns that no one else tends to look for, owning and expressing his uniqueness, created NLP in the first place. Terrence McClendon (1989), in *The Wild Days: NLP 1972-1981*, makes it abundantly clear that Richard started out weird. And do we not usually think of geniuses as being weird, strange or odd? And what about those pictures of

Einstein with his hair looking as though he had just put a knife in an electrical outlet?

Richard has often said, "NLP is an attitude, backed by a methodology that leaves behind a trail of techniques." Considering this succinct statement, I think we can well consider the practitioner training as taking someone along that trail of techniques as well as introducing them to the procedures and components of the methodology. Here one learns the content of NLP.

The next step after acquaintance with the methodology and techniques of NLP brings us to the process of becoming fully immersed into the NLP *attitude*. This means learning the very attitude of the NLP founders and developers. Accordingly, Master Practitioner training takes people through a process of learning to adopt that spirit. The attitude of looking out upon life and our experiences from an entirely new and different perspective. This involves an attitude of curiosity about possibilities—about what we have not yet tried, about what we have not yet tapped—and of a ferocious resolve to make our ideas, representations, and dreams become real.

The NLP spirit includes adopting Bandler's surprising positive attitude regarding any problem or difficulty:

> "This problem is great! What can I use it for? What else would it be good for?"

To what extent would you say that you now have the spirit of NLP? To what extent would you like to adopt this way of orienting yourself in the world? If you wish to learn more, you have come to the right book.

On the surface, it will seem that the following chapters will offer you much academic information about NLP. I have included information that Bandler and his associates taught on one particular summer in a Master Practitioner training. Yet beyond that surface level, going deeper, you will find here many reference experiences for expanding your own map of the world. You will find instructions for exercises, using thought experiments, and by exploring new mental worlds of possibilities. I have incorporated these in order to evoke and/or create more of the core attitude that characterizes Richard and which enabled him to create this domain.

On another level, I plan to do what Richard, for the most part, does not do and I don't believe that he believes in doing, and perhaps wouldn't want me to do, namely, to put the intent and design of the training into words. So regarding this aspect of the material, the words that follow may or may not offer an accurate representation of Bandler's training. My creation here might be nothing more than pure unfounded mind-reading. You will have to hold me responsible for all of the conclusions that I have drawn in this introduction and in the pages to follow.

A caveat as we begin. What follows reflects my understandings of an experience that I once had with a true master. Therefore, everything you will find here arises from my perspective and my model of the world, not Richard's, nor that of his associates. Not only did I probably miss some of the most significant things and mishear others, but I probably kept on distorting it over the years. So they obviously suffer contamination from many of my own deletions, generalizations, and distortions.

Becoming a Master Practitioner

To reach a level of mastering NLP, participants usually receive between 150 to 180 hours of intense training. Such training may occur in intensive three week seminars, or a dozen intense weekends, or some other format. Practitioners usually have to have at least 150 hours of direct training.

What happens during this time? A great deal of learning about NLP. Presentations about advanced strategies, sensory systems, pacing and leading, hypnosis, modeling, calibration, the Meta-Model, etc. In the Master Practitioner course, people learn in details about Meta-Programs. Meta-Programs refer to the sorting patterns by which someone sorts and attends to information. One also learns 'Sleight of Mouth' patterns which refer to the linguistic patterns which enable us to use the distinctions learned in the Meta-Model for engaging in conversational reframing and swishing.

On the Master Practitioner training one gets multiple opportunities to go and visit some new and more resourceful states of consciousness. Such experiences, in and out of trance, enable people to experience NLP in themselves and to program themselves with the kind of states that allow them to become their best.

We need to master both intellectual and experiential learnings to become a Master Practitioner. Perhaps emphasis should be placed on the experiential learnings. Why? Because the states that we must learn so thoroughly consist of those very states that I am calling *the spirit of NLP*. These characterize and manifest the basic NLP presuppositions, they elicit the representations and sensations that allow us to adopt the very mindset which the originators of NLP had.

The NLP Master Practitioner states include the following:

1) *Perseverance:*
   "There is no failure, there is only feedback."

2) *Curiosity:*
   Curiously explore everything.
   "What allows this to exist as a possibility?"
   "What else can I use this for?"

3) *Creative suspiciousness*:
   Always suspect that more exists.
   "What else lies out there that I can discover?"
   "What else does this experience offer that I can use?"

4) *Desire:*
   Develop a passionate attitude toward life.
   "How can I make this mine?"

5) *Creativity and productivity:*
   "How can I make it better?"

Various unresourceful states can prevent us from accessing this kind of mindset or attitude. States of frustration, hesitation, indecision, fear, impatience, etc. keep us from actualizing all of our potentials.

What solution does NLP provide in order to deal with negative unresourceful states? We can chain the unresourceful states so that they will move us naturally and automatically to the resourceful states. When someone finds themself frustrated, that feeling will automatically swish and anchor that person to the state of anticipating something new. Then that state will trigger yet another, even more resourceful, state.

With such *chaining technology* we establish a *direction* for consciousness and neurology to go. Then when we find ourselves in an unresourceful state, we will automatically shift our thinking and feeling so that we go into a little more resourceful state. Each state will steer us a little further toward the ferocious state. States in which we feel stuck and limited can themselves become automatically connected to the process of moving us to one of the NLP resource states (learning, curiosity, desire, etc.).

Do you like this idea of directing our states? What a truly great idea! Imagine it. Whenever we find ourselves in a limiting state due to some circumstance in life, the real master in NLP will immediately begin to access NLP resources. In this way, chaining gives us an automatic chain of anchors that moves us from hesitation, frustration, impatience, or whatever to other states such as wanton desire and 'totally going for it'. This presents *the NLP attitude* par excellence. This reflects and expresses the attitude and state which the Master Practitioner training aims to install.

Bandler has several ways of alluding and referring to this total NLP resource state. At times, he refers to this as an ultimate ecstasy state, at others as 'Totally going for it!' He also calls it 'ferocious resolve.'

The Content of the Master Practitioner Training

If you have incorporated the content of the Practitioner level, there remains some, but not much, of new content to master. The specific content of NLP that the training focuses on involves many things basic to NLP. In fact, some NLP Master Practitioner training programs run simultaneous to the Practitioner training, with the participants hearing it again and working as coaches with the new Practitioners.

What matters most at the Master level? Developing the attitude and spirit of NLP so that we begin to think and feel and operate from this. What counts most?

- Learning to boldly and ferociously 'meta-question' everything, to passionately want to understand and apply the Meta-Model distinctions and challenges as well as the Milton model distinctions and language patterns.

- Honing our skills in the field of making submodality distinctions and even learning to read them from the outside.

- Developing more openness to feedback, more flexibility in responding, more aptitude in running our own brain, getting more fun in the process, in fact, learning that the fun lies in the process of getting there!

- Mastering NLP means experiencing more ecstasy in life, in relationships, and in our basic orientation through life.

Given these understandings, at the Master Practitioner level we should have the ability to design individualized interventions with a client, on both the remedial level and the generative level in such a way that it enables the client to become more resourceful. The one who has mastered the NLP model should always think in terms of ecology for new designs and constructions. This, of course, presupposes the ability to shift to meta-positions when working and to be able to move from content to context, form to process, etc.

The new material for the Master Practitioner includes the Meta-Program filters and the 'Sleight of Mouth' patterns. It also includes a further tuning of our ears to linguistic markers so that we can hear values, criteria, complex equivalences, etc., in everyday conversation. The Master Practitioner should have developed the ability to do much more refined work with submodalities. They should demonstrate the ability to automatically hear submodalities in everyday language and recognize the effect of submodalities on both speaker and listener.

At the Master Practitioner level, we should have expertise in multi-level communications, utilizing agreement frames in negotiating, utilizing and transforming beliefs and presuppositions, and identifying Meta-Programs.

All of this suggests a multitude of new learnings and discoveries, many new avenues of development, and much refinement of the materials learned at the Practitioner Level. So if you feel ready now to tackle all of these new learnings and to have the very attitude of NLP installed within you, then hang on to your seat and get ready to have a propulsion system installed in your mind-body.

L. Michael Hall

Author's note

I originally wrote the following pages at the time of the training. That effort resulted in sixty pages of notes which I immediately made available (in 1989) to both Richard Bandler and Eric Robbie. In the years that followed, I expanded the notes with a text in order to create a readable account of the training. Having no audio or video records to consult, and therefore no transcript of the training, the following pages reflect the fallible memory of the author.

What follows here is therefore what I heard and wrote at the time, not verbatim quotations. I have always appreciated and used the NLP Communication Guideline, "The meaning of your communication is the response you get." We have long said that this leads to a no-blame frame and should rather activate the feedback frame. What did you hear? The following represents what I heard.

Part One

Programming

Chapter One

Developing an Internal Propulsion System

For Richard Bandler, a propulsion system in human personality has two directions. It has first a compulsion (→●) and it has an aversion (●→). This energetic system has both *an attraction* toward something valuable and important and it has *a disattraction* away from what we disvalue and dislike. While so many talk these days about getting over compulsions and compulsive behavior, with this pattern we explore a process for installing a good, strong, healthy compulsion.

In this case, this pattern builds a compulsive direction toward something very positive, attractive, and enriching. In this sense, it is in the same order as Dr. William Glasser's work *Positive Addictions* (1968).

In the case of learning to think, feel, perceive, and experience life as an NLP Master Practitioner, this propulsion system offers a compulsion toward NLP learnings, skills, and states. This refers to the spirit of a strong compulsion toward more effective understanding and more effective use of the Meta-Model of language and of noticing Meta-Programs regarding how someone sorts information. This spirit seeks to install an internal grid for reading people and communicating with them effectively. It means feeling compelled to the Milton model, and to the various Sleight of Mouth patterns by which you can induce positive hypnotic states and positive reframes.

A propulsion system, however, also has a counter-direction built within it. We design it so that as someone moves away from the new and positive compulsion they will get less and less enjoyment, ecstasy, reward, etc., and more and more discomfort and dissatisfaction. On the surface the following chapters may impress you as simply about NLP content. But don't be fooled. If you move to a meta-level, you'll discover a way to build a Master Practitioner propulsion system into yourself or another person. The counter-direction in this system consists of all of those things that you should find disgusting. Then you can feel a strong aversion to mediocrity, self-satisfaction, pseudo-compliments, bad feelings, giving up, dislike, etc.

A logistics problem I have struggled with in writing and presenting this process was how to communicate this pull/push, toward/away from propulsion system without using tonality, tonal embedding, volume shifts, and other non-verbal processes. So how can I notate this propulsion system?

The solution I came up with, and have incorporated in the following pages, involves the use of arrows. So when you find arrows pointing toward an object →●, this indicates that within the text you will find some toward values, states, learnings, etc. You can think of them as part of the NLP model toward which you should feel compelled.

Similarly, when you see the arrows pointing away from an object ●→, this indicates that within the text at that point you can find some away from values, states, thoughts, etc., which will decrease your enjoyment.

Now as you read, study, and meditate through these chapters, I recommend that you immediately stop whenever you come across such arrows. Stop and take a few moments to note and experience the attractions and aversions referred to in the text. Take a moment to allow yourself to go slow enough to access the experience, evoke the state, or construct the experience in your imagination. Then, you can begin to let the arrows become for you a visual anchor to re-establish this bi-directional propulsion within you.

As a student of NLP, you know that written words, at best, can only provide an auditory-digital (word/language) account of the training of the experience, and not the experience itself. In reading this text, you will necessarily tend to operate at a dissociated level... unless, of course, you allow yourself to vividly imagine and experience the words and exercises as you read them. And I would like you to feel completely free to get together with a partner and do the exercises as you read them. And with that, the time has come for you to catch the vision.

Catching The Vision

How to become an inquisitive Master Practitioner

[The following section has been primarily derived from Richard Bandler.]

Let's begin with the question that will guide much of this training, namely:

> "What difference separates an NLP Practitioner and a Master Practitioner of NLP?"

A Practitioner, by definition, is someone who knows how to take the learnings, the formulas, the techniques, and the methods of NLP and use them. They can use them with clients, with customers, and they can use them on themselves. What then distinguishes someone who has become a Master Practitioner?

Well, suppose as a therapist, a depressed person comes to you. What do you do or say to that person? What would be a classic NLP response to that? You could ask:

> "What do you see, hear or feel that allows you to feel depressed?"
> "How do you know you feel depressed?"
> "If I should take your place for a day, what would I need to do to experience this depression?"

All these responses are basic NLP maneuvers, which will get you some answers. Some of them may be quite useful ones. That expresses how a Practitioner thinks. But would a Master Practitioner do such? If not, then what?

We want to understand not only what distinguishes a Master Practitioner, but also what it means to be one. What does the M.P. stand for? Perhaps the M.P. stands for 'Mostly Pissed-off'? or perhaps 'Missed Possibilities'? ●→

Master Practitioners will be asking themselves questions right out of the gate. This means that if you have begun the process of mastering NLP, you will be using your sensory awareness to ask questions: good questions, hard questions, surprising questions, wild questions—all kinds of questions to understand this phenomenon and not assume that you know all about it. And you'll be doing that from the word go.

For instance, suppose you use the NLP presupposition that says that "People work perfectly and are not broken." What would you then ask? For example, you might ask:

> "What does this really mean"
> "How else can I frame or perceive this behavior or response?"
> "What could someone use this for?"
> "What can I learn?"
> "Can I do this?" →●

A Master Practitioner does not just take the Practitioner level materials and use them over and over. A Master Practitioner will rather use a meta-pattern of questioning everything from the word go. You will not just go through a list of questions that you have memorized. Rather, you will begin to ask questions about the questions you ask. You will ask questions about what questions you do not ask, and what questions yet remain for you to ask that you haven't thought of... yet. You will begin to ask questions about what could possibly exist as true about whatever you or another now experiences. →●

One of the stories that Richard frequently tells has to do with a young schizophrenic named Andrew. "Years ago I was brought a schizophrenic young man named Andrew by two psychiatrists. Now Andrew saw little men come out of the TV show he was watching. As he watched a TV show called 'Little House on the Prairie', the snippy little bitch named Mary would come out of the TV and chase him around and bother him. And of course, he was a paranoid schizophrenic. Well, these psychiatrists brought him to me and wanted me to cure him. But my first thought was 'Now there's a skill! If I could market this, I could make lots of money!' "And of course, when I found out what he was watching I asked

'Why aren't you watching the Playboy channel?' That's where my mind went." →●

Here then stands one of the great, and often neglected, NLP secrets. Namely, at the heart of NLP lies the art of asking questions. This means learning to ask good, hard, unpredictable, stupid, and even unanswerable questions.

Asking yourself and others questions plays a central role in NLP methodology as a process of information gathering, brainstorming, exploring possibilities, expanding alternatives, etc.

> "How can I use this?"
> "Where else could I plug this into and use?"

This passion to use everything you receive from the world in order to learn expresses the spirit of functioning like a Master Practitioner.

> "Do I find this useful?"
> "What can this person teach me?"
> "Of what am I now not aware?"
> "What else is in this experience that I may not be noticing?" →●

In Practitioner training, the art of questioning plays an absolutely vital role. Now we want to allow it to play an even more significant role as we move into mastering this discipline. And given the place of meta-levels in NLP, let us call this pattern 'meta-questioning' so that we can use it to question our questions.

During my Master Practitioner training, Richard presented these ideas at nine o'clock on a Monday morning on Day One of the training. I remember that many of the participants did not respond with the eagerness that he must have expected. So Richard shifted gears, altered his voice tone, adopted a deep and rough tonality that we more generally associate with anger, attack, and intimidation. Then in that voice he said, "Do I have to do the motivation pattern on you to get you to say Amen? I'll just install a motivation program so you can respond with motivation." →●

Now for Richard to have pulled off that response in the middle of a presentation tells me that he must have done some meta-questioning himself.

> "Where do I stand with this audience? Where do they stand with me? Where do I want them to stand with me? What would evoke some response potential to wake them up and get them responding?"

Even in the middle of presenting Bandler could suddenly make a mental shift and throw in an apparently unrelated piece. I am presupposing that he was using the strategy of asking empowering questions.

In NLP we know that the structure of every experience has syntax —order and structure. Syntax is also fundamental in linguistics. When you read the sentence, "The sun rise down," you intuitively know that the speaker has created an ill-formed statement. If you read the sentence backwards, it becomes even worse: "Down rise sun the."

So what? What does any of this mean? Well, what direction does all of this suggest to you? It suggests that we ought to pay attention to sequences. We need to keep asking ourselves:

> "How can I make it work if I change the sequence? What effect would syntax have on this or that experience? What would be some truly empowering meta-questions to gather even better information?" →●

Richard then asked,

> "How many of you here only want compliments when you perform? Have you ever performed a piece of music, or created a piece of art, or generated some piece of behavior, but you felt and judged you were having an off day? And you knew it. But then someone came up to you and said, 'You were great!' Well, I've got a question for you. Did that help you? Did that make you better? Did that sharpen you? No! It did not!" ●→

"Now suppose you go somewhere and you wear some clothes that you simply hate. Then someone compliments you, 'You look great in those clothes!' Do you need to hear that? Do you find that useful? Actually, the feedback—even negative feedback—helps you improve. That's what you need. And that indicates what you need to be looking for, doesn't it?" →●

Later Richard told another story. "Once I had five people who brought a woman to me who was hallucinating sexual dreams. And these therapists, psychiatrists and husband decided that this was a serious problem! They really thought it was serious since she was waking people up with her dreams. And they wanted me to fix her. Of course, I fixed her husband so he could do it too!" →●

What do you have to have before you can ask good questions? To ask good questions, you have to hear things. Do you hear the language? Do you hear the presuppositions in the language that people use? These are the questions you need to address before you master NLP. →●

Shortly thereafter, when someone asked a question about self-esteem, Bandler responded: "Sometimes people have asked me, 'How do you deal with self-esteem?' I respond by saying, 'In other people. I go to other people, beat them up, and then I feel better.'"

Now on the surface, that comes across as a very gruff response, does it not? At the content level, it might even seem downright mean. But what does it mean at a meta-level? What does it mean in terms of the previous statements about questioning, presuppositions, and syntax? What questions would you need to pose about that exchange that would provide you insight and give you some useful answers?

To answer that, we should first recognize that because meta-levels exist as statements about lower levels, they always influence and control the meaning and significance of lower levels. This provides the structure of paradox. (For more about meta-levels, see Bateson (1972) *Steps Toward an Ecology of Mind*, or Hall (1995) *Meta-States*).

Notice how you think about the meanings evoked in you if I make the assertion "The statements I'm making to you are false." On the content level you may come to the conclusion that this means, "I'm lying". Now, if I have indeed been lying, and that is the truth of my statement-making, is the second statement also a lie? If I lied when uttering the second statement, then it is a lie that I have been lying. Therefore, in those statements, I have been telling the truth! Ah, paradox!

When we recognize the first statement as a meta-statement (as undoubtedly Richard intended it), then we understand it as a statement about other statements. Consequently, we cannot apply the statement to itself. It exists and operates exclusively as a meta-statement. And as a meta-statement, it controls, influences, and determines the lower level statements—the statements that it comments upon.

Suppose then that Bandler's earlier statement about self-esteem functioned as a response, at a meta-level, to the questions about self-esteem at the primary level. Suppose we take his words as words of exaggeration. For, after all, do not a lot of people try to feel better about themselves by winning out and competing with others? And doesn't that exist as a form of beating them up to feel better? Yet won't most people respond negatively to putting that idea in such a brazen way? I think so.

To the subject of trying to feel good about oneself, Bandler then said,

> "What am I saying? Well, feelings keep changing, do they not? How long do you ever have a sustained feeling? Think about good feelings. Do you have things in your house, which when you look at them, they give you good feelings? Do you also have things in your house which give you bad feelings? The question that I wonder about is, 'Why do you keep anything that gives you bad feelings?' Do you keep it because it gives you a bad feeling? What does that do for you?" ●→

Just as there are behaviors that make us feel good, there are behaviors that can make us feel bad. Anchors exist for both sincerity and insincerity, seriousness and humor, confidence and doubt, and so on. Our lives are so conditioned in this way.

Yet if we now engage in some meta-questioning and meta-thinking, we will want to begin to ask ourselves questions about which direction we want to head in, which states we want to evoke, which experiences we want to make possible for ourselves. If we want to run our own brain, we will necessarily have to engage in self-management and self-direction.

Richard tells the old joke about a psychiatrist and a schizophrenic. It begins with a question, "What is the difference between a psychiatrist and schizophrenic?" The punch line is, "The schizoid learns how to get well and so gets to go home." Now try your turn at this kind of thinking and go meta to the joke. What messages could Richard attempt to communicate through that joke?

NLP has a great deal to do with direction, with life orientation, and with focus. Even with the subject of running your own brain for a change we ask the questions: "To do what? To go where? To accomplish what?" As a Master Practitioner, would you not answer, "To accomplish things of importance that bring out the best in myself and others!"? No wonder Richard Bandler constantly recommends that instead of looking for what is wrong in yourself or other people, look for what works.

Learn to master the art of meta-questioning. Keep asking yourself:

> "How can I make this more useful?"
> "What would be some resourceful states that would enable me to function at my best when in situations of conflict?" (Stress, incongruity, obnoxiousness, etc.)
> "How can I access such states with greater ease?"
> "What ideas or reference experiences would put more—passion in me for life, for love, for living fully?"

Later Richard told this little vignette. "Once a lady said to me, 'I really feel bad for you.' So I said, 'Good! Now I don't have to.' "

Now what could you ask about that? What are you aware of? Certainly it demonstrates a skill to feel bad for or about someone else and about their behaviors. Richard seemed to take that piece and run with it. In fact, he reached a surprising conclusion: "Now I don't have to." Now was that the intent of the lady? I think not. Yet Richard assumed that positive intent, even though it probably did not exist when she first made the statement.

I made a powerful learning, at a meta-level, about this and many other such things that Richard presented. Namely, I don't need to waste my negative emotional energy on going around feeling bad. If that is my orientation and focus, I will, of course, find it everywhere I go and turn. But what will that do for me? Looking for and finding the positive, and the positive intent in things (the basis of reframing) offers a far more empowering resource, and one that provides much more fun and enjoyment.

This reminds me of another refrain that I heard Richard say on numerous occasions: "Some people need phobias!" He explained that if they had only thought about the divorce court, their children feeling torn apart, people yelling and treating each other like shit when they began showing contempt or making judgments on each other—they might not have created and endured such experiences. A good phobia of such things might be something worth having. "And others could stand a good self-enhancing deception."

So we have more 'bad' things reframed as having possibilities one could use for good. After all, we do not deal with reality, but only with reality as filtered through our cognitive maps and perceptual grids. The key to enjoying life and demonstrating resourcefulness lies in developing the most enhancing cognitive maps possible.

So even in the midst of otherwise negative stimuli, why not choose to have more fun, and to laugh more? After all, laughter brings healing and dissociation. So why wait? Laugh sooner, and get over the hurt quicker. This is an old refrain in NLP. Let's use our resources in a resourceful way rather than create or perpetuate limitations and problems.

Beginning to Install The Spirit of NLP

A Hypnotic Induction to Recover your Natural Passions

Ready for some installation? Then right now I want you to close your eyes and think about some things that would truly make your life a better place to live. What do you need in your life for it to be a safer, saner and more exciting place to live? What ways of thinking, feeling, and behaving would increase your sense of becoming resourceful? Fully identify a set of resources.

And now you can allow yourself to begin to see some of those resources as you relax in a comfortable way. And you can hear them, feel them and allow any and all of the resourceful thoughts, behaviors, etc., to come into your consciousness, now, as you wonder, really wonder what your life would begin to become with such empowering resources at your fingertips, because you can. And you can take all the time you need to do this exquisitely and thoroughly, because with this you have begun to master this art more fully than you have ever thought possible. →●

Practicing Hearing Language
Once you have done that then you can use the following exercise to master this level of NLP. This exercise has to do with increasing your resource of hearing language patterns. It has been designed to assist you in tuning up your hearing. This is an essential prerequisite to having true power with NLP or any kind of language elegance. After all, language functions as the mechanism that propels our experience of reality. So if you tune up your linguistic ears, you will learn to hear your own internal reality as well as that of others. And I want you to become hungry for this, and to really want what you want. The funny thing about brains arises from the fact that they can do all kinds of things: they can distort time, hallucinate new and different kinds of realities, and accomplish all kinds of things, some useful and some not so useful. →●

Age Regressing to Rediscover Passions
In a group, take some time to practice eliciting another person's strategies and submodalities.

1) A identifies a skill (#1) that s/he does very well; something that s/he feels good at, and enjoys doing.

2) As A accesses that, B anchors it. B then does a transderivational search to its source.

3) B assists in age regressing A to the time when s/he first began learning that skill. This will help you rediscover some of their original passions along with all of the presuppositions within it.

4) Now B asks A, "What made it worth learning for you? Something existed there before you found it interesting to you. Now allow yourself to discover that value and motivation."

5) As B finds those initial triggers, s/he now elicits the submodalities of that state in which A felt drawn to something worth learning.

6) B now amplifies those submodalities to evoke the most intense response.

7) Next, A identifies another skill (#2) that s/he finds interesting, but something that s/he has up until now judged as not worth learning. B asks A, "What have you never taken a lot of interest in?"

8) B elicits the submodalities of this experience in order to compare with the first one.

9) Now B changes the submodalities of skill (#2) to match those of skill (#1), and tests by noticing whether these submodality shifts change A's response to the second skill. B can now 'steal' this behavior by adjusting the submodalities of A's first skill.

Building An Internal Propulsion System

From Beliefs and Internal Fetishes

As we move through the world we develop hundreds or even thousands of generalizations about life, ourselves, other people, and so on. When these become preserved in our minds, they function as our programs. They become our mental expectations, beliefs, understandings, etc. Our generalizations, as mental concepts or constructs, enable us to become functional organisms in the world.

An example of generalizing at the level of perception occurs in the process of stereotyping other people or their behaviors. Once we have witnessed an initial event which had some kind of emotional impact on us, we thereafter tend to project those feelings onto any new situation that provides us with the appropriate triggers. We do not see what is actually there, but instead we see what we want to see. Such perceptions operate as generalizations.

Colin Turnbull tells us about some Pygmies in Africa who had not learned to see perspective. Surrounded by close tropical rainforest, they had not experienced far distant objects, and were therefore unfamiliar with the effects of perspective—how things a long way away appear to be smaller, and so on. They had not made the generalisation that things stay constant regardless of the size they appear to be. Turnbull recounts an incident where he took some of the tribe to a vantage point, where they could look out over an almost treeless plain where buffalo were grazing down below. When one of the men saw the buffalo several miles away, he asked, "What insects are those?" (Turnbull, 1961).

If those examples illustrate how someone creates generalizations, and the far-reaching ramifications of beliefs, then the question arises: how do we break up those generalizations and create new and more empowering beliefs? One powerful process for breaking a limiting generalization is by using counter-examples.

A single counter-example can sometimes be enough to break a generalization and create an openness to new beliefs and experiences. Of course, experiences that match your beliefs, ideas, and mental constructs of the world, will tend to verify your generalizations. Consistent examples will in fact build up your generalizations. And the effect of further examples becomes less and less.
●→●

Suppose you wanted to change something which you think and feel neutral about. Suppose you wanted to turn it into a like or dislike. This structure of push and pull forms the basis of building a propulsion system into someone's motivation strategy. →●

In discussing this process, Bandler told the following story. Notice what goes through your mind as you hear it. "I once met a compulsive man who was extremely fearful in his approach to life. He worried so much that he had literally seen one hundred doctors, and had written up long lists of his symptoms. When I first met him, my first thought was, 'This man has an extremely effective propulsion system within himself. Now just how can I turn it around and use it for him?' That's the question." →●

Now, did that question arise in your mind as you thought about a man who had seen one hundred doctors? If it did not, then what shifts and reframes do you need to make within yourself in order to learn to think that way more frequently? After all, that kind of thinking and questioning represents the spirit of NLP, an attitude that will make you a master at it. At least it expressed the kind of questioning, framing, and presupposing that took John and Richard places. This kind of questioning drives the process of mastering NLP.

Engage your thinking along the lines of: How do you build a propulsion system within a human being? When you think about a man who had already seen one hundred doctors, who had written out many pages of his symptoms, and who still looked for help.... This describes a very powerful dynamic within this man, does it not? So what kinds of generalization had to be there for this person to become so organized in this way?

More questions:

"How could you take a compulsion like that and re-channel it?"
"How could you re-direct that kind of energy so that you could turn it on and off at will?"
"How can you use an operational program within someone like that and give it more constructive pathways and objectives?"

We discover an important secret in that story. When you think about a propulsion system, it helps to think about it as a form of the swish pattern. After all, you have to admit that the pattern of compulsiveness certainly reveals a psychological mechanism of absolute thoroughness, does it not? I mean, a hundred doctors! Now that shows thoroughness in my book! Everything about his fear, his worry, his dread, everything about that state swished his brain to making lists, writing out details, thoroughly exploring his symptoms.

We use submodalities to drive the swish pattern. Swish patterns work by using a key quality or distinction of some modality which, in turn, drives a generalization as an understanding or mental idea. This means that the person will start with some representation of a cue, which then shifts, thereby revealing or creating a less attractive picture, sound, feeling, etc. At that point, the person will simply feel less compelled about it. ●→●

Conversely, when we shift the submodalities in the other direction, it creates a greater attraction which increases the compulsion. →●

Bandler noted that "When you deal with a phobic person, you should ask, 'How much fear do you have left?' In other words, make sure that they don't leave your place with their compulsion to become phobic in the world. Because I think I might just stand around in the hallway, and give them phobias back! You went in there to have them work on your compulsion? Doesn't that really, really s c a r e you?"(Hear that in a very loud and harsh tonality!) ●→

This describes the process of actually creating a phobia: You evoke the state with your words, tonality, volume and so on, and then connect it to whatever you choose.

In automating any system, you have to develop a V–K synesthesia, do you not? A V–K synesthesia is a see-feel connection in the nervous system. One half of the swish pattern is about creating the condition whereby the person is repelled from eating chocolate, and thus has a phobia of it. Their entire nervous system would then automatically and systematically have them avoid it. ●→

The other half of the swish pattern involves the creation of a new and more enhancing compulsion, so much so that the person develops and experiences a fetish toward it. →●

We could create a new compulsion such as having a sense of choice about feeling good, while still pushing you toward the choices that you have programmed in. The consequence would be experiencing a shift away from the old torture to instead feeling compulsive about not getting to make good choices! Or feel compulsively driven to always making the choices that bring out the best in you and that fulfil your long-term needs.

Eliciting the Submodalities of Propulsion

Has that given you a clear understanding of the two parts of a propulsion system? If so, then you have become ready to begin to do the submodality elicitation for it. With that piece, then you will become ready to install a propulsion system in yourself and/or others.

1) Pick an aversion. First, identify something to which you feel a strong aversion. To elicit this you might want to answer the questions: "What do you move away from?" or "What things do you feel revolted by?" Notice what comes to mind with these questions. Explore that with a partner.

2) Identify the driver submodalities. Find one or more driver submodalities that run the aversion. When you have one, crank it up, amplify it so that it becomes more powerful.

Whenever you work with states of consciousness, always test them in reality. Bring your partner out and see how they respond to the object. You want to make sure that the phobia still exists. After all, the brain will follow directions. But you have to provide those directions, which we know from doing the submodality elicitation and shift. We build in the directions for their nervous system to follow in terms of what they move toward and away from in life. ●→●

3) Pick a compulsion. You should now feel ready for the next part of the elicitation. Let us do an elicitation of something that you feel compelled toward. Pick something juicy. Think of some fetish that you have. This actually has the same structure as a compulsion. It is something toward which every fiber in your existence automatically and quickly moves, something about which you have no questions.

In a properly constructed propulsion system both of these dynamics will co-exist and co-operate. This means, you will feel and identify energies that move you away from one thing while simultaneously other energies move you toward something else. For instance, on the one hand you may feel phobic about being ignorant and not learning something important while simultaneously you may feel compulsive about reading, studying, learning, and thinking.

When these things work together, the energies become synergistic in nature. This means that out of the whole something emerges and becomes something greater than the sum of the parts. Simultaneously you feel powerfully drawn toward something positive and enhancing while you feel powerfully averted from something else. When you have not correlated these items enough so that they do not fit together as polarities, you end up a terribly conflicted human being. We call this Inner Conflict. ●→

This explains the crucial role of thorough preparation work in this particular pattern for building a propulsion system. As you pick your phobias and compulsions, do so with care. Also, thoughtfully target the end states that you want to achieve.

In doing this, you will discover how to build an internal mechanism in yourself or another person from the structure of your submodalities. The overall propulsion system operates from the energy and power of the driver submodalities. How do those drivers relate given your structures of phobia and compulsion?

When you are ready, you will use those driver submodalities which will most push the person toward their compulsion and away from their phobia. This creates a place where we can make that other person's inner reality 'sensorama land.' So make it intense, three-dimensional, intensify its color, have the picture panoramic wrapped around them, give it angles, explore smells and tastes, etc. Keep asking yourself, "What else is missing from this list of submodalities? What items are not here? And what would happen if I used some of them?"

Swishing to a Compulsion/Aversion

Are you ready for this one? You will need to use the standard swish pattern for this. The purpose in doing this exercise is primarily to give you an opportunity to practice designing a compelling behavior.

Away From: B elicits something that A moves away from. B should then gather extremely detailed information in order to discover the driver or kicker. B should ask many questions about aspects of A's consciousness that s/he does not typically focus on. As a Master Practitioner, B should keep asking him/herself, "What is missing here?" B should have A change each submodality a little to check for differences.

Toward: When completed, B should elicit from A a very powerful moving toward experience, and in the same way find its driver submodalities. ●→●

All of this so far serves as a thorough preparation. So, as B, do commit yourself to doing a thorough job. Then, when you have completed it, do the following:

4) Anchor and amplify. B begins by anchoring the first experience (#1 Away From/Phobia) and amplifying the submodalities. B anchors this Move Away From state very strongly. S/he can establish a revulsion by anchoring and amplifying (exaggeration). In accessing the state of aversion, s/he aims to pace it so that s/he can get a full 4-tuple of it: "Show me how you do it." Amplifying the state will also take the person into some very strong emotions. That is what we want, and also frees us from fearing them. In fact, B goes ahead and asks for it directly, "What do you experience as your reality right now?" ●→

B now anchors the second experience (#2 Moving Toward/ Compulsion) and amplifies its driving submodalities. B gets A into a powerfully Compelled Toward state. →●

5) B now anchors curiosity and elicits a state of curiosity in A, and anchors it. When that anchor is set, B has A open his/her eyes, and instructs him/her to turn up the submodalities of the Revulsion Driver of the phobic state. ●→

   B now turns up the submodalities of the drivers of the compelling state. →●

   Make sure you use a different language tonality for each of these drivers. The programmer, B, should establish mixed state communication with A by looking behind A's eyes. This will induce an altered state. To do this, B should tell A, "Remember a pleasant activity. And as you fly forward (use whatever driver you have) you can allow your pleasure to increase more and more. The more you hesitate, the worse you feel. And the more you go toward your activity the better you feel. →●

Debriefing the Process

Aim to pick a really intense experience, something that you find irresistible. As you do this with a partner, allow yourself to begin noticing how their Meta-Programs operate on them as part of this process. Typically your world will most likely turn into high comedy when you play around with this pattern.

Now you can answer the question: "What turns pleasure into pain?" Whenever you take an experience to its threshold, the experience changes. It has to. Remember that submodalities usually work in non-linear ways. So as you play with this there will probably come a point where they will cross a threshold, and something unexpected will happen.

The thrusting power in this pattern comes from developing a driving mechanism which coordinates two forces in personality. Many compulsive people already have most of this pattern, although some only have the compulsion and not the aversion. Aim to remain in a state of curiosity as you work.

Now consider the attitude of functioning with absolute tenaciousness in your work. Bandler says, "In my sales seminar I say 'The only reason they're not buying is that they don't understand!' So allow yourself to become totally drawn! Let the thought of not talking to your client or customer become really repulsive to you!" ●→

When you pick something you want to feel more compelled to do, allow yourself to feel that you have missed out on it, and continue to do so. And you can feel a complete revulsion about hesitating. At the same time, feel yourself drawn to your object in a compulsive way. Remember, you will have two images: one of aversion; one of attraction. One pulling, one pushing. ●→●

Set the stage for this work by doing some 'mixed state communication.' Pace the person to induce a mild altered state. De-focus your own eyes by looking at some distant object. Then reinforce both states. Now lock in the driver and keep cycling between aversion and attraction. Anchor both anchors together (#1 + #2). You may want to think of this construction as multi-layered, because there will be a backward movement and a forward movement at the same time. "You feel bad/worse as you move away from your attraction and feel good, great, better and better as you move toward it." This combines the push/pull parts of motivation. ●→●

When you use this process, you are aiming to build a direction for someone to go in rather than an end to arrive at. Therefore use analog distinctions for creating this direction. If you think of this direction as one that leads to more and more personal development, then the attitude to adopt involves believing that getting there provides us with most of the fun. Create a representational code that cues you to think and feel, "There is always more! What more lies out there? I've got to know! How much more resourceful can I become? How much more skilled? How much more elegant and successful in my use of language?" →●

I remember hearing Bandler once say, "I like the comment Einstein once made. He said that he believed that the universe is a friendly place, and that it is becoming more and more predictable." Imagine your orientation if you adopted a point of view like that. Or if you imagined that anything exists as possible if only you were to go searching for it. And I should remind you that mathematics itself functions as a behavioral science. This means that equations work by feelings, and that without human beings math doesn't work." →●

Installing Internal Propulsion Systems

Use the following question to ponder the degree to which you have so far mastered the NLP model, its methodology and technology:

> "How do you install a strategy in yourself or in someone with whom you work? What process do you use for programming a new learning, a new decision, a new belief, a new compulsion into a human being?"

Within the NLP model, we generally think of the following as methodologies of installation.

1) Trance induction. We could install a new program in someone by putting that person into a trance state and then walking them through a step-by-step procedure of the ideas, learnings, and feelings that we want them to have, while at the same time future pacing them with the various contextual cues with which they will have to deal.

2) Thresholding process. Or we could use the threshold pattern. We take someone to the point where we blow an old behavior through the roof. People do tend to become very receptive at this point. They become wide open for a new program to replace what we have just pushed over threshold.

3) A chain of states. We could create a chain of states that we had previously anchored. Then we could have them repeat the firing of the anchor until the process becomes a completely auto-

matic response to a specific environmental cue. Then when the cue occurs, it sets off the entire chain, sending the person to the new outcome. This describes every strategy anyway—a sequence of representations (internal and external) that someone goes through to create a piece of subjective experience.

4) Submodality feedback. We could anchor the specific submodalities of the new experience and then feed those very submodalities back to them. In this way, it would begin to evoke that experience in them. →●

How many of those did you come up with? Did you come up with some other installation methods? These are some of the key ways to do programming. And of course, as a NLPer, you need to have the ability to program yourself and others. If you do not you will just know a lot more stuff, but be without the corresponding ability to do things. In which case, that would make you either an egghead or an incompetent! And really, does the world need another incompetent egghead? ●→

Thresholding Patterns of Pain to Keep Building Up the Aversion

As you well know, there are certain moments in life when most of us feel blocked from our resources. We all experience such times—often more frequently than we desire. We become stuck in some negative pattern that keeps looping and preventing us from accessing our resources. What do we do in such a situation? How do we help someone in that kind of state?

Suppose at this point you turn up the submodalities of that compulsion (of being limited) until it goes over threshold, so that something snaps within them which stops them from feeling and functioning in a stuck way. After they have crossed that threshold they will find it extremely difficult to go back.

(A word of caution: We want to move the person to the place where they become sick and tired *of their limitations*. Take care here. Aim to increase the state of pain and aversion to feeling sick-and-tired of feeling limited. This describes a meta-state. We do not want to increase the pain and aversion to the limitation itself. We want them to feel motivated toward change, not to move away from noticing their limitations. If we did that we would put the person in a very unresourceful state.)

The same principle applies as when you bend a piece of sheet metal. At first, if you bend it back and forth, it returns to its original shape. But if you continue bending it back and forth, the metal eventually passes a tolerance threshold and the sheet breaks.

We use this threshold principle to gain leverage over a less-than-useful pattern. And when we get someone to go over threshold, we can then slide in all kinds of things. Generally speaking, at the point of going over threshold, they access a great state of receptivity. Crossing the threshold creates a kind of void which we can then fill with something better.

Bandler tells this story about a fellow he once worked with. "I once dealt with a man who had a really stupid belief. He believed an idea about relationships that created limitations for him. He believed that 'Relationships start out great and then go downhill.' How about that? So guess how he had been experiencing relationships in his life!"

When you amplify a state beyond what it allows the experience to be, then it cannot be the same. If you do it hard enough and fast enough, this can be the straw that breaks the camel's back. We call that 'going over threshold.' →●

Consider also the state that Bandler calls 'More Ecstasy Right Now!' For a moment, just in your mind, pick a point where you would like more ecstasy, but where you do not currently have it.

Bandler told the story: "One man I knew did not distinguish between what you find and what you create. So he went out trying to find the perfect relationship, and never could. It just never dawned on him to create it. But you can! You can create an ecstasy loop in life so that you always, with most everything, keep evoking more ecstasy now! At least that holds a certain appeal to me. →●

> "Another man I worked with complained bitterly that he always had difficulty getting what he wanted. As it turned out, he only had one strategy. In his case it was creating what he wanted. Think about that one. This strategy of creating things, making them happen, made him highly innovative and productive in business. And financially successful! But he was lousy with relationships. Can you guess why? He was always trying to change his partners. And for some reason or another, they didn't seem to like that."

As a Master Practitioner, what would you do? Bandler simply added a new auditory-digital line to his strategy. He formulated it as a question, and installed it to run at the decision-point: "Do I make one or find one?" Now in the context of relationships, his focus lay in finding a partner that he liked, rather than re-creating every partner into his liking. This actually saved him a lot of grief and conflict.

We can create a decision-point like that in someone's mind by pushing an experience to its threshold. Just take the feeling of wanting something and push it until the person gets to a decision point. Perhaps it will be something that the person externally sees [V^e] to which they then say, "I want that!" Then keep pushing the V–A–K until it goes over threshold. Repeat this process, each time anchoring the feeling of going over threshold. When you get to the blow-out point, put in the new behavior. →●

You can also program in empowering ideas whenever you find or create a good strategy that you would fit into the vacated decision-point. For example, if you meet someone who continually says, "I tried and failed," and they use that to excuse themselves from continual effort, reframe them with, "Oh, have you ever experienced constipation?" (!) (Another classic Bandlerism). As you do this, remember to keep operating from the NLP presupposition: "There is no failure, only feedback."

Use the driver submodalities that you find in someone to amplify their experience until it blows out. Thresholding it in this way allows you to then immediately anchor in their strategy and state for ecstasy.

Using Time Distortion for Programming in the Propulsion System

While there is no right way to do anything, some strategies, procedures, and technologies function more effectively than others. The following process can richly contribute to this pattern.

1) Elicit representations and feelings of slow and fast time. Begin with the elicitation of how the person represents 'fast' and 'slow' time. Also create an induction signal.

2) Worst case scenario. Next, select a worst case scenario to work with. If you work with clients, create a representation of your worse client. If you work with customers, elicit the 'customer from hell.' Then run the simulation of this representation in their time distortion.

3) Identify the key structuring submodalities. The kind of time distortion you want to work with here is the feeling that 'time stood still' for you on the outside while simultaneously it seemed to speed up on the inside. Test this by finding some reference experiences for yourself, and notice which parts of the image move at different speeds. This kind of time distortion experience will always involve different parts of your pictures moving at different speeds. This characterises the distortion of your sense of time.

4) Anchor the trance and the experience. Obviously, doing this takes someone into a trance state. Here your internal time will seem to move very fast while the external time will seem to move very slowly. As you experience this state and this sense of time, set an anchor for it.

5) Practice in fast time. Most of us already have the realization and generalization that what allows someone to become good at something requires much practice, and sufficient time for practicing.

   Therefore, pick something that seems hard for the person and then have them begin to practice this skill or activity over and over in their imagination. But do this in the accelerated time distortion state so that they feel as though they now practice and have practiced the new skills and behaviors to the point where they have begun to get really good at them.

Remind them, that as they do this, to practice at super-speed in their time distortion. Then they will not have to waste of lot of external time. And you can have them light up and glow as they discover themselves experiencing this.

Overall, you can use and design this time distortion exercise to give you plenty of practice at installing an ecstasy anchor into the altered state of time distortion to preview and problem-solve a future experience. Have B elicit from A an altered state of time distortion in which A's internal time becomes speeded up. Then anchor it.

6) Fast timing the worst client. B should then have A run through ten minutes with A's worst client experience in just ten seconds. In this state, A will see everything that s/he would see in real time.

7) Set a sliding anchor. C, the meta-person, can build a sliding anchor along A's midline that induces trance within the time distortion state by pushing, shoving, and amplifying the ecstasy anchor as A runs pictures. C gives A suggestions to run the scenario and to try something new until A's midline zings with ecstasy. The more it zings, the more ecstasy the person experiences, both in and out of trance. Test. →●

Mastering the Practice of the Spirit of NLP

As we continue to pull together all these understandings, exercises, and experiences, you should be gaining a clearer idea of what it takes to become a Master Practitioner in the art of NLP. NLP involves far more than just the academic learnings about representational systems, strategies, Meta-Programs, the Meta-Model of language, anchoring, swishing, reframing, and so on. More important is having that special kind of attitude which reflects the beliefs, values, and passions of Richard Bandler and John Grinder.

These beliefs, values, and passions, as far as I can tell, are the disposition and supporting beliefs which led Richard and John and which are represented by the following statements:

- There is no failure; only feedback.
- Be delighted when you discover something that you have been doing wrong—now you never have to do it again.
- There is no point in giving yourself a bad time or feeling bad.
- Feel good! It's important to be flexible.
- When facing a barrier, instead of going "Yecch, I messed up!" tell yourself "I find this interesting!"
- Life is now, so go for it.
- Develop a ferocious resolve; maintain an insatiable curiosity.

Summary

Now, given those kinds of beliefs and values, states and perceptions, the essence of Master Practitioner training and the spirit of functioning as a master of NLP lies not in paper-and-pencil testing efficiency, but rather in the ability to master your own states by running your own brain.

The essence of any reputable Master Practitioner training involves providing a systematic guide to a series of states and learnings. And it does this in order to elicit and anchor those very resourceful states that make you live and think and breathe NLP as part of your personal model of the world.

When fully established, these processes and programs then provide us with an automatic chain of anchors which could then move us from a state of hesitation, frustration or impatience to wanton desire and totally going for it. Now would that enhance your life? In recent years, the idea of 'walking your talk' has become more prevalent in many fields. And in a field whose content involves managing your own consciousness and neurology, this should be one of our key concerns, should it not?

Without question, mastering NLP involves a great deal of intimate and detailed knowledge and skill with using the Meta-Model, knowing the Meta-Programs, handling the techniques and patterns for change, utilizing the Milton model, and so on. The passion and motivation that drives us to learn NLP must be large and intense enough for us to persevere, no matter what life throws at us.

Could we become intimately familiar with such material without incorporating the spirit of NLP? No. The spirit of NLP operates as a prerequisite for Master Practitioner. It necessitates having the ability to use NLP in a spirit of curiosity, wonder, passion, commitment, exploration, creativity, and so on; and in having access to all the resource states that we build and cultivate in the trainings. Being so propelled lies at the heart of the design and intent of the 'propulsion system' itself, which automatically installs compulsive and aversive elements that drive us to achieve excellence with passion.

Studying Hard

The Art of Applying Your Brain

One myth circulating about NLP says something to the effect that the only kind of training and learning that truly counts arises from experiential learning. Another myth says that only unconscious installation really counts. I completely disagree. We can learn much from experience; yet much learning must come from using the brain to encode ideas, insights, understandings, models, patterns, etc.

As you will discover in the following chapters, NLP does not represent a discipline for those who lack the passion for studying and expanding their consciousness. To expose yourself to the academic depth of NLP, just read Robert Dilts' first three books *NLP, Volume I, Roots of NLP, and Applications of NLP.*

In fact you will need the spirit of NLP as described above precisely because this discipline does not represent a simple (or simplistic) black-and-white model. The NLP model is characterized by systemic, cybernetic, and holistic qualities, which involve the entire mind-body (linguistic-neurology) phenomenon. It addresses the complexity of human neuro-linguistic functioning.

Exercising your conscious mind, studying hard, thinking with precision, living consciously, and so on, all play a central role to Master Practitioner training. Count on it. This describes part of the process of moving from unconscious incompetence to conscious incompetence to conscious competence to unconscious competence. This third step plays a necessary role. And if later you want to teach and train this material, you will need to move to a fifth stage after unconscious competence, namely, to an even higher level of conscious competence.

In the Master Practitioner work and training I did with Richard Bandler in 1989, Richard and his associates provided many out-of-class assignments. In that master track experience, I felt 'baptized' in this NLP mindset by all of the presentations, demonstrations, exercises, and assigned homework exercises. Later, when I worked on the manuscripts of the master track and the trainers training, I felt a sense of immersion into the discipline and the attitude was confirmed and amplified again and again.

At that point I decided to begin looking for this component of installing human propulsion systems in the subtext and in the syntax of the experiences. And then I began to see it everywhere. Did that occur because I had developed the appropriate perceptual filters and beliefs, so that as I perceived, so I discovered? Or did it occur because I happened upon something that Bandler had incorporated into his trainings? Did it accurately represent a key component of becoming a Master Practitioner which he had designed into his program without ever communicating it in so many words? And if you asked Richard, do you think he would tell you directly?

One of the most powerful hypnotic suggestions lies in the slow building up of response potential and of gradually seeding ideas until suddenly, eureka!—something new and synergistic pops into awareness.

As you can no doubt tell, I firmly believe that this spirit, attitude, predisposition, or world-view drives the power and passion of the NLP model. And I believe Practitioners often acquire this spirit as they learn the presuppositions of NLP.

In other words, the ultimate mastery of the art of NLP comes from taking on board the NLP beliefs and values within those very presuppositions:

- The map is not the territory.
- There is no failure, only feedback.
- Never give yourself a bad time or engage in bad feelings.
- Be glad you learned what not to do!
- The fun lies in the process of discovery and traveling, not in arriving.
- The universe is a friendly place and becoming more and more predictable. (Einstein).
- There are books to write, negotiations to make, money to be made, so go for it!
- Get more ecstasy now!
- You can put yourself into a joyful state anytime you want to.
- If you meditate, induce yourself into a state of ecstasy.
- The person with the most flexibility will have most choices.
- Mind and body exist as part of the same system.
- Magic has structure and we can learn it and replicate it!

I think that this spirit of NLP comes through crystal clear if you listen to the themes that Richard constantly emphasizes. First and foremost you will hear his emphasis on passion. Who has heard him and hasn't heard the refrain "Go for it!" again and again? Who hasn't heard him speak about the need for an absolute passion for ecstasy? I have heard him say, "'Just enough is not enough!' is my policy."

Then you will hear his emphasis on building up a ferocious resolve. Who was it who developed The Decision Destroyer by using a time-line pattern to blow out old and limiting decisions that get in the way of people experiencing empowering resolve? Richard Bandler. Further, if you have been to his Flirting Workshop then you know what it feels like to have the state of 'sizzle!' introduced into your neurology. →●

In one training Richard began, as he frequently does by inviting someone in the audience to come up and let him work with them to demonstrate a pattern. To make his invitation, Richard asked, "Who here needs a swift kick in the *a-a*-attitude?" (Another classic

Bandlerism.) What does this mean here in this context? It indicates what it takes to become a Master Practitioner, namely, an attitude adjustment, a bold new way of thinking about exploring, feeling curious, going for it, responding with boldness, etc.

For many, adopting this spirit of NLP necessitates a tremendous shift of attitude. How about you? Would looking out on the world as a 'piece of cake for your enjoyment' represent an altered state for you? Or how about looking out at the world and saying inside your mind, "Your ass is mine!"? This Bandlerism undoubtedly provides a shift from thinking and feeling like a victim to the ferocious state of really "Going For It!" (Of course, some have taken such metaphors and statements literally and assumed that Richard advocates manipulation, control over others, etc.—not so.)

How far will you have to go in order to access the spirit of NLP as described here? In this book, if you look closely enough, or if you go meta to it, you will find numerous ideas designed to elicit and anchor this state within you.

Another point by Richard Bandler (if you will bear with my mind-reading some more) that exemplifies the true spirit of a Master Practitioner, is the ability to question. Questioning provides a potent technology for adventure, exploration, and discovery. And questioning everything 'right out of the gate,' and then asking another five questions—epitomizes the unquenchable attitude of NLP. When you are doing this, then start meta-questioning. A master in the art of NLP has deeply installed in them a questioning attitude:

- "What is still missing?"
- "What else could I find this useful for?"
- "What skill can I infer that exists within this?"
- "How can I make this mine?"
- "How can I make this better?"
- "What may I not see, hear, feel in this experience?"
- "What do you see, hear, feel, etc. that I do not?"
- "What would happen if I put procrastination together with depression?"

- "What would happen if I took the wide-eyed wonderment of a child with the rote behavior of someone on an assembly line?"

Master Practitioners live in an ecstasy state and feel an absolute compulsion toward using and living the NLP model because they so much want to live their lives to the fullest. This means:

- They have a passion toward more effectively understanding and using the Meta-Model to speak with precision.
- They feel passionate about hearing and discerning the Meta-Programs people use to sort and attend information.
- And they feel a thrill about using the Milton model 'Sleight of Mouth' patterns to induce more positive hypnotic states in themselves and others.

The Hypnotic State of being a Master Practitioner

The Propulsion System as a Hypnotic Induction

How does Bandler structure his trainings so as to enable learners to master the material? By essentially creating the whole thing as a hypnotic induction into states of excellence and passion. In the trainings I have experienced, not only did we experience constant opportunities for 'trancing out' and using our full powers of imagination to dream about using the NLP Model with more precision, elegance, and power, but there we also experienced many little pieces (demonstrations, exercises, and so on) also designed essentially to function as hypnotic inductions.

Those who have received training in the Bandler workshops will attest that the training sessions function primarily as hypnotic inductions. He has designed them to build into the participants a kind of propulsion system of attraction to NLP attitudes and methodology, And if truly a propulsion system, then also an aversion to anything less.

Such training not only takes participants into new and enhancing experiences in self-discovery, resourcefulness, altering limiting beliefs, decisions, and scripts, it does even more. It also moves participants through a series of states which substantiate the new orientation. Such training not only gets them to study and use NLP, it also gets them to 'breathe' NLP. In this way, the model becomes an intuitive set of tools and procedures which enable them to make the most of their life.

In those trainings, I believe that Richard also sought to create a community of people hungry for ecstasy and passion in life, in love with people and living, and compelled to grow and develop their understandings and skills.

Now all of the basic NLP techniques which we generally use in change work can be the means for installing these states of ecstasy. Included as part of the repertoire are: trance, threshold patterns for blowing out old programs (hesitation, holding on), installing new programs of excitement, curiosity, and exploration, and so on. We could use the process of developing chains that anchor resource states to hesitation states (or other limiting states) which can then prevent someone from staying frustrated.

We could use submodality anchoring, communicating, and amplification. Doing so would thereby create internal drivers for the compelling future. We could use some of Richard's favorite interventions such as rehearsing in time distortion and thus improving exponentially by practicing so much faster.

We could 'rehearse in play'—which I think explains Bandler's style of 'testing' his Practitioners. In his NLP trainings and certification, participants do not take paper-and-pencil tests. Instead, they play games. So when the time comes for testing, they will more likely hear, in the manner of the Roman call, "Let the Games Begin!" Then in that context, you can expect your skills, knowledge, and ability to get tested.

In describing this, I am reminded of a teasing process that I detected in his presenting. He would often suggest without stating, and he would often tease the conscious mind in ways that some found torturous, by simply leaving things out in his descriptions, storytelling, listing of steps, etc. He would not tie up loose ends or bring his subject to a point of closure. And of course this would inevitably drive some participants crazy! Eric Robbie would do similar kinds of thing. For example, on one occasion he ended a session with this question: "How do you know to draw the next breath?" Even my brain, which can stand a lot of non-closure, felt like interrupting and saying, "Say, would you mind elaborating on that a bit?"

Homework assignments also tend to play a big part in the trainings. These served, I think, as metaphors of the Master Practitioner propulsion system itself. In the training I received we were given the following homework assignments:

1) Design and create five exquisite chains so that you can move from a limiting state to a much more resourceful state. As I did this for myself and created a set of states by which I could achieve increasing resourcefulness, it personalized things for me to a greater extent.

2) Transcribe and analyze a hypnosis session. To assist with this we each were given a tape of Bandler doing a hypnotic induction with a workshop participant who wanted help in dieting (See Chapter Three). We then transcribed that tape and identified the Milton model patterns which we found in it. At the same time, yet without declaring it, this provided a model of a propulsion system. If you examine it, you will find that he took the lady who wanted assistance with dieting through a series of states. He then tied those resource states together (anchored with words and tones), anchored them, and then fired them all off at the end. He thus used a stacking anchors pattern to create a super-anchored state. And of course, Richard amplified all of this with his words and music at the end of the workshop.

The hypnosis tape teasingly provided a micro-model of the entire Master Practitioner induction or training. It functions isomorphically to the workshop experience in the kinds of states accessed and anchored and to the kind of propulsion system he was building into the participants. Bandler invited everyone to become compelled toward becoming excellent, healthy and rich NLPers!

Accessing Master States

If you have made a ferocious resolve and have developed 'an eye of a tiger' motivation and passion for mastering NLP so that it becomes part of your spirit—part of the way you think, part of the resources that you bring to bear on the world as you move through it—then the following resource states will facilitate this process of accessing and installing the spirit of NLP. By doing this, you will indeed become a master of this art and science.

Obviously, an auditory-digital presentation and analysis of NLP training offers a poor substitute for the training experience itself. But if you do want to master NLP and incorporate its spirit, then please take the opportunity to access and install the following resource states as fully as you can, because doing this will move you towards mastery.

1) An intense, and perhaps even shocking, state of challenge. Do not grow complacent. By all means avoid any thought or attitude that you 'have it made.' Stay open. Stay alert. Keep setting passionate and exciting desired outcomes for yourself in order to keep yourself challenged to *"Go for it!"* Expose yourself to something new, different, strange, and weird on a regular basis. Never, but never, take life for granted. If you want to keep the mystery and wonder in life, then expose yourself to one provocative idea or person every day.

2) An intense wide-eyed state of child-like fascination.

Personally, I found the formatting of the Master Practitioner training captivating and absolutely fascinating. Since I like things sequenced, I enjoyed the non-sequencing because it challenged me to do that for myself.

It did seem that many participants felt totally disoriented by the workshop experience because neither Richard nor any of his co-trainers ever informed them about the process, what their intentions were for any of the pieces, what any particular piece meant, what would come next, and so on. Never once did any of them provide a big picture of the processes occurring.

Now as someone who thinks in gestalt configurations, I had no problem with any of that. My own brain sorted for and constructed all kinds of global understandings of the trainings. So the fact that we received none of that information only teased the daylights out of my mind all the more and kept me in an intense wide-eyed state of child-like fascination.

What puts you in such a state? Does the idea of reading submodalities from the outside intrigue you? What other possibilities exist for NLP that we have not yet invented?

3) A learning state for more advanced state-of-the-art NLP. NLP continues to keep moving and developing. Learners in the field constantly invent, discover, and create new patterns, processes, and models. They make more and finer distinctions about the sensory systems, the Meta-Model, and the rest. So consider:

    How well do you feel that you keep updated?
    How much more informed and skilled have you become with the Meta-Model today?
    How much more attuned do you feel to nominalizations, presuppositions, etc?

Remember, a Master Practitioner has a compulsion toward such learning. Do you? Consider:

How much have you developed at becoming a creative mind-reader?
How much more skilled are you at strategy elicitation?
How much better are you at understanding the structure of beliefs?
How much more facility do you have with going meta?
How much better are you at understanding the role of presuppositions in language?
How much better are you at realizing that every abstraction beyond experience involves a belief (criteria, values, generalizations)?

4) A strong aversion to mediocrity. How much distaste do you have for functioning at a mediocre, average, and a conformist

level? Do such things really revolt you? You don't have to be around Richard very long to sense the rebel within him. Both he and John, as outsiders to the field of psychology, created a new paradigm. Actually, this precisely fits the model of a 'paradigm shift' that Thomas Kuhn (1962) described in his work. It is frequently the case that those on the outside discover what those within a field cannot see.

Richard and John came up with NLP, in part, due to their ability to mismatch. After all, they looked for things that didn't fit the current theories and explanations. They sorted for things that never crossed the minds of others. And many have, in fact, argued against the NLP model for this very reason. Yet it was this very spirit of rebellion to the assumed and given knowledge which initiated this model. So how much creative and balanced rebellion do you have in your life? To what extend can you mismatch, step aside from the need for approval, and head up a rebellion to the traditional? You have to have a bit of the rebel in you in order to practice NLP and especially if you want to help invent it.

Allow yourself also to be determined not to use the Meta-Model in a rote and unthinking way. As I will quote from Richard later, even if you use the Meta-Model challenges for unspecified nouns and verbs in a conformist way, you may only develop a Pavlovian dog-bark to language:

"I'm depressed?"
"About what?"
"I feel rejected?"
"Rejected by whom? Rejected in what way?"

Engaging in such indexing plays a critical role in good information gathering, but we should not do it in a rote stimulus-response kind of way, as a dog barks to the ringing of a bell.

5) An advanced ability to go into a trance state at will. NLP has contributed much to the area of demystifying all the hocus-pocus about hypnosis. NLP has brought the state of trance away from the mystics, charlatans, and kooks, and into the modern era by identifying the linguistic and non-verbal structure of hypnosis. NLP also suggests we all engage in all kinds

of 'everyday hypnosis.' The difference lies in this: we neither understand what we do, nor do it very well, and, more often than not, we misuse it!

In NLP, we use the hypnotic trance state primarily to develop greater receptivity to events, to tune our ears to language and language experiencing, to tap into our natural unconscious powers, and so on. Developing quick trance capacities further empowers us in developing higher levels of self-mastery because it enables us to quickly access our resources both consciously and unconsciously.

6) A highly motivated and turned-on state. Practitioners who do not apply the skills and resources of NLP to themselves and who therefore keep getting stuck in limiting and unresourceful states present a sad picture of the NLP spirit. These people stand in stark contrast to those who have mastered NLP, who have created for themselves a chain of anchors which will reliably take them from states of hesitation, indecision, fear, worry, etc., to totally going for it.

Having applied the art of NLP to themselves gives them resilience power. Now they can quickly bounce back from discouraging responses and defeats. This does not mean that we never have such experiences. We do. But we do not use these occasions to pay long visits to states of guilt, anger, frustration, hesitation, etc. Rather we quickly access our resources, get up again and get going. We learn from our mistakes and feed that information back into our updated strategy.

Having a motivational strategy with this kind of internal bounce means we can move on without getting stuck in some negative state. This truly demonstrates that we are gaining mastery. It shows that we live as if in a resourceful universe and that we are running our own brain.

7) A state of aiming and experiencing excellence every day. With a good resilient motivational strategy we can quickly move from holding onto old securities, fears, dreads, etc., to letting go of them and moving towards a more exciting future. We do not confuse aiming for excellence with perfectionism. In fact,

excellence has nothing at all to do with perfectionism, but has everything to do with giving it your best, enjoying the process, and optimizing what you can without feeling compelled to make everything absolutely right.

NLP began when John and Richard decided to study three 'therapeutic wizards.' By identifying their strategies and replicating them through reframing, anchoring, swishing, and other techniques, NLP Practitioners have learned how to understand the structure of excellence more deeply. This refers to replicating the high quality that results when someone has a streamlined and elegant strategy. It has nothing to do with wanting to avoid every mistake at all cost. True excellence, in fact, does not only stand and endure mistakes, errors, and failures, but exults in them, because the process of moving toward excellence means using those mistakes for learning and further development.

8) A state of persuasiveness. Like all subjective experiences, there is also has a structure to excellence in persuading others. At the heart of that structure lies the ability to enter into another person's world, pace that reality, become aware of that person's values, and then package your message using those qualities. Doing that will involve identifying, and then using, their submodalities to amplify your subject or product. It also involves using that person's driver submodalities in order to amplify their ability to respond. It means using the Meta-Model and Meta-Programs to read the person accurately enough to know how to communicate with them in a persuasive way.

9) A state of feeling totally compelled towards growing mentally and emotionally. What structure can we expect to find in the state of a healthy compulsion? For one thing, the person will have learned how to use and adjust the submodality distinctions in such a way as to make the things they want feel even more attractive.

Have you done this yet? Have you accessed a state in which you feel totally driven toward something of positive value for you and totally averted to the opposite qualities? When you do, you will have some real thrust power in your motivational engine. And it will operate as a turbo-charger in your personality. It will drive you forward in a truly empowered way. It will give a direction for your mind and enable you to sizzle!

You might want to master the kinesthetic time-line pattern (Chapter Fourteen) so that you install these feelings at the kinesthetic level in your body. Then you may just discover that you can walk into your future with all of your resources at hand, or at foot. You may also want to master the kinesthetic continuum pattern. Doing this will empower you to generate new behaviors on any personality quality continuum.

10) A state of total persistence with a 'no-quit' clause in it. What Meta-Programs contribute to allowing yourself to give up something that you find difficult? Which Meta-Programs allow you to stick with something (a project, idea, person, and so on) even though you find it difficult? Have you ever run an NLP contrastive analysis and then used your discoveries to develop even more refinement in your ability to persist? Would you like to do that now? You can.

Conclusion

Mastering the NLP model means becoming compelled to move toward excellence, health, resourcefulness, etc. It means adopting an empowering attitude toward life, incorporating the NLP presuppositions, and taking on a truly ferocious attitude toward all the things that lie within the realms of possibility.

Now may the spirit of NLP, and the genius of Richard Bandler and John Grinder, go with you as you journey through the following chapters. May you have a ferocious attitude that will enable you to learn these distinctions and apply them with a passion in all of the areas of your life.

Chapter Two

Learning the Art of Trance

[Derived primarily from both Richard Bandler and Don Wolfe]

What we have traditionally labeled 'hypnosis' or 'trance' plays a central role in the communication model of NLP. If hypnosis sounds scary, then as you begin to realize that it is nothing more than "the misunderstood nature of communication" (Hall, 1994), you can then relax in understanding how this part of communication works in human mind-and-neurology.

After all, going inside one's own mind and accessing or reaccessing internal representations—pictures, sounds, words, actions, sensations, smells, tastes, and so on—simply describes the experience that we call 'trance.' We all do it. We go inside by directing our attention, not to the things we see, hear, or feel on the outside, but on the inside. And we do this all the time because in this way we make sense of what someone else is saying. It describes how we think.

Now within the domain of experience called hypnosis there are many phenomena that we describe as 'hypnotic.' Actually there is no human skill or power that you can do in trance that you cannot also do in the waking state. Trance simply makes it much easier and quicker. One such phenomenon within this domain is 'time distortion.'

What question would a Master Practitioner ask first about time distortion? What other questions at both content and process levels could you come up with? Time distortion can provide someone with a tremendous personal resource.

Using Time Distortion for Mastering NLP

You will need practice in distorting time in order to have this as a resource which works to your benefit and which allows you to induce a state in which your experience seems to slow down. To do this, take the experience of motoring off an interstate highway doing 70 mph. Driving along the off ramp the car is now moving at 30 mph and it suddenly seems as though you are creeping along and everything seems to go o o so o o o s l o o o o o o w! →●

Presuppositions operate as some of the most important drivers of hypnosis. In fact, communicating by connotation often evokes states more effectively than attempting to communicate directly by denotation. The following exercise is designed to enable you to practice utilizing presuppositions so that you can alter your own state or the state of someone else. Notice the effect this exercise has on others.

Presupposing Trance

1) Write ten statements that presuppose that someone has begun, even now, to experience going into a deep, comfortable, and relaxing state of trance. Stuff these sentences with semantically packed presuppositions that will enable the person to become relaxed. As you do this, remember that we use language as the doorway to the unconscious, as it is part of our genetic wiring. So go ahead and use it to the full in order to utilize this resource.

2) Read the sentences. Once you have your sentences, get into groups of four and do the following: B reads two of his/her sentences to A, using a tonality in which voice inflections go down at the end of each sentence. Have some nice trancy music playing in the background, and B should practice speaking at the tempo of that music. When B has finished reading the two sentences, s/he then points to person C, who then reads out two sentences, using the same beat. D then completes this by reading two sentences to A.

3) Change places so that everyone has a go. When you have finished reading to the first person, rotate places to allow each person to have the experience of being the subject. In this way everyone accesses a pleasant and mildly relaxed state for the next exercise.

Debriefing

What kind of statements presuppose the experience and the development of trance? What states did you find worked best for you, and best for the others in your group?

One group generated the following:

> You can wonder how deeply you will experience the sense of relaxation this time.
>
> Your unconscious mind can access a pleasant memory of a place where you experienced feeling warm and comfortable, and felt at peace with yourself.
>
> And your eyes will only blink as often as the sense of comfort deepens in your deepest self.
>
> And you will sense your breathing with more awareness as you allow the images in your mind to become softer and softer in hue.
>
> And your sense of serenity within will allow you to deepen your comfort ever so gently.
>
> And with every growing awareness of your arms you will become comfortable in the comfort that you can take within yourself, and trust your unconscious to give you learnings from this experience.
>
> And the sounds and vibrations of the music in the air around you will also enable you to flow into the music, as you let it enter into you, and then float down even deeper.

> And as you become aware of your breathing, that awareness will increase as you continue to breathe in and out, in and out, and allowing you to progressively breathe in the learnings that you need, and breathe out those ideas that do not fit within yourself.
>
> For as your fingers slowly touch each other, you can sense the warmth and let that warmth penetrate into you deeper and deeper.

Developing a Strategy for Quick Trance

By giving yourself the gift of trance you provide yourself with a resource for personal empowerment and management of your own states. Taking the time to learn these trance induction skills will enable you to develop a much deeper rapport with yourself and your unconscious mind. It will enable you to become more congruent with yourself, since, after all, your unconscious mind runs your body and generates all of your behaviors.

Further, we need to avoid the trap of thinking of trance as some kind of hocus-pocus. In NLP we use the term 'trance' to refer to a heightened state of consciousness. This happens whenever someone becomes highly focused, and it can occur whether they have their eyes open or shut. In this heightened state we find that we actually have more control over ourselves than usual, and as a result we can also create more resources for taking more charge of ourselves and our life. This gives us more choice, not less. →●

NLP has numerous strategies for going into trance. And because of our individual differences, we need alternative ways of doing it. If you elicit the strategy of someone who can already go into trance quickly and effectively, then that will offer you some new possibilities to try for yourself. If you know a lot of 'trancy' people, then think of all the quick trance strategies you could gather from them.

One person I knew who had an effective trance strategy would always begin with visual external (V^e). She would defocus her eyes and look to her upper right (where she made constructed images). As she did that she would shift her breathing (kinesthetic external), and with that movement her body would relax. This would then release any muscle tension in her body and simultaneously begin to turn her head in a clockwise motion ever so gently. And the more her head would turn, the more she would go deeply into trance.

This would continue for several minutes during which time she would utilize some auditory-digital words and sentences (A_d). She would make statements that would essentially give herself permission to go into trance and to enjoy the process. With positive statements and affirmations of the value of trance itself, she would then use those words to relax as her head continued to move clockwise.

Eventually, she would begin to create internal visual representations ($V^{i,c}$) of things that she wanted to see and focus on. This would depend on the content of the given trance. In her positive and resourceful trances, the visual images would increase to a point of threshold. Her pictures would become very large and at a distance. Then, kinesthetically, she would have the sense of zooming right into the pictures and getting into them as they simultaneously became even larger.

Then suddenly, from the position and sense of being within the images, everything would begin to become broken, strange, weird, slow, and so on, in an Alice-in-Wonderland kind of a way. It resembled a lucid dream, except that she felt a more personal control over it than she typically did with her dreams. The images would then become increasingly defocused as they became surreal and coded in soft pastel colors.

After that, the images would come closer to her, becoming larger in size, macro-zooming at her, coming all the way up to her face. And with this she would begin to feel the images with her skin because they had become so large and bigger than life. This created a V-K synesthesia for her.

At the same time, she would access some kinesthetic internal sensations by feeling warmth and heat in her body, and her breathing would shift to become much higher and faster. The sense of heat would then begin to swish to all of her body, inside. This was the heart of her trance. She might stay there for just moments, or for an hour.

When she felt ready to leave the trance state, she would experience a fluttering of her eyelids as if closing the cycle or recycling her thoughts. And then her head would begin to move in a counter-clockwise direction as though she was going through a process of rewinding.

How did that feel? Surely, you tried this strategy of trance as you read it, did you not? Now for some practice in the wild and woolly art of hypnosis. The following exercises describe ways to elicit, unpack, install, and 'steal' various deep trance strategies from others.

Trance Exercise 1

1) Choose someone in your group who goes into the most exquisite and pleasurable trance state (person A). B begins by eliciting A's state, "And as you access this trance state, no matter how deep you go, you will always have the ability to hear the sound of my voice." B can then begin the process by asking, "How do you go into trance?" Calibrate to A's physiology.

2) Observe A in trance. B then instructs A to come back out of trance and inquires, "What goes on inside as you go into trance?"

3) As B elicits A's strategy, take notes of the submodalities involved in the experience. This will enable you to amplify the submodalities as you elicit them.

4) Afterwards, test by eliciting the strategy step by step using the same sequence and submodality distinctions.

Trance Exercise 2

To add a little more refinement, the following exercise allows you to practice doing a double induction elicitation. Practice utilizing deep trance to access various hypnotic phenomena.

1) Find out about A's hemispherical organization. Ask questions that elicit his/her auditory construct representations.

2) B and C then lift A's arms up at the same time, with A's right index finger and arm outstretched and left hand cupped (left palm facing up). They then gently lower the arms and position the left hand with index finger pointed and right hand cupped. They raise the arms, then lower them, and raise them a third time with both hands cupped. They release the arms and tell A to "allow your arms to go down only as fast as your unconscious mind allows you to go into an exquisite, deep trance...."

3) B and C then begin a double induction on A for cerebral overload (tempo-counterpoint). B speaks on A's right side saying nursery rhymes, using rhythm and melody with voice, pacing A's breathing. B leads A into pleasant memories of past experiences, and pleasing songs. C speaks on B's left side, using a complex syntactic form, giving specific instructions (such as using a Time-Lining to lead A into a complete age regression). C should have A try each one of the varieties of hypnotic phenomena. Check which ones A can do.

Enhancing One's Skill with Hypnosis

People have many different beliefs about what it means to experience hypnosis. Yet many of these beliefs are myths or misleading ideas which either completely fail to present the case accurately, or at least do not assist us in any useful way. For instance, some people think that in hypnosis you cannot hear in your mind. Others think such nonsense as, "You make your mind blank when you do hypnosis." "Hypnosis is just hocus-pocus." Of course, none of this is true.

In fact, when we experience this wonderful state of hypnosis, we develop a limited focus of attention that turns inward. Furthermore, in hypnosis we become so emotionally absorbed that we begin to adopt an uncritical and therefore very receptive mind. This explains why we find the hypnotic state one of high suggestibility and receptivity. Sometimes such an altered state arises because we may begin to use a representational system that we do not usually use, and we may become aware of ideas outside of our normal thinking. Typically in a state of hypnosis we begin to use the unconscious part of our mind to accomplish deep trance phenomena.

Hypnosis operates primarily as an unconscious process. In some ways it resembles sleep (the Greek word for sleep is 'hypnos'), although if we are aware of sleeping, then we have not developed a very deep state of sleep.

So what do you think about hypnosis? What frame of reference do you have for this phenomenon? Do you consider yourself good at or skilled in hypnotic states? For some of us, we will need to do a belief change with some of our limiting ideas about hypnosis before we can develop skill and expertise with it. We will have to utterly turn around such ideas as "I don't believe I can go into trance." ●→

To achieve this we need to do a belief change pattern and install another idea. "I can go into a profoundly altered state in which I can access more and more of my unconscious resources. In fact, I believe I can go into a deeper trance than I have ever gone into before."

Trance Exercise 3

One method that I like to use for dealing with these kinds of possible limitations is Rapid Hypnotic Induction. The rapidity of this method, like the speed in other NLP techniques such as the phobia cure and the swish pattern, makes this procedure very impactful. Here the rapidity does not give time for the old negative programs to rise and block it.

If you want to practice this in small groups, it is important to practice acting and responding with speed. In other words, do this quickly! This means that you must eliminate any small talk and take action in the group as soon as you get there. So get into the group and go for it… now! Quickly overload your subject's conscious mind—and feel free to do that in any way you desire. If you get resistance in the process, simply fall back on the old NLP technique of giving them new and different frames. →●

A truly enhancing and supporting belief for you to adopt is: "Hypnosis can happen as quickly as any other emotional state." If you can quickly fly into a rage, or into a state of self-pity, confidence, wonder, or anything else, then you have all the neurological equipment you need to fly into a trance! Add to that belief which says: "If I use hypnosis it can lead to a state of strong receptivity where emotional changes can occur rapidly either for myself or others."

We have several techniques for rapidly inducing an hypnotic state. You could begin by doing something shocking or unpredictable which totally interrupts the person's present state. Actually, we use this process all the time for inducing states of amnesia in people. Quickly touch them on the head or shoulder, give them a push that momentarily takes them off balance. Use quick movements when you do this. Or just fire off some trigger that you believe will interrupt all of their actions, such as giving them a push.

The purpose in doing this is simply to create a shock effect. When they receive a sudden shock they go into a confused state where their critical mind goes on hold and their perceiving mind looks for meaning, looks for a program. And of course, this is your cue.

You may have noticed that this process occurs naturally and spontaneously to all of us in everyday life anyway. And when it occurs, do we not spontaneously go into a strong emotional state of confusion? In fact, 'going into a state of confusion is the gateway to new learnings'!

There is another thing to do with this pattern. Once you have provided the initial shock, quickly follow it up by giving the person an idea or a suggestion as to what to do to replace the missing program. Give them the next step in the process instead of the one you just removed. Supplying this next step offers them something solid to grasp while they inwardly sway from the confusion.

Next, create a biofeedback mechanism with the person, using the arm as an external sign for the internal state. This means that the height and movement of the arm gives you a way to gauge the other's ongoing internal experiencing. Offer the person a suggestion such as;

> "As your arm goes down in tiny movements, it will enable you to increase your depth of trance. And it can only go down as slowly as you continue to drop into a trance state."

During this time, make sure that you pace the person's beliefs. Think of resistances as providing you more information about the person's beliefs and understandings, and about what the trance must mean to that person. Then, as you hear the resisting comments, utilize them by incorporating them back into the experience:

> "And as your body jerks a bit it is seeking how to find just the right kind of relaxation that will allow you to relax even more in a way that makes this experience authentic and fully convincing."

Simultaneously, think about getting the person to want to experience a trance. Do this by saying words that validate and establish the importance of going into trance—by adding value to it:

> "And does a resistance to letting another person guide you... to trusting another... assist you in finding those unconscious resources that will enrich your life and facilitate those resources that will make you more...? And you can allow such thoughts to simply exist there, but off to the side... further and further so that you can more fully experience this state."

Trance Exercise 4

The following exercise will allow you to practice amplifying and controlling trance states.

1) B facilitates A in going back to the deep trance state elicited and anchored earlier. As A begins to go into trance, A notices and tells B what s/he is aware of first, for example feeling pressure on chest, or whatever.

2) B now shifts the submodalities of A in order to intensify and amplify the experience, thereby allowing A to experience an even deeper trance. B continues to notice submodality changes as the trance deepens and utilizes them to take the trance even deeper. B should use the trance to effect any deep trance phenomena that A has previously agreed s/he wish to try.

3) B now picks one or two types of hypnotic phenomena in the following list and seeks to generate them with the person once s/he has accessed a fairly deep trance. Hypnotic phenomena that can be played with are as follows:

   anaesthesia (partial and glove), paraesthesia, hypesthesia, synesthesia, amnesia, positive hallucination, negative hallucination, hyper-awareness and selective awareness, deep trance identification, eidetic (total) remembering, eidetic recall, eidetic physical sensing, catatonia, catalepsy (arm catalepsy), time expansion, time contraction, pseudo-orientation in time, pain control, various psychic phenomena, seeing auras, clairvoyance, clairaudience, telepathy.

Utilize this list to see how many you can elicit with your partner.

Time Distortion Elicitation and Installation Exercise 1

1) Begin with B using the hand-shake interrupt on A as a quick trance induction.

2) B should then set one anchor to induce trance state, and another to return to waking consciousness. B sets one finger signal for Yes and one for No with Person A, after firing the trance anchor.

3) B requests A's unconscious mind to first organize time in a way to enable A to enjoy, in full detail, a movie that s/he found enjoyable and do it in exactly two minutes; then give a finger signal when his/her unconscious mind has completed that organization of time. When B gets the finger signal from A, s/he should say, "Begin the movie, now."

4) After A breaks state, A identifies a simulation they would like to run (for example, presenting a speech, practicing an instrument), while B fires the trance anchor and instructs A to run the simulation with the same time distortion utilized in watching the movie. When B sees A's completion signal, B fires off the waking anchor.

Time Distortion Elicitation and Installation Exercise 2

1) B chooses to use either the soft touch (on shoulder, forehead), the shock touch (unconventional pattern interrupt), or the biofeedback induction (behavior of arm moving down as a biofeedback for internal state) for trance induction.

2) B sets anchors for relaxation, deep trance, and fully alert state. B should lead A first, by talking rapidly and giving many different directions about going into a deep state of relaxation. B continues to lead A into deeper levels by using sensory overload of touching on different areas of body. B should pace any of A's conscious resistance and build it into the induction, validating any discomfort, and lead into relaxation. After giving the induction for a relaxed learning state, B should fire the waking anchor. Rotate.

Accomplishing Positive Results Through Trance

[The following has been derived from Don Wolfe]

What practical results can you achieve with trance? How can we use this altered state to access resources that would assist us in living more effectively? If you recall the statement in Trance- formations, Richard and John said that they could not find a trance phenomenon that they also could not create in the waking state. The converse also seems true. There is nothing that we do in the waking state that we cannot make even more effective in the trance state.

Let us apply the context of trance to weight loss. The following demonstrates the value of the trance context for creating lasting changes by using trance. Don Wolfe presented this model as an example of the effective changes that he had accomplished in his workshops on weight loss.

Once you have gotten someone (or several people) into a comfortable trance state, you can use the following format as a guide to working with them to lose weight.

1) In trance elicit the person's reasons for eating. While they listen to you in trance, you can generate a whole list of ideas of typical reasons why people eat and why they overeat. Note some of the reasons people engage in 'psychological eating.' They may do so for: comfort, relaxation, nervousness, frustration, anger, to escape, to feel a sense of protection, to reward themselves, to assuage their guilt feelings, to clean the plate as a program left over from childhood, to satisfy their hunger, to take a break, because they see food, because they feel bored, because they smell food, to feel nurtured, to feel loved, and so on. Voicing these ideas using the receptivity of hypnosis provides a context for someone to search for their individual reasons. You might want their unconscious mind to raise their hand, or effect some other ideomotor response, to indicate what stands out as operating as motivating them to eat.

2) Elicit their reasons for maintaining the overweight state. Next offer some suggestions that will help them explore those ideas

and reasons which specifically allow them to continue being in the overweight state. Use the reframing presupposition:

"And you can begin to wonder, really wonder what this behavior seeks to do for you that would add positive value in your life? Does it provide you with protection, humility, a reason for not asserting yourself, a protection from others noticing you, from feeling embarrassed, from fear of taking front stage, of not looking good, of hating exercise discipline, or work, or whatever?"

The reframing presupposition puts the answer in a positive light—something to feel good about, rather than something to feel bad about. It underscores the crucial point that the person just doesn't have enough of the right resources... yet.

3) Explore and amplify the person's motivation to lose excess weight. One problem that we have to deal with in this realm of losing weight, concerns the issue of delayed satisfaction. So explore with the person:

"What would happen if you did delay gratification?"

"What would compel you to delay immediate pleasure so that you can attain a long-term pleasure?"

Now crank up the person's motivation in carrying out those behaviors which are inevitably involved in losing weight, and which simultaneously allow s/he to maintain his/her gains. You need to aim at integrating both negative and positive motivations. What negative and positive values does this person have in regard to losing weight? Once s/he has identified them, use them to bring the person into a state of "I want it really badly... now!" Set it up so that the push-and-pull strategies of the goal of weight loss will balance each other.

4) Raise and support the person's ability to have self-esteem about him or herself. The question with this behavior, as with so many behaviors, is how to start, given the place where the person is currently in his or her thoughts and feelings. Is s/he

wondering, "How do I get the momentum going?" This is of crucial importance.

If a person feels so disgusted with him/herself for his or her history of defeats and humiliations, s/he can probably go into a very powerful and negative trance state called Total Self-Contempt at any moment. This may indeed be one of the critical restraining forces in that person's life. After all, if s/he feels like crap, s/he will act accordingly and will not bother to take care of him/herself. That kind of a state of mind works in an absolutely counter-productive way for weight loss or any other kind of behavior change.

Take care then not to activate such programs. You will find that overloading the person with more self-disgust and hatred will not work, so do not go in that direction. Those are the kinds of disempowering thoughts that got the person to overeat in the first place. Instead induce in him or her a state of self-acceptance. This will involve building up an empowering identity, by having the person develop his or her resources to increase self-esteem. (Remember that the nominalization 'self-esteem' represents a 'hidden' process of 'esteeming by the self.')

5) Identify and future pace the specifics of losing weight. While the person remains in trance, communicate to him or her about some of the specific details involved in losing weight so that s/he can create a vivid representation of it in terms of his or her own life situation:

"This process may focus, for you, on the matter of eating less food, of having smaller helpings, or it may be learning to eat the right foods, or of finding it okay to leave food on the plate, or of eating something truly nutritious rather than junk food, or of eating slowly, to taste and savor the food. And you can see yourself tomorrow and in the weeks to come eating a small portion, putting your cutlery down after every bite, and enjoying it, really enjoying it, as food, tasting it and savoring every bit of it. You can see yourself eating at the right time and at no other times."

Rehearse these basics with the person in trance, making sure that s/he begins to build compelling pictures within his or her mind of the kind of lifestyle that accords with losing weight.

6) Assist the person further to change the qualities of the representations of food so that s/he feels supported in his or her goal of losing weight. For instance, you may want to alter the person's experience of the taste of chocolate, butter, red meat, or whatever gives him or her particular problems. Work on setting up within the person an emotional idea that makes the new program compelling and attractive. Keep swishing his or her mind from the old to the new until the changes become deeply accepted inside and become an intrinsic part of him or her.

   Here you could do a submodality shift with the taste of chocolate so that it becomes an overly sweet taste in the mouth. Then when it goes down the throat it will hurt, or at least not taste good. Replace the sensation with the idea:

   "You now want a glass of fresh water. And you can make this new idea a part of yourself so fully and completely that it can become a new way of orienting yourself in the world when you want to put something in your mouth. You can receive it into yourself."

Conclusion

The trance state represents a powerfully receptive and open state in which you can do new programming. It gives you the opportunity to install into your deepest part of mind various values, suggestions, ideas, and beliefs that you will find empowering for living. In such a state you can install the NLP presuppositions themselves, and the states for being a Master Practitioner of this art. Use trance purposefully and systematically to install such learnings and energies which will enable you to master NLP and enable you to run your own brain at a higher level. Then you can alter your state and go into a state of passion, ferocity, and curiosity, and be able to do that any time you so desire.

Chapter Three

Formatting the Language and State of Trance

[Derived primarily from Richard Bandler]

Once upon a workshop Richard Bandler invited a woman to come on up to the front of a workshop so that he could zap her into a trance and assist her in developing the personal resources she needed to achieve her ideal weight and maintain it. A transcription of that trance induction follows. Because Richard distributed audiotapes of this trance without any explanation, I do not know where it occurred. I do not know when, or even with whom. I only know that it occurred 'once upon a workshop.'

During the Master Practitioner training we received a copy of the audiotape with instructions to transcribe it. The female subject said that she wanted to learn how to lose weight effectively and to keep it off in a balanced way. I have included this verbatim trance induction here because it wonderfully exemplifies the process of building a propulsion system, doing so within the context of a trance, and Bandler's genius in using hypnotic skills.

Instructions

To train your intuitions about the language of hypnosis, take the following text and transpose it, sentence by sentence into a thin column on a sheet of paper (Column I). Then next to it, in Column II, identify the Milton model distinctions that you find in the text. In Column III identify the analog markings (verbal and tonal) (this necessitates having an audio-recording of the text whereby you can then identify the tonal anchors and embedded commands). In Column IV, identify the presuppositions incorporated in the language itself that propel the trance and the dieting state.

I Text	II Milton model	III Analog marking • Tonal • Embedded commands	IV Presuppositions	V Anchors • Words • Conceptual	VI Chain

Figure 3.1: Propulsion system

In Column V, identify the linguistic anchors built into the presentation, words, refrains, and concepts. Then in Column VI, identify the chain of states induced, anchored and tied together which flow throughout this process. Doing this will provide you with some hands-on practice in looking at a propulsion system model.

Transcript of the Tape: The Induction

You—come on down… no need to be nervous. Ha. Ha. Ha. That's the establishing rapport part! Well that's all right; you don't need to breathe anymore. I'll take care of that for you. Come a little closer now, come and get close—within striking distance—and just sit back and relax, and we'll let the rest of you…. For our general purposes here, what I am going to do, is not so much important; and some of you will understand some of it and some of you won't.

Basically, what it boils down to in a nutshell is that everyone who has ever tried to diet in any way realizes that it's hard. And, you know, it's like the people who don't have any problem dieting say it's easy. And, you know, I have friends who can go out and eat everything in Orlando. Right? And they would never gain a pound; and they always say that dieting is easy. I don't know why they diet though; that has always surprised me.

But there is something that a friend of mine figured out, a guy named Don Wolfe, a pretty good hypnotist. He was a student of mine when I actually taught at the university. He has really concentrated on dealing with one thing, namely being able to do weight control in one day, now a waitress told me that. I thought, "You've got the weight off in one day? You can only do that with an axe!" Just axe me any question, and I'll axe you any answer.

Now after all the research which has been done about weight loss and management, what I found most important about this subject of controlling one's weight has to do with controlling one's metabolism. That, to me, is the most important thing.

There is also the matter of understanding four basic principles of what to eat in order to lose weight. Namely, you only eat fresh foods, period. Nothing packaged, nothing canned, nor anything dried. But only eat food which is fresh. And, of course, you eat only a smaller helping of it. Furthermore, you should eat at the right times and you know when those are. Other than that, you can learn how to feel full from eating and exercise some. You don't have to go out and kill yourself about exercise. Just walk a few blocks every day, you know, get up off your duff and move around. Take the stairs instead of the elevator a couples of times a day. And the other thing is to be able to change your metabolism....

Of course, when my friend told me these basic principles, I roared with laughter because they are so simple and are such common sense knowledge. Now some time later, he and I got together and went into the studio because we wanted to make a tape based on the fact that he does a group once a month and bats 80% success with doing weight control in hypnosis, and the amazing thing is that he only sees people once and that is in a group. Now that's a pretty good batting average. And this is what he installs in people.

Now, the only difference in all of this is the difference between telling the conscious mind something and dealing effectively with the automated programs that run the metabolism of the body. Don says it is one thing to say, "Only eat fresh food," but then you walk by a candy counter and your brain goes *bbrrrhhhrr!* Here the conscious mind knows one thing, but your unconscious mind has an entirely different response. Well, we need to change this.

Because the problem is that all your unconscious processes have automated the compulsion to eat other things—so that when that box of Godiva chocolates calls out to you, "What is your first name?" Millie. The box of Godiva chocolates calls out to you ever so seductively. "Millie, you buy a box! You will only eat one… at a time… after each other." And when you walk through the house and the refrigerator calls out and goes, "Millie, there's something in here, and it's just for you. It will make you feel better." Now when I go home, my microwave talks to me. I'm not too schizee. I'm fascinated.... I'll cook anything in the microwave, I put towels, oranges, I'm just fascinated that it goes rrrinnnngggg and it's hot.

I can't get over these things. How many of you have a microwave in your kitchen? I'll stick anything in that box. I don't care what it is, especially if it says, do *not* put aluminum foil in it. And what's the first thing that Richard puts in it? And talk about a light show! I got one microwave just to put aluminum in it. The one built into the apartment I rented. Beautiful light show! You turn all the lights out, throw a TV dinner in, leave the foil on top, and you get a light show and dinner!

Of course the microwave doesn't last long. But then I bring it back in and go, "It's broken—under warranty. Haaa Haa Haaa! Fools that you are giving me something under warranty!" Because you see, I'm afraid it'll break after warranty, so I make sure that it breaks under warranty.

It's like that guarantee thing you get when you rent a car. When you go to rent a car, they have you take out insurance on the car; then of course you get to wreck the car... for free. Do any of you have kids to teach to drive? Well, don't use your own car, man. Just give them one of those rentals; let them take one of them out and have them demolish the thing.

I mean, I think that's one of the best deals. It used to be six bucks — they upped it to ten. But for six bucks you can go out and wreck a car, you know. I mean, you know, I think... that these ace people....

"You mean, if I buy insurance and if I wreck the car I don't pay anything? If I pay six bucks, I don't have to pay anything if I damage the car?" And they would go, "Yeah!" So I used to take them out, and just smack into poles and things. I'd bring them back in, there'd be nothing left but the chassis and doors hanging, and they'd go, "What happened?" And I'd say, "I don't know, I parked by the Seven-Eleven over there. And when I came out, it was like this."

Now, the point is about realizing what is going on because, you see, the car rental people don't think of it that way. But if you realize that it is a licence to do what you want, then the thing that they're counting on is that you have automated processes that go, "Don't wreck this car!" Right. It's not in your nature to get into the car, and say, "I'm going to wreck this car." Except every once in a while. ●→●

But you have automated processes that tell you to do things like not eat and follow those principles. Those four principles are not new to you, are they? You eat fresh food, you eat at regular intervals, you exercise a little bit and you eat stuff that is good for you, and you don't eat too much of it. You don't have to be a rocket scientist to know that. You have to be a rocket scientist to do it. Right! Because rocket scientists have no conscious mind. (You can't laugh, you have to leave the room, or you have to go into trance too.)

Now, what we're going to do is to have a little talk with your unconscious. Because, see, your unconscious knows how to control compulsions. Because you know what weight you would like to be, right? Okay. →●

Can you make a picture in your mind of where you would like to be? Clear, focused, rich image. Now what I want you to do is to keep looking at that. I'll tell you when to open your eyes. You'll know. You'll have no doubt. You will not need an interpreter. And don't be nervous. Be terrified… of not getting what you want. ●→

Because if you don't learn to control your own life, and your own happiness, it's not just about whether you lose ten pounds or gain ten pounds. It's about at any moment in time changing your ability to make a decision and to stick to it. →●

Because if you quit smoking and gain weight, and then you start dieting, and you smoke, you are playing ping-pong with your life. Now if you want to smoke, smoke; if you want to eat and be fat, eat and be fat. But if you don't want to, you shouldn't have to, as soon as you learn to control the unconscious portions of your mind. ●→

Because the behaviors that you learned, you learned only because you were born, and grew up. If you weren't born and didn't grow up, you wouldn't have problems. But since you did you learned to do things. Everything from walking and talking, and speech and language, learning to make clear images in your mind, learning to read and write, learning to do a whole cluster of things, and some of them are so automatic. They're as automatic as a hand-shake. When somebody walks up and extends their hand to you, your hand lifts up like this to shake their hand. And it doesn't take any knowledge and understanding to do it because your unconscious mind knows how to do it in such a way that learning stays with you for the rest of your life.

Now, what I want you to do is to begin a new learning, a new understanding such that at the unconscious level, you can begin to make changes that will last and satisfy you and delight you. I want your conscious mind now to begin to run memories of times and places where you have eaten right, and dealt with food in an intelligent and a productive manner. And keep those images, bits and pieces of past times where you had a learning that hadn't stayed with you yet, in just the way you want it. And allow me to speak privately with the parts of you that understand only the things that count.

"Because what I want your unconscious to do is to allow this hand to slowly go down, only at the rate that your other hand begins to lift up, involuntarily. That's right. Very slowly now and unconsciously. And no faster than your unconscious begins to make shifts that will stay with you for the rest of your life. And slowly begin to take that furnace inside you and turn up the temperature, and turn up the burning sensation of digestion and food in such a way that while your health remains perfect, in fact, while you get healthier, you begin to dissipate unwanted fat.

Because your unconscious knows how to set a weight in the middle that you can float up a little bit, and way down from, and it's just set it somewhere that's not satisfactory to you.

It's now time to turn back through the pages of time, and let your unconscious readjust the compulsions that are inside you, such that when you look at food that you know is not the best food for you to eat, your unconscious is going to say, Not today! So when you start to eat at a time that you know is not the right time, your unconscious will send a message to you that will make you feel in your whole self, "Not now". So that, instead of your world revolving around the struggle with food, it begins to become more comfortable for you to make the decisions that are the right decisions that will begin to change your relationship to food in such a way that, as your compulsion to eat the wrong foods diminishes, your pleasure and lust for life will increase as proportionately as your hands are moving now.

I want your left hand slowly to begin to feel attracted to your face—almost as if there is a rubber band between your hand and your nose that can grow stronger and stronger. But I want you to get stuck in the process. I want it to be difficult, if not nearly impossible. And I want you to begin to try in vain to touch your face, while that attraction grows stronger, as strong as the attraction to what it is that you want to learn. →●

I want you to feel that struggle in your arm growing because, as that struggle grows and intensifies, I want your unconscious to make all the necessary adjustments for you at the unconscious level to begin to get exactly what you want: to change the feelings you have about foods, and to change your metabolism in a way that allows you to keep your weight down to where you want it. And as that struggle grows more and more intense, as the attraction grows stronger at the unconscious level, you've been making changes, now, changes that will stay with you for the rest of your life; And as that struggle intensifies, I want your hand to proceed up toward your face at the rate that your unconscious has thoroughly made adjustments to allow you to have the ones that you want and need for yourself, and no faster. That's right! Such that when your hand does touch your face in a moment, then and only then, you will feel an explosion of confidence and vigor spread throughout your entire body. Now. That's right!

And enjoy that feeling and realize that every time you make the right choice you are going to have that feeling and it's going to intensify and intensify, and spread and you're going to enjoy the process. Because each good choice you make is going to feel that wonderful. And it will take all the pleasures in your life and intensify them, tenfold. That's right! There you go.... Enjoying it more. Because your unconscious leads your own life and controls your neurology in such a way to help you make choices. It doesn't have the value to know what choices are good or bad. But it is always more than willing to cooperate.

Now, your unconscious knows just how to spread good feelings; you can do it right now. There it comes. And feel that feeling spread throughout your body and know you'd rather feel good! Now, your unconscious can remember a time when you felt so full you couldn't eat another bite. And I want a memory such as that to fill you right now. So much so that you couldn't think of eating another bite. And I want your unconscious to give you this feeling every time you stop eating.

When you look at a plate of food at the beginning of a meal I want your conscious and your unconscious mind to decide together how much of it you should eat; and at the moment it's eaten that much, I want you to get this feeling of fullness and stop eating and suddenly start feeling good! Because the minute you make a right choice, what happens? That's right!

And that's the power of unconscious learning. People always really learn unconsciously. When you learned the letters of the alphabet, you didn't realize they'd make up a whole domain of reading and writing that would stay with you forever; you didn't realize how many ways you would use it.

But these are the building blocks of having the choice that you want. Knowing how to feel full and knowing what happens if you make the right choice, now. Your unconscious is learning a lot. That's right! And it's showing you and convincing you how powerful that learning is.

So I want you to let your hand move away from your mouth for a change. That's right! →●

And that feels awfully good, doesn't it? Because each time your hand doesn't go to your mouth and you make that choice, you're going to get that good feeling. That's right! You don't need to smoke it and you don't need to swallow it—you just need to enjoy it. It's Richard's hedonistic way of changing the problem into a pleasant distraction.

And to focus that energy on something which would be more useful. Because I want you to drop now even deeper and deeper into a trance. Let your unconscious be your guide, and float on the waves and you can feel yourself float down a little bit and up a little bit and while you continue to float down, you're learning even more and your unconscious is now making changes, to adjust your metabolic rate to replace the feeling of hunger that was necessary in the past with a smaller amount of hunger only when it is appropriate to you and taking all those extra feelings and turning them into wanton pleasure.

And desire to be more energetic to walk upstairs and exercise in whatever way gives you the greatest pleasure, no matter what comes to mind. That's right! Burning calories at every moment; and while you drift down deeper I want your unconscious to realize it is responsible and to take responsibility for making these changes last and stay with you because the process of taking building blocks and making them into new compulsions, more useful ways of supplementing your behavior, and utilizing them in such a way to build a solid foundation for behaving in a way that satisfies you.

Because I want you, now, to begin to see, off in your own future, tomorrow, a few weeks from now, and I want you to see yourself sticking diligently to your diet, and then failing utterly in five days. And then going back on your diet, and then failing utterly once in two weeks and then going six months into your future and make another mistake.... And then as you look into the future, you will realize the whole time you got thinner and thinner; because, instead of going from one diet to another to another, you'll realize that if you make a mistake, you just go back and continue and you don't give yourself a bad time. You just realize that it didn't feel as good as it was supposed to, so it's not worth doing again.

Instead you go back to what really feels good, and do it a lot more. Now, I want your unconscious to take that new feeling you had before and multiple it by ten just to remind you. And when you see yourself in your mind in the future, going back on your diet I want it to give you that good feeling... now. That's right! There you go! And to realize how good it feels to know that you can make a mistake and enjoy fixing it. There you go! Because the practice of learning doesn't require perfection; only tenacity.

Now what I want your unconscious mind to do now is to slowly begin to involuntarily lift this hand up and to make all the adjustments and all the changes that it needs to make guarantee that there'll be no more waiting around for a solution to this problem.... That's right.... Honest unconscious movement when your unconscious is thoroughly ready to take full responsibility for making sure that these changes are there in the days and the weeks ahead so that every right choice feels intense pleasure and every mistake seems inconsequential and does not get dwelt upon.

Then, and only then, will your hand be once again touching your face, but this time it will be empty, and ready to feel good in a new way. Now I want you to take your time so that your unconscious thoroughly does this with completeness and intensity... so that, any time in the future, if it begins to become a problem... you just simply sit down in a chair and remember how to touch your face in just this way.... That's right!.... There you go! And feel good.

Now very slowly, at your own rate, I want you to realize if I touch you like this you can go right back into a trance any time you need to and, of course, you know what this means.... That's right!... And remember it and use it wisely. Now. Take a few moments at your own rate, and I want you to slowly float out of the trance, so that I can speak to the rest of you, take your own time. There's no hurry, and feel yourself come up, alert, refreshed and ready for lust, life.

How do you feel? Good. I'm hungry now. How about you? Well, life's like that. You just get your way and there is nothing you can do about it. What do you all look so bleary eyed for?

Conclusion

Because this trance induction exemplifies the process of building a propulsion system within the context of a trance, the more you use it to learn the Meta-Model and Milton model distinctions, and how they come together as here, the more it provides a way for training your intuitions as a Master Practitioner.

Part Two

Linguistics

Chapter Four

Mastering NLP Linguistics (the Meta-Model)

[This chapter was derived mostly from the presentations given by Eric Robbie, along with some from Richard Bandler (Belief Change) and Chris Hall (Linguistic Markers.) It also contains many of my own ideas.]

NLP began with language distinctions. Richard Bandler and John Grinder got together in the first place because Richard discovered he could produce the Gestalt language patterns of Fritz Perls from hearing Fritz on audiotape and from reading a book about the subject. Although he could imitate or model the patterns, he did not know *how* he did it. Later, when he ran the recording equipment during a weekend seminar held by Virginia Satir, he quickly recognized that she had used seven patterns, mentioned this to her, surprised her, and then demonstrated them.

As a mathematics and computer science student, Richard believed there had to be some kind of structure to this modeling skill. He had already become highly attuned to structure and patterns during his studies in computer programming, and from his passion and skill as a musician. To discover how these linguistic patterns worked, he turned to his professor, John Grinder, who had already made contributions to the field of Transformational Grammar.

In this way NLP came into being—given birth in the womb of language (linguistic patterns)—starting with their creation of 'a Meta-Model of language in therapy.' In fact, they entitled their seminal work which began NLP, *The Structure of Magic, Volume I.* Richard apparently wrote it (or had John write it for him) and then submitted it as his thesis for his master's degree. About the same time they produced *The Structure of Magic, Volume II,* as they began to turn their attention to the hypnotic language patterns of Dr Milton Erickson.

I do not exaggerate when I say that language is at the very heart of NLP—in linguistic distinctions and patterns, and in the Meta-Model. Therefore it makes sense that in order to truly master NLP one must thoroughly master the Meta-Model. One must know it to such an extent that its distinctions become one's very own perceptual filters. Accordingly, let me now ask, "Just how conversant are you with that model?" What happens when you are asked: "Identify the twelve linguistic distinctions in the Meta-Model"?

Let the Linguistic Games Begin!

On Day Two of the Master Practitioner Training, Richard, Eric, and some other trainers showed up wearing coaches' shirts and brandishing whistles. They divided the participants into four groups, who then invented names for the groups such as The Meta-Monsters, Transformational Derivatives, The Towering Generalizations, and The Formidable Distortions (or some such names). After that, the groups began to prepare themselves for The Games. This involved each group huddling in one of the four corners of the ballroom at the Holiday Inn.

Then, when the starting whistle blew, the first four designated players, one from each group, would run to the middle of the ballroom and gather under the great chandelier. A coach/trainer would then call out an ill-formed sentence. The first one of the four people at the centre of the room who thought they knew the largest level Meta-Model violation would yell that they would take the challenge. Immediately one of the trainers asked that person to identify the violation, and to offer a Meta-Model challenge to that violation.

Now would you learn the Meta-Model if you played that game? A few hours later, after the end of those Games, I noticed that another game had begun. Self-initiated, too! I saw that not a few participants were making a beeline for the NLP book table. I saw credit cards and fist-fulls of cash being laid down to purchase copies of *The Structure of Magic*. What was happening?

As I explored this phenomenon (you've got to have a bit of nosiness to do NLP), I discovered that many had taken an NLP

Practitioner training but had actually received no training whatsoever in the Meta-Model. A few others admitted that their trainer did try to teach the Meta-Model, but they "just didn't get much out of it." But now they suddenly had a great deal of motivation and passion to use it, because they now had a reason for learning it. Never again would they sally out to a joust with an ill-formed statement in English and not have their lance ready!

The Meta-Model

A Modeling Tool Par Excellence

[Derived primarily from Eric Robbie]

Let us begin by considering the presuppositions inherent in the language when people use mind-reading statements. These distinctions (presuppositions and mind-reading) are two very powerful and important Meta-Model distinctions.

You can think of it this way. Before NLP we lived in a world where people freely projected their hallucinations. Everywhere you went you could find people presenting their hallucinations, pure and simple, and it seemed that they did not even know they were doing it. People simply hallucinated and projected their ideas, beliefs, interpretations, and evaluations of reality onto the environment, other people, and circumstances. Then they would go their merry way, completely unaware of what they had done. Furthermore, many of them absolutely and totally believed in their hallucinations and could not conceive of them as being anything other than reality. They doctored these hallucinations up by calling them 'beliefs.'

Then along came NLP. And with the NLP Practitioner level there arose a linguistic understanding that began to open up awareness of how language actually works. At this level of using the Meta-Model, people began to recognize the difference between their 'maps of reality' and the 'territory.' They began to recognize that there also exists a distinction between the descriptive level of language (sensory based language) and the evaluative level that Korzybski called 'higher levels of abstraction' (*Science & Sanity*, 1933).

Suddenly NLP Practitioners had the ability to hear mind-reading and presuppositional statements in everyday conversations. It seemed like a magic spell for them. They even began noticing these distinctions in their own talk. And since they knew that the surface sentence statements they heard from others were only the tip of the iceberg of the deeper structure, they went about seeking to elicit from others more of the deep structure. By meta-modeling them, they put such speakers back with the experience from which they had made their mental maps. Of course, many times they would often forget to run that pattern when they actually conversed with others. (Put the palm of your hand to your forehead and say, "I could have meta-modeled that!")

So what happens to a person who has moved to the Master Practitioner level in terms of understanding and using the Meta-Model? How do they experience life differently at this stage of development? How does a Master Practitioner differ from a Practitioner?

Before NLP Pre-Practitioner:	**NLP Beginnings Practitioner:**	**Master NLP Level Master Practitioner:**
Hallucination "Yeah, I know what you mean."	Sensory specific "Specifically what?" "Specifically when?" "Specifically who?" "Specifically where?" "Specifically which?" "Specifically ..."	Mind-reading on purpose! Specificity/Precision
	Challenging Mind-reading	Hypnotically communicating empowering means
My Map Interior	Your Map Exterior	Shared Map Synergistically co-created map ●→●

Figure 4.1: Moving to the Master Practitioner Level

By way of answering that, let us begin by considering a question that takes us from the ordinary response of challenging a mind-reading statement to a Meta-level, namely:

> "Under what conditions would you consider mind-reading to be a very useful violation?"

Think about that for a moment. The basic Meta-Model suggests that we will not typically find mind-reading very useful, but rather that we will find it an ill-formed and therefore not productive pattern in communicating. Do you agree with that assessment, or do you consider that the Meta-Model does not suggest that? What precisely does the Meta-Model say about the usefulness of mind-reading statements?

When you have little sensory awareness of a given person or a particular context, if you have not yet done your sensory acuity work, then any mind-reading you attempt with that person will probably fall flat on its face. As it should. Do that kind of mind-reading, and it will not work, as this is an uncontextualized mind-reading and sure to miss its target.

So when does mind-reading become useful? Only after you have used your sensory awareness and sensory acuity. Then you can develop the awareness that offering mind-reading statements may accurately and usefully serve you. Then you can pace someone by your mind-reading.

The basis of master level hallucination, then, is in using your own map to determine someone else's thoughts or emotions. To avoid the trap (and ineffectiveness) of merely projecting your own map onto others you will need a meta-awareness. Mind-Reading can be useful only if your map includes your own awareness that your map is filtering their map. (Did you catch all of that?) Then you can use that awareness to offer accurate insights for the other person and to invite him or her to create enhancing new maps by means of your communication.

The process whereby everyone creates his/her model of the world works this way: First, we have some raw experience. Then, out of that raw experience, we map out (or abstract) our understandings, conclusions, learnings, beliefs, values, decisions, and so on, about the world. Other people create their maps in the same way.

Our individual maps are based on the 'real world'—the territory that exists beyond our skins and sense receptors that provide us with awareness of that territory. And yet that territory never is contained in or by our maps. Korzybski put it succinctly, "The map is not the territory." The map does not exist on the same logical level as the territory and so can never be identical to it. How in the world then can these people ever communicate anything in common? Their individual realities inevitably and always differ. So how can they relate? How can they connect? How can one truly know what another person's internal experience feels like?

The answer to these questions lies in the redundancy in our mapping and in how we communicate our mapping. After all, each person has also conducted his/her modeling (map-making) in a similar context, using the same kind of material the current materials of the language at hand (in our case English), and the same basic kind of nervous system (neurology). Also, each person has used the same modeling processes (deletion, generalization, and distortion). And at the meta-level, these same unifying processes operate. Hence we have a model of the modeling.

Furthermore, once a Practitioner knows the Meta-Model and how language reflects any given person's model of reality, knowing that model enables him or her to 'know' or 'read' (to use that metaphor) another person's 'reality.' The Meta-Model thus provides a kind of window or process by which an NLP Master Practitioner can engage in effective mind-reading. This means that when we use this model systematically and methodically, it drops into our subconscious and can inform our intuition so that we have a much more accurate way of entering into another reality and hallucinating it with some precision. This apparently describes the skills and intuitions of those three therapeutic wizards that first captured Bandler and Grinder's attention.

The 'meta' in Meta-Model means that we are moving to the model of the model, to exploring the actual process of modeling. Using the Meta-Model, while simultaneously ensuring we have plenty of sensory specific awareness, enables us to stay out of our own map while we gain accurate, useful, and precise information about the other person's model of the world.

As you do this as a Master Practitioner, take special care lest you become overly caught up in the auditory-digital channel. Auditory-digital language is a vital part of NLP, but only a part. There are also non-verbal aspects of communication. Do not take this as an either/or case, but rather consider it as a both/and situation. If we become overly dependent upon the auditory-digital dimension, we could begin to live in a world of words and miss experience. If we do that, we will necessarily miss a great deal that other people offer us. Similarly, if we live in a world of gestures, sighs, signs, movements, etc., we could miss all of the information conveyed by their words. We need both channels.

The Meta-Model

Within the Meta-Model we have understandings, distinctions, and challenges with regard to ill-formed surface statements. By detecting these—knowing what they mean and how to respond to them—our questions or meta-modeling can take us to the more useful deep-structure statements of that other person. It further helps us to get back to the experience out of which s/he created his or her maps.

A's model of the world	B's model of the world	C's model of the world
Linguistics Abstractions Sensory awareness	Linguistics Abstractions Sensory awareness	Linguistics Abstractions Sensory awareness
The territory of the world – experience in the world		

Figure 4.2: Going Meta to the Mental Mapping Process

After we develop competence with the Meta-Model, it then becomes unconscious, so that we no longer have to keep it in mind. It becomes part of our intuitive knowledge. Our mind-reading of others will then make our Master Practitioner work possible, enjoyable, streamlined, and highly practical. This is a key level of skill for everyone at Master Practitioner level.

Remember, here we have a kind of mind-reading based on a vast amount of sensory awareness, elegance with language patterns and distinctions, and experience with understanding and utilizing how the Meta-Model distinctions, such as presuppositions, actually work in the human map-making and modeling process.

Masterfully Focusing on Presuppositions

By definition, a presupposition in language consists of 'what comes before that which holds up statements, understandings, or beliefs.' A presupposition, thus consists of all those essentials required for a statement to make sense in someone's reality. It refers to what has to exist for the sentence to make sense to the speaker.

Now take a moment to consider:

- Just how is this distinction important for us?
- What can we do with this understanding?
- What value would this have in conversation?

If you wish to find what is presupposed in the world around you, begin by explicitly using the semantic environment form: "There is..." and "It is possible that...." Use these semantic forms in every sentence that someone offers you. By doing so you can ferret out the presuppositions (or assumptions) lying within or behind those statements. This will also train your language intuitions about the connotative level of language.

Practicing Presuppositional Awareness

The following exercise is further practice in developing your skill at mind-reading.

1) Make a list of statements that you use regularly, or that you hear others use.

2) Now generate a list of possibilities as to what has to exist for those statements to be true or be true for someone. This means imagining what has to exist in that person's mental world. Generate as many kinds of possibilities as you can.

3) Let your imagination go wild and allow yourself to make up all manner of possibilities about what might exist, or must exist, in the conceptual world of the other person's mind. Let yourself be really creative, especially if you do not have the foggiest clue about the other's mental world.

4) Now begin to test those possibilities with the 'left hemisphere of your brain.' Run a reality check on your imaginative alternatives to make sure you did not just make them up out of nothing. Check it out.

5) Finally, ask the other person to collaborate on your guesses. In doing this, remember that you will get better at mind-reading when you have tested your intuitions many times. Both of your accurate guesses and wild misses will provide valuable feedback, helping you to develop your skill at 'getting out of your own map' and accurately tracking the other person's reality. →●

Here are two group exercises for three or four people.

Group Mind-Reading Practice 1

For a group experience in practicing to identify presuppositions.

1) A generates a simple sentence. The other people practice identifying the presuppositions in the sentence. "What has to exist for the statement to exist meaningfully?"

2) Change roles when you have exhausted all of the presuppositions in their statements.

Group Mind-Reading Practice 2

This exercise is for practicing eliciting two different kinds of presuppositions: the presuppositions of language and the presuppositions of experience.

1) A describes a piece of excellence from his or her personal experience: something s/he enjoys doing, has developed proficiency at doing, and feels strongly attracted toward.

2) B and C backtrack A to the beginning of that experience, to his or her 'moment of inspiration' when the thought of that experience first arose in consciousness. B and C should keep

asking A, "What had to exist for you at that moment in order for you to feel and judge this experience as wonderful? What else had to exist to judge it as that?"

3) B and C now back A up to the presupposed experiences and language descriptions within that experience of excellence, and should not be satisfied until they have enough information to fully understand how it worked.

4) D should pay attention to the presuppositions that showed up in A's language. For instance, "What has to exist in order for A to say that sentence?"

5) Conclude with everyone comparing impressions of A's experience.

Presupposed	Beginning of	Language	Piece of	Moment of experience	an Idea
Linguistic	Excellence or thought	Inspiration Distinctions			
The skill/ aptitude	Memory of first interest	Meta-model Meta-programs	The event	First ideas and dreams	

Figure 4.3: Backtracking to an experience of excellence

There are two kinds of mind-reading at Practitioner level. The first kind is catching people offering mind-reading statements and using the Meta-Model to challenge them: "How do you know that?" When you use the Meta-Model challenges in this way, you are seeking to identify the person's source of information: "What lets you know that?"

The second kind of mind-reading is offering mind-reading statements quite intentionally. You do this when you seek to induce in someone a state of trance and, when doing this, you have shifted to using the Milton model, the 'reverse' Meta-Model.

Now a third kind of mind-reading also exists. We could call this 'creative mind-reading.' This truly reflects working at Master Practitioner level. It enables us to develop our intuitions about what has to exist in other people's models of the world (linguistically, conceptually, and neurologically) and to state those presuppositions to them. And when we do that, magic occurs. They feel absolutely understood, paced, and validated. We know their reality.

Imagining how this might prove exceptionally useful, would you like to fine hone this skill? →●

Getting Beyond Barking Meta-Model Challenges (Ruff! Ruff!)

What is a central skill for everyone interested in mastering NLP? It is the ability to question.

- How good are you at asking questions?
- How well do you direct your mind and state toward new and wondrous possibilities that no one has yet explored?
- How much curiosity do you bring to the people, events and situations of your life?
- How many new questions have you planted in your consciousness today?
- What other things do you evaluate as worth knowing?

Questions can function like a knife into consciousness. The questions we use can often cut right through someone's reality (model of the world) and gather the highest quality information about his or her maps, psychological organization, presuppositions, hallucinations, evaluations, beliefs, values, and so on. Knowing how to gather such information helps us in facilitating the transformations that we seek for ourselves.

We can also use questions to cut through the chaos of the world and divide it into more manageable amounts. We can chisel information down into the chunk sizes (big and little) that prevent us from becoming or feeling overwhelmed, in order that we can mentally contain and handle the phenomena before us. The value of such questioning when conversing with a client or customer enables us to cut out much unnecessary data.

Furthermore, the questions we use with people arise from our purposes, i.e. our 'reality' will inevitable manifest itself to those 'who have ears to hear.' This is due to the fact that, along with our questions, come presuppositions and other structures. These presuppositions drive our language and our experience.

Bandler asked the following question in one of his Master Practitioner trainings. "Suppose," he said, "someone shows up in your living room and says to you, 'I'm depressed…' What do you say to that?" If you know the Meta-Model challenge, then you might reply with, "About what?" "How do you know specifically that you are depressed?" "How specifically do you do that?" Do you know what a barking dog sounds like? As you imagine a dog barking, imagine an NLP Practitioner barking those Meta-Model responses: "About what?" "How do you know specifically?" Hear it with a 'woofing' effect. (That is as close as I can get in a written form to representing the tone of voice that Richard used in talking about 'barking back Meta-Model responses'.) ●→

In responding like this, Richard set up a tonal anchor for the words "About what?" "Ruff, ruff!" By barking it out in a manner similar to a dog barking rapidly, he gave a strong impression that to use the Meta-Model in this Pavlovian way (pun intended) does *not* represent his idea of elegance with this language model. He commented that people who always come back with that challenge behave "like a dog barking off the Meta-Model challenges: Ruff, ruff! About what?" ●→

I think (*my* mind-reading) that Richard was saying that to move beyond the NLP Practitioner level of using the Meta-Model and to actually think like a true Master Practitioner, we need to increase our questioning skills and powers, and to learn to even question the questioning, to question the meta-frame, etc. Consider, "Do I even require this small piece of information at this point from this person? On many occasions (perhaps most of the time), we do not.

Master Practitioner questioning involves asking much more: →●

> What size of information do I go after?
>
> What size of information do I need to do good work with this person?

> What kind of information do I want to gather?
>
> What is the desired outcome I am seeking to achieve?
>
> What kind of state do I wish the person to induce himself or herself into by answering the question?
>
> When that person responds to this question, where will that put him or her in relationship to what s/he wants?

We need to ask these kinds of questions rather than just automatically using one pattern, "Who or what specifically?" Thinking about such questions takes us to a meta-level. The specificity questions in the Meta-Model consist of ones that presuppose we need and want some small chunk size information. Did you know that? Had you ever noticed that? These questions can cause us to get lost in a mass of details if we ask too many of them.

On the other hand, the Meta-Model allows us to examine language from other points of view than by chunking down to specifics. Now without doubt, the specificity patterns in the Meta-Model assist us wonderfully in gaining precise detail for responding to someone giving us a lot of fluff.

As you continue to master this model, you can also respond to the person in your living room who says, "I'm depressed…" by asking for some larger level chunks. You could ask a big chunk question, "What are you doing in my living room? Why did you come here? What do you want?" Do not questions like that help you discover the person's purpose in standing there and talking to you and saying those things? Do you not think that such questions would get you some pretty vital information? I do.

In asking for larger chunks we move up the Meta-Model to the larger level pieces within it. To acquire this sort of information we can ask some 'when' questions (not in the sense of the 'when specifically?' Sometimes this might work, but usually 'when' questions will trigger information from a person about when in time an event occurred and how it started. After all, no experience occurs all the time. Rather, it occurs at certain times. 'When' helps us to identify those times so that we can then generalize about possible patterns regarding the contexts that elicit such behavior.

The Logical Levels of the Meta-Model

As a Master Practitioner, embrace the realization that there are multiple levels of statements. For example, in the surface structure that you hear in a sentence, you will comprehend the actual *content* of the sentence, the subject.

Yet if you explore behind that statement, you will find another level of meaning (designated as 'Deep Structure', or 'D-structure' by Chomsky in Transformational Grammar). Here you will hear the transformation of the person's meaning in terms of a higher level abstraction. Therefore, you can expect to find in it many deletions, generalizations, and distortions. You have now moved to another level, the level of process which concerns the structure of the statement. Such a level may deal with the syntax or arrangement of the statement or what that suggests by connotation (see Figure 4.4).

Deletion: Simple deletions Comparative deletions Unspecified referential index (Unspecified nouns) Unspecified verbs Nominalizations
▼ operates on ▼
Generalization: Universal quantifiers Modal operators Possibility/impossibility: necessity/desire Generalized referential index (Verbs/nouns)
▼ operates on ▼
Distortion: Lost performatives Mind reading Complex equivalences Cause-effect statements
▼ operates on ▼
Presuppositions

Figure 4.4: Operational levels of the Meta-Model
(Shown here in reverse order. See Figure 4.6)

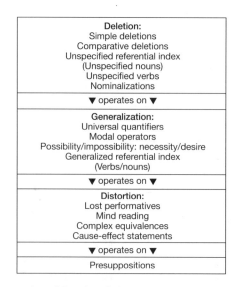

Practicing Meta-Model Questions

The following exercise will assist you to practice training and recoding your intuitions about language. By using it you will discover which Meta-Model patterns provide you with the most information in the shortest time.

1) In groups of three or four people, elicit sentences from each other in turn.

2) Then, by asking Meta-Model questions, determine which modeling category (deletions, generalizations, distortions) provides the most information in response to your questions. When Person A makes a statement, the rest of the group should each ask one question that they think will provide them with the most crucial information. They should seek to Meta-Model A for the larger chunks, not the smaller ones.

3) As a group, examine the statements and questions afterwards asked to become clear about which question elicited the most information.

Recognizing Presuppositions

There is more. Every sentence contains presuppositions beneath or beyond the content and structural levels. These represent very much larger chunk information. In the Meta-Model these larger chunk levels of information occur in the modeling area of 'distortions,' which are the distinctions of mind-reading, cause-effect, complex-equivalence, and presuppositions. Among generalizations the Universal Quantifier and Lost Performatives can carry large amounts of information.

For clarification, I should mention that in NLP we have several different kinds of presuppositions. Briefly we have:

- The Meta-Model presuppositions which refer to those that occur in every sentence in our natural language.

- The introductory 'Presuppositions of NLP', which are those principles or assumed beliefs that govern the epistemology of NLP as a discipline—the actual "Theory" of NLP.
- The 36 syntactic environment presuppositions which offer many different kinds of trigger words which, in turn, allow us to set up presuppositions in sentences. You will find them in the back of *The Structure of Magic II.*

Now the presuppositions of language, which the Meta-Model highlights, provide highly valuable information—if you know how to use them. Tuning your ears to them enables you to hear more than just the words that someone actually uses. You can hear his or her higher frames-of-reference. Thus, learning to hear and identify them in everyday language exchanges truly governs our mastering NLP. →●

Presupposition Training Exercise

For practice in this skill of identifying presuppositions in natural language:

1) Get into a group of three or four people.

2) Let each person in turn generate sentences with presuppositions included from the syntactic environments.

3) Ask each person to systematically go through the sentences and identify all of the presuppositions they can.

For example:

- "I enjoyed running in the park this morning."

What things does the speaker presuppose here? Simple presuppositions include:

> the existence of the person, the emotion of joy, the activity of running, the park as a place, the time-related words 'this morning', and so on.

More profound presuppositions about the person's reality include:

> the person having a set of criteria whereby s/he can judge enjoyment; the person now consciously choosing to exercise because s/he has linked pleasure to that experience (a complex equivalence).

- "The more we practice presuppositions the better we will get."

The simple things presupposed:

> a class of learners, the process of repetition, improvement over time, time moving into the future, etc.

More profound presuppositions:

> 'the more... the more...' pattern, a belief in the cause-effect relationship between increasing one thing and having an increasing effect on something else.

- "Listening to music is enjoyable."

Simple presuppositions:

> the existence of music, people, the process of listening and receiving, the auditory channel, the experience of enjoyment, etc.

Profound presuppositions:

> the person has connected in a cause-effect relation between the external behavior of receiving auditory stimuli and the internal state of enjoyment; the internal criteria that allow for this kind of judgment to be made, etc.

Now explore the presuppositions in the following statements:

- "The one who does this quickest, wins."
- "Never speak first."
- "The idea of mastering NLP and developing its very spirit will enable me to experience a higher level of empowerment than ever before."

Meta-Modeling our Meta-Modeling

Since questions set the direction of our information gathering, this following exercise enables us to learn to handle presuppositions with greater efficiency:

1) With two other people, create a context between you for some language exchanges. Identify some specific content to talk about.

2) As A speaks, B listens for presuppositions in the sentences, and then asks 'cutting questions' which will allow B and C to get to the meat of the statement.

3) C, as the meta-person, should interrupt from time to time and ask the questioner, B,

   "What one piece of information are you going for?"
   "What operational level of the Meta-Model are you using?"

This will help them to identify and become conscious of the difference between crucial and trivial presuppositions.

> "What presupposition do you hear?"
> "How do you plan to inquire about it?"
> "With what question or set of questions?"

In this way, you can even begin to question the presuppositions in your own questions.

Targeting Procrastination

Suppose for example, that someone makes the following statement,

> "I want to stop procrastinating."

What questions in response to that could you ask that will get you the largest chunks of information?

Suppose you challenge the universal quantifier, "Do you *always* procrastinate?" the person may simply say, "No." So how much information did that exchange yield? Suppose you seek to discover the context markers of the statement. So you ask, "*How* do you know *when* to procrastinate?" And the person says, "When I feel frustrated," or "When I feel overwhelmed." Now that might get you a somewhat larger chunk.

But suppose, instead, that you challenge their attribution of meaning, "How do you know you procrastinate?" Ah, that would get you even more information. Or suppose you go for the complex equivalence, "What does procrastinating mean to you?" Or a modal operator: "Do you *have* to procrastinate? Do you have the power to stop it?" "What prevents you stopping?" "Have you ever stopped procrastinating?" Or a cause-effect challenge: "How can I help you to stop procrastinating?"

At the Master Practitioner level, we move to thinking about and working with larger patterns. In the following set of statements you will find the 'scope' of a word and its effect on an entire sentence illustrated. In linguistics, 'scope' refers to the amount of effect a word can have on a syntactic environment. Eric Robbie provided an example using the following sentence:

> *Only* I can tell you the way to do this now.
> I *only* can tell you the way to do this now.
> I can *only* tell you the way to do this now.
> I can tell *only* you the way to do this now.
> I can tell you *only* the way to do this now.
> I can tell you the *only* way to do this now.
> I can tell you the way *only* to do this now.
> I can tell you the way to *only* do this now.
> I can tell you the way to do *only* this now.
> I can tell you the way to do this *only* now.
> I can tell you the way to do this now *only*.

Here we have merely played around varying the position of *only* in the same sentence. Read through each statement slowly, putting the emphasis on the word 'only,' and take your time savoring the effect that has on the meaning of the sentence.

How does the Meta-Model Relate to the Structure of Beliefs?

Once Eric Robbie started off by saying something on the order of the following,

> "I think it is appropriate to say to anyone who is learning to master NLP that 'I don't even want you to think about hesitation without going to **go for it**.' "

What presuppositions did you hear in that sentence? What patterns or levels did you discern in it?

Let us now take another step in furthering our understanding of the Meta-Model and add more depth to this exploration by asking the following questions:

> How does the Meta-Model relate to the structure of a belief?

> "How does a person move from the level of experience (say at the sensory-based level of the 4-tuple) to the level of experience that we call 'belief'?" (Belief actually functions at a meta-level inasmuch as it consists of a filter about experience.)

> "How do we relate sensory-based level experience to the more generalized level of abstractions about experience (beliefs)?"

To answer these questions we need to look again at the Meta-Model in terms of the size of the chunks of information with which it deals. But before we do that, recall the linguistic pieces that comprise the twelve distinctions that we have come to recognize as the Meta-Model. Let us make sure you know them. Close the book, grab a blank sheet of paper, and jot them down. When you have completed that, compare your answers to those in Figure 4.5.

Meta-Modeling Practice

Now let us exercise your intuitions about this model. The following exercise will give you practice creating, recognizing and

The pattern of deletions

1. Deletions: Simple and Comparative (We may also describe Comparative Deletions as Unspecified Words: Unspecified Nouns, Unspecified Verbs)
2. Unspecified Referential Index (Unspecified Nouns)
3. Unspecified Verbs
4. Nominalizations (hidden Verbs as Nouns)

The pattern of generalizations

5. Universal Quantifier (all, nothing, never, none, everyone)
6. Modal Operators (necessity, desire, possibility, impossibility)
7. Generalized Referential Index (labeling, global verbs, nouns, pronouns)

The pattern of distortions

8. Lost Performative (Who in the world came up with this?)
9. Mind Reading (Projecting our hallucinations onto others and then believing our second-guesses as totally accurate!)
10. Complex-Equivalence (A meaning equation, equating an external thing with an internal association, equating things that exist on different logical levels)
11. Cause-Effect Statements (Constructions about causality coded in causation terms and present-tense verbs)

The pattern of presuppositions

12. Presuppositions

Figure 4.5: The patterns of deletions, generalizations, distortions and presuppositions

responding to Meta-Model violations of distortion, and other large level chunks of information:

1) In a group of four or five, Person A generates a sentence that contains multiple Meta-Model violations. For instance, "I'm depressed. I don't think I can go to the movies because once I get there I'll think of all the things I haven't done."

2) In response the other people offer various Meta-Model challenges to the distortions, generalizations, and deletions that they hear within the statement.

One of the greatest things we can learn through such Meta-Modeling of language is the realization that we all need to run regular checks on our own thinking. By doing this, we can learn to identify our own systematic (habitual) Meta-Model violations in the patterns of our own thinking.

The person who does not check out his or her own filters will, inevitably find that s/he cannot see or hear those very patterns in others. We can thus think about the Meta-Model as providing a way to run a 'diagnostic' on the 'software programs' in our head and neurology. It enables us to check for any 'bugs' and 'viruses' (thought viruses) coded in our language as we use our maps to operate in the world. The Meta-Model distinctions and questions provide a basic model or process for improving our critical thinking skills.

Cognitive Effectiveness Exercise

To use the Meta-Model as an effective way of checking your cognitive effectiveness, your critical thinking skills, and using the operational levels in it, do the following:

1) First, send your consciousness to the largest level of structure and meaning within any given statement.

2) From there begin to chunk that information down into smaller pieces. Do this by first dealing with presuppositions; then with the distortion patterns (mind-reading, cause-effect, complex equivalence, lost performative); next with the generalization patterns (universal quantifiers, modal operators, generalized referential index) and finally with the deletion patterns (deletion, unspecified verbs and nouns, nominalizations).

3) As you do this, keep the following principle in mind: the larger levels 'operate' on the smaller levels.

A metaphor for this process may give you a better feel and sense for what this means. Think about the way an airplane *'operates'* on all the passengers it carries: The passengers are contained within a space which is carried by the plane. In the same way, the wind currents 'operate' on, or carry, all of the planes that fly through them thereby affecting their path.

If we let the passengers stand for the linguistic distinction of deletion, the plane for the linguistic distinction of generalizations, the wind for the distinction of distortion, and the turn of the planet for presuppositions, then we can readily recognize just how the larger levels 'carry' the lower levels. In other words, within the larger levels we have a level that carries all of the lower levels (it organizes, governs, and modulates every lower level. (See Hall, *Meta-States*, (1995, 1996) and Bateson (1972) for a fuller description of this.)

In the Meta-Model, the higher level patterns 'transcend and contain' the lower levels. Figures 4.4 and 4.5 present this schematically. Accordingly, at the lower levels we find the smaller chunks. At the lowest level we just have deletions (unspecific nouns, verbs, simple deletions, and so on). As we go up to the higher levels, we have generalisations (universal quantifiers, modal operators, generalized referential index). At the highest levels of this model, we get into more complicated neuroses and discover the place where psychotic behavior primarily occurs: in the distortions (lost performatives, mind-reading, cause-effect, complex equivalence).

Now try training your brain to go first to the larger chunks (presuppositions, distortions), and then to the smaller chunks:

> "Every time Russell returns to our group, I get really nervous when he looks at me with that smirk on his face. I can't believe he keeps doing that when he knows how I feel about it."

What large level chunk would you go for first? What presuppositions first jump out at you here? Would you go for the complex equivalence—the 'smirk on face'—with the creating of some negative feeling? Would you go for the cause-effect presupposition—his smirk causes this bad feeling? Would you go for the mind-reading—he knows he does this and continues to do it anyway?

Notice how those chunks elicit a very different response than if you asked for smaller chunk—"Does this happen every time?" "Has there ever been a time when he did not do this?" Asking about the mind-reading elicits a pretty big chunk—"How do you know that he knows what is going on inside you in response to his smirk?" Think of several questions that go for even larger chunks.

Or again:

> "I hate it when this group chases rabbits all over the place."

The largest pattern among the distortions would be the cause-effect statement, 'chasing rabbits creates (causes) the emotion of hate to arise in speaker'. But an even more important piece of information to elicit would consist of the complex equivalence. 'Chasing rabbits' serves as a metaphor for 'running around in circles', another auditory-digital phrase that serves as a metaphor for 'not getting to the point', which serves as a linguistic metaphor for 'not being direct.' That would be a fairly large piece to go after and it certainly seems to carry a lot of meanings.

> "He is my friend, but he put the presuppositions in the wrong places."

One large chunk here is the complex equivalence that makes friendship equal to agreement. This is one of the presuppositions of the sentence itself: We cannot stay friends without agreement. To disagree would mean or cause (CE) there to be no friend. To Meta-Model the unspecified verb 'put' (where specifically did he put the presuppositions?) would comprise a very tiny chunk, wouldn't it?

> "When someone tells me that they don't want to do something, I know what they mean. So to show myself as a polite person, I stop."

What mind-reading is the person demonstrating here? What cause-effect presuppositions are operating in this statement?

Using Meta-Modeling Skills for Changing Beliefs

[The following is mostly derived from Richard Bandler.]

NLP enables us to understand how we all take the sensory experiences that we have in the world and turn them into the mental abstractions i.e. beliefs, understandings, learnings, decisions, etc. that we create within our nervous system as we move through the world. This is the map-making (modeling) process which we use to create our personal paradigms, or mental constructs.

A meta-pattern in NLP involves taking our abstractions, nominalizations, language patterns, and so on, and tracking them back to the sensory-based experience. To do this, we first track back to the process words that describe various actions and responses, and then to the sensory-based referents from which they came. We call this process (an NLP skill) of identifying, locating, and finding the hidden verbs/processes that someone has nominalized, 'denominalizing the nominalizations.'

When we track back the nominalization 'failure,' you find the unspecified verb, 'to fail.' This allows us to assist a person to index more precisely when, where, how, according to what standard, etc., s/he makes his or her judgments, evaluations, and maps about 'failure.' By rediscovering the original 4-tuple experience, that person can then more effectively abstract again from that experience and create new beliefs that s/he will find enhancing rather than limiting. This process facilitates re-mapping.

This essentially describes the reframing process. When you think about the person who has experienced a lot of what s/he calls 'failure,' and considers 'being a failure,' this represents much more of a challenge than working with someone who has merely 'failed to pass a test,' or who has 'failed to understand someone else's communication.' With specific failings we can engage with the person in problem-solving thinking. But with globalized and overgeneralized nominalizations, we have a much larger semantic problem on our hands! When we are dealing with people at a level of their more abstract models of the world (e.g. 'failure'), they give us a very large semantic reality to handle. And when they do, we can expect to find a whole lot of fluff in their formulations.

So although we can change beliefs with various NLP Belief Change Patterns, why take take them on at a mega-level? Why not first chunk them down, de-nominalize their abstractions, blow out the unnecessary fluff in them, and then deal with them after we have gotten them back closer to the reality from which they came. As an NLP meta-strategy this makes considerable sense, does it not? It also makes the forthcoming transformations much easier as well. NLP offers several procedures with which we can change and alter beliefs. The following is an example of one such process.

A Belief Change Pattern

1) *First, identify a limiting belief.* What do you believe about the world, people, yourself, finances, health, etc. that creates problems for you? What do you believe that limits the way you feel and respond? Think of an event, person, environment, subject, etc. about which you have some negative and limiting emotions.

   Do this very quickly. Identify the very first thing that flashes across your mind when you entertain those thoughts. What other thoughts, judgments, ideas, beliefs, understandings, etc. immediately intrude into your consciousness?

2) *How do you know that you have that belief or those thoughts?* What lets you know that you think such things? Asking this question invites us to become more aware of beliefs, and their component pieces (their modalities and submodalities). Knowing these enables us to explore the submodality distinctions of the beliefs, and thereby identify their structure.

3) *Identify the place where you have stored your strong, limiting, and 'don't care' beliefs.* In this step you will explore the submodality structure of three different kinds of beliefs. Identify the location submodalities of where you put strong beliefs, limiting beliefs, and 'don't care' beliefs. Notice also how you code the representations that make up these thoughts.

   A Strong Belief: Pick something like "I believe the sun will rise tomorrow."

A Limiting Belief: Pick a belief that you don't like and wish you didn't have but which definitely limits you as a person. For example, "People who use a harsh tonality are mean and dangerous." "I can't learn very well." "I'm not a good hypnotic subject."

A Don't Care Belief: Pick out a belief that doesn't matter to you one way or the other. For example, "It really doesn't make any difference which shoe I put on first when I get dressed."

In this exercise we focus primarily on the location submodality of your beliefs. Identify where you put or store each of these kinds of beliefs in your mind. Do you have your strong beliefs in a position 'down right' in front of you? Are your limiting beliefs perhaps to your left, in your past? When we discover the coding that you use, you can then use the configuration within your mind to make an internal shift that will give you more control over yourself and your neurology. As a result you can take an important but limiting belief and put it where you have the don't care beliefs located. Would you like to have that choice?

4) *Next, allow yourself to imagine, fully and vividly, a gigantic slingshot right in front of you.* Into the leather pouch of that slingshot (you see it now, do you not?) put the limiting belief (in just a moment) which you want to go somewhere else. At this point, take care to just notice where that belief will go when you change its location coding. Pay careful attention to where you locate your "I don't care," beliefs in your mind. Okay? You will have had to elicit enough "don't care" beliefs so that you have a strong sense of where you store them. Good. Now, notice that place that defines where you want your limiting belief to end up.

5) *Practice stretching the slingshot pouch.* Now allow yourself to imagine your limiting belief being pulled back, all the way back in that leather pouch, and, as you imagine this, you can feel the rubber-band or elastic material pulling and straining, more and more. You can hear the rubber-band stretching more and more until it reaches its limit. And in just a moment... when we ask you to let this limiting belief go, you will sense it shooting out and flying out from its location of limiting beliefs

and landing in that place where you have your "don't care" beliefs stored which don't bother you at all.

Remember that since your unconscious mind runs your neurology you can trust it completely. Your job, with your conscious mind, is simply one of providing the program of what to do. Your unconscious mind will take care of the feelings. And since your beliefs can severely limit your possibilities, it is a good idea to be aware of what you believe. →●

6) *Let it go… now!* Putting your limiting belief into the pouch of the gigantic slingshot in front of you, you can now let it go. Feel it as it rams into the place of your "don't care" beliefs. Now take a moment to notice just how that old belief settles into there, as you hear a bolt locking tight, which means that the old limiting belief has become locked in there so that it stays stuck there as a "don't care" belief for good.

7) *Now install the new empowering belief.* Undoubtedly, you will have noticed that this belief change technique involves a spatial anchoring process. Because when you have cleared out an old limiting belief, you find yourself feeling much more open to having some new and more empowering belief put in its place. If you know where you store your strong beliefs, then you can go for it right now. You can now install a new belief about your increasing resourcefulness, your ability to access enhancing states, of staying clear-headed and calm, of maintaining a presence of mind, etc. So put the new belief into the strong belief place.

Belief Change Exercise

To make this really useful for yourself, identify three beliefs that you now have, one for each kind of belief:

- A strong belief that you have about yourself or the world, such as "I believe the sun will rise tomorrow."
- A limiting belief about yourself, such as, "I'm a slow learner."
- A belief about something of lesser importance such as, "I believe I will eat at home tonight."

When you do this elicitation, don't rush it. Once you have your three beliefs, pair up with another person.

1) A tells B where s/he has located his or her limiting belief.

2) A then follows B's hand movements and puts the belief in the slingshot position. As B uses words to direct A's experience of pulling back the slingshot, B can also use hand movements to anchor the slamming of that belief into the new position.

3) B then asks A to pull up the new empowering belief s/he wants installed, using hand movements to locate that space for A. Have the new belief move from the ambivalent belief position with a 'whoosh' sound to a 'thwack!' sound (to break through threshold) as B's hand stops in the strong belief position.

B should repeat this pattern three to five times with A, then future pace him or her and test by eliciting only the new empowering belief.

Distinguishing Cause-Effect and Complex Equivalence

We began this exploration with several questions about mind-reading at Master Practitioner level:

> "How can we use mind-reading in an appropriate way?"
>
> "How does mind-reading differ at different stages of development?"
>
> "When and under what circumstances does mind-reading become justified?"

We also looked at the abstracting process and how we create abstractions:

> "How can we move from experience at the level of 4-tuples of sensory experience to our 'beliefs' as abstractions of words and language at a higher logical level?"

These questions crucially focus our mind on modeling and abstracting. It is no wonder that such questions bring us to an exploration of the structure of belief itself. So let me pose some more questions, namely,

> "How do we come to recognize a belief at the non-verbal level?"
>
> "How do we get in rapport with a belief?"
>
> "How do we pace a person in a strong belief state?"

Presuppositions
Covert beliefs, Mental constructs, Assumptions

Distortions
Perceptual filters, Values
Overt beliefs, Meaning constructions about causations, significance, etc.

Generalizations
Conclusions & abstractions about classes, categories, etc.

Deletions
of Details, specifics

Figure 4.6: The operational levels of the Meta-Model

You now know that the precision model part of the Meta-Model, the part that asks the *specificity questions* (i.e. indexes who, how, which, what, in what way, comparatives, etc.), covers only deletion and generalization areas. This means that it gathers only small chunk pieces. The problem lies in that it does not deal with the larger level chunks of distortions and presuppositions. This makes it limited and less useful.

Learning to deal with the larger operational units of the Meta-Model empowers us to effectively handle higher level mental constructions. Doing so also makes for more personal resourcefulness. This brings us to two important distinctions in the Meta-Model, cause-effect and complex equivalence.

When we ask about the relationship between experience and the complex equivalence that we construct about experience, we initiate paradox. For the linguistic distinction of a complex equivalence involves both a *process* and the *result* of the process. And with this we come face to face with *logical levels of thought*.

Think about the verb 'select.' This verb refers to 'a process of selecting.' From this we then create the nominalization 'selection.' This nominalization may also refer to the result of the process of selecting, namely, 'the selection.' This means that the process of doing something and the thing done eventually becomes one in language and one in the way we represent them in our thinking.

This same confusion process occurs with complex equivalences. At first we make the equation explicit:

> "You always put me down and insult me because you never look at me when I talk to you as you do with your friends."

Here we equate the external event 'not looking at me' with the internal significance we give it 'insult,' 'put down.' Then things become more complex:

> "You communicate in an insulting way when you talk to me."

> "Our relationship suffers from your contempt."

These words present a level of abstraction, do they not? Someone has encoded a map with these abstract words regarding the experience. When, without hesitation, we hear and effortlessly process these kind of words as meaningful representations we have fully entered into the land of generalization and fluff, without even noticing. We have lost our senses and come to a particular state of mind. This takes us into the land of auditory-digital definitions about auditory-digital definitions. Korzybski (1933/1994) described this as 'intensional' meanings (see Hall, 1998, *The Secrets of Magic*).

The problem with relying too much upon auditory-digital representations (words, language) involves how it then initiates us into secondary, and therefore derived or vicarious experience. We begin to live through words by deleting primary experience (sensory experience) and believing in the reality of the words. Yet the

NLP model informs us that words are not real in the same sense as their referents are real. Words function as only as symbols of some referent (real or imaginary).

The auditory-digital representational system, as a high level of abstraction, codes the territory beyond our skin, digitally. Called 'digital' in NLP as much of this coding of things is in all-or-nothing terms, either/or terms, and on/off choices. As such it lacks the ability to effectively convey the range of processes or choices within reality. For this reason auditory-analog language works much better using graduations to represent such experiences.

Identifying Behavioral Complex Equivalences

The following exercise is designed to assist in tuning your linguistic ears to hearing and dealing with complex equivalences. In this exercise you will identify a complex equivalence for 'trust.' You will learn to answer the questions:

> "How do you know when you trust someone?"
>
> "What does this word trust signify for you?"

1) In a group of at least three people, invite person A to evoke an experience of 'trust' by fully remembering or imagining it.

2) B meta-models the experience that lies within and behind the word trust. "How would it look, sound, feel for you to trust someone?"

3) As B then backtracks A to the experience (the 4-tuple) from which A derived his/her complex equivalence. Identify all of the behavioral equivalents you can between the external behaviors and the linguistic code 'trust.'

4) B now models back those behavioral equivalences to A, with C (the meta-person) observing and checking for modeling accuracy. Does this now evoke the sense and emotion of trust in A? Use the 'Teach Me' frame or the 'How would I do that?'

frame to generate questions that allow you to obtain a complete list of the sensory-based evidence of 'trust.'

5) Finally, test the work. B models 'trust' for A, and then asks, "Do you trust me now?" B is looking for both the ingredients that make the pattern work and the process involved in doing this.

6) As B takes on the other person's external behavior and gestures which he or she regards as meeting the linguistic label 'trust,' B should access the state (as s/he has imagined it) and become aware of when A recognizes his or her complex equivalence for this auditory-digital code of 'trust.' What does B now feel awareness of, intuit, etc. from this state?

We can use this same process with other high quality words (values and criteria) such as 'loyalty,' 'love,' and so on. Watch for the "Aahhh!" experience in A. After the initial rush of awareness, there will come an easy familiarity.

As you engage in this kind of discovery (modeling) process eliciting another person's complex equivalences for various nominalizations, use accessing questions such as the following:

> "How do you know you feel X?"
>
> "What represents X for you?"
>
> "Show me with your face, posture, breathing, gestures, etc. what X looks like."

Do all of this covertly in a natural way so that it does not appear obtrusive.

Distinguishing Cause & Effect

You will now begin to recognize and appreciate that inside every cause-effect statement lies a complex equivalence construction. Since you need to clearly distinguish between these two linguistic phenomena, seek first to understand what each refers to.

In a complex equivalence you have a nominalization that someone has equated to a behavior, or another nominalization.

> nominalization = behavior; or,
> nominalization = another nominalization

Here a static 'state' takes the form of an equation; the '=' represents Korzybski's 'is of identity.' (Korzybski, who originally founded neuro-linguistic training in the 1930s invented several linguistic terms that Bandler and Grinder did not use in their original formulation of the Meta-Model. For those see Hall, *The Secrets of Magic*, 1998).

In a cause-effect statement, we typically find some activity (verb) which implies a causal connection between two events. Somehow the earlier event creates or causes something to happen as a result. Sometimes we may code this using nouns or pronouns.

> "She *makes* me angry"

> "Her *tapping* that table always *leaves* me with a headache." (Figure 4.7)

Typically in cause-effect statements we have some non-static or dynamic process which implies a temporal connection between two separate events, presupposing the idea of causality.

> Some A causes some B; A $\rightarrow$ B

The arrow represents a causal linkage through time.

You can develop your ability to detect a cause-effect statement by listening for causation words, such as causes, forces, makes, and so on. We use different words to represent the degree of causation (implied or explicit), and these vary along a continuum. One attempt to give these words a score between 0% and 100%, between implied and overt, occurs in Figure 4.8. Although people may be more or less consistent within themselves, there is less agreement between different people. More general agreement occurs about the higher the words in the scale, since these more explicity describe a cause and effect connection.

The Structure of a Complex Equivalence
I.S. = E.B.

Internal Significance or State = External Behavior
Nominalization = See, Hear, Feel Referents

On the screen of the mind we code the external event or referent which we typically represent as an action or a set of actions. By contrast, we typically map the meaning as a still picture, a semantic interpretation, hence the static code involved in nominalization—selfish, trust, love, etc.

The Structure of a Cause-Effect Statement
S → R (Stimulus Response)
This Object/Event → Causes This Event

On the screen of the mind, we typically map out an object or event (a noun or nominalization) as causing, making, or leading to another object or event.

Figure 4.7: The structure of a complex equivalence/cause-effect statement

It will help you train your intuition about causation and cause-effect statements if you prepare a list of verbs and implicatory words that match the notional scale in divisions of 10%: For example, you may decide that 'tends' is 50%; 'allows' is 20%, 'forces' is 90% and so on (see Figure 4.8). Once you have done this, you can begin to play around with matching and mismatching the level of causation in various statements that you make or that you hear others make.

Complex Equivalence		
	100%	Is, am, are
	90%	Causes
	80%	Forces
	70%	Makes
	60%	Controls
	50%	Generates, affects
	40%	Molds
	30%	Influences
	20%	Lets, allows, permits
	10%	Tends toward
	Cause-Effect	0% Approximates

Note: This is an illustration only. Your list will probably be different. Generally speaking, people vary a great deal in this kind of allocation.

Figure 4.8: Causation words

Cause-Effect Recognition Exercise 1

As an exercise for matching or pacing implied cause-effect statements,

1) In pairs, A identifies a problem and tells B in a single sentence.

2) Once A has stated their problem, explore the level of causation involved in stating the problem as in Figure 4.8.

3) Next, take turns matching and then mismatching the experience as a way of testing it.

4) Finally, offer a counter-example to it. For example, suppose someone says,

   "I can't stand criticism. It makes me worry about being rejected."

A match at the causational level might involve a response such as,

> "So criticism forces you to worry?"
>
> "You have to worry when you hear a communication of a criticism!"

To mismatch, you could say something like,

> "So you feel allowed to worry at criticism?"

Pacing causation matches someone's beliefs about how the world works and what causes things to happen. Shifting them from those kinds of belief, especially if they create limitations, problems, stuckness, and so on, will involve leading them to the new ideas having first paced the old ones.

Cause-Effect Recognition Exercise 2

This exercise allows you to practice detecting and utilizing the hidden and semi-hidden cause-effect relationships within language.

You can use this both to gain rapport as well as to set up a mental frame in which change becomes possible for that person:

1) In a group, A should offer a problem that he or she currently experiences.

2) B listens for that problem and the driving beliefs within it. In doing this, B internally marks out the complex equivalences in A's description.

3) B then marks the related cause-effect relationship on a notational 0–100% scale. If desired, B can then check the level of implied cause-effect with person C (the meta-person).

4) Finally B should feed back to A sentences which contain the same level of cause-effect implication.

Reading Complex Equivalences and Cause-Effects on the Outside!

[The following is derived from Eric Robbie]

As Master Practitioners we expect to be deal only with complex equivalences and cause-effect statements as linguistic entities. While they are linguistic processes, they also involve much more, so we need to deal with these structures in the terms of their non-verbal implications.

For instance, suppose someone says,

> "My magic ring helps (cause-effect) me to think (unspecified verb) more clearly."

Central to this statement, the person has perceptually built in a cause-effect structure. Now more important questions arise:

> "What effect does this statement have on the person's neurology?"

> "What effect does this statement have on the speakers posture, gesturing, breathing, and so on?"

> "How does this statement contribute to creating that person's physiological reality?"

Why do we ask these questions? We do so for for several reasons. They can assist us tremendously in developing our intuition about hearing language while simultaneously seeing the non-verbal structure of the language. These questions direct our attention to noticing the behavioral equivalents (in someone's gestures, movements, etc.) of the nominalizations they use. We make new learnings as we explore the effect of language structures in terms of how they affect our neurology.

After all, for an NLP Practitioner, the structure of intuition arises from total sensory awareness. First is the ability to identify complex equivalences in language as they occur; and second is the ability to notice the effect such language has on physiology. When we so train our intuition, we have even more choice about how to respond.

To do this, make sure that you have all your sensory channels open, so that you can see, hear, and feel what someone semantically equates to whatever nominalization they may use ('a good time,' 'flirtation,' 'love,' etc.). Now begin to explore that relationship with the question:

> "What would you experience if you were having a good time (felt flirtatious; operated from a loving state, etc.)?"

Asking questions that elicit the person's behavioral equivalents of the nominalization and opening up all of your sensory systems to notice the shifts, changes and responses in their physiology, will give you much high quality information about their psychological world.

As you do this, remember that sometimes someone will use a part of an experience, or of a statement, to represent the whole. One part of a complex equivalence of a behavior has, for that person, come to represent the whole of it. In hermeneutics (the study of interpreting literature) this phenomenon of using 'the part for the whole' is called synecdoche or metonymy. In terms of personality the use of metonymy indicates that the person is streamlining their strategies and beliefs, that s/he has reduced a whole experience to a term, a phrase, a nominalization, or even a gesture. This can be framed as anchoring as well. S/he has anchored the strategy of the complex equivalence to a word, gesture, phrase, sound, symbol, or other coding.

Perhaps, at this point, we should go back to the original question with which we began this process of exploration, "How then does experience relate to beliefs?"

	Neurology	Linguistics	Meta-Level Gestalts
Experience an event in the world →	Mapping the process in the mind and neurology →	Complex Equivalence →	Beliefs Meanings Values

Figure 4.9: How beliefs relate to experience

In NLP, we talk about criteria as the rules or standards which enable us to operationalize our values. 'Operationalize' means the way we put our values into practice. Criteria often contains the modal operators e.g. must, may, should, etc.

If someone has 'timeliness' as one of their values, this will show up as a belief. It will express itself along the lines of, "I deem it important (valuable) to produce this product on time (in a timely manner)." That belief will also show up in various causation statements and equations of meaning:

> "To arrive on time indicates or means high integrity of character." (Complex Equivalence)

> "Being on time with something makes me more credible and trustworthy." (Cause-Effect)

With that, let us ask the physiology questions again:

> "What physiology goes along with these values and beliefs for this person?"

"What physiology do they use to anchor an internal conceptualization such as the abstract concept of 'time'?"

"How can we see or detect 'timeliness' as a value within the way this person moves, breathes, acts, responds, etc?"

A Master Practitioner principle, when you are working with people, is always to go for their values first, and then for the criteria and rules behind those values. Values usually consist of nominalizations that you will hear as single words or short phrases (e.g. timely, an on-time person, punctual, excellence, powerful, productive, and so on). When you next ask for a person's complex equivalences for this value, you essentially get him or her to track back to the experience (a sensory-based 4-tuple) from which it came. This will then typically activate his or her physiology.

Remember that a complex equivalence may indicate the process or the result of the process. The person may offer their answer in a static form ('punctuality') or in a process form ('arriving/delivering on time'). So you may have to go through the process of questioning several times until s/he begins to de-nominalize the value. As you do this you will begin to identify the pieces and relationships between his or her experience, belief, values, criteria, and so on.

Throughout this process, keep your eyes and ears open for detecting the person's naturally occurring physiological anchors. These cues will tell you when s/he has accessed the belief state and when s/he has begun to utilize those constructions for orienting him or herself in the world.

How do beliefs become structured within us as our programs? How do they show up in our physiology and behavior? In searching for these answers, learn how to fish elegantly in the pool of another person's experience and understanding. Learn to use the Meta-Model with great elegance. For cause-effect statements, listen for the word "because" and for implied becauses, as these words will alert you to the cause-effect relationships within someone's thought processes.

Programming (Meta meta-level: More habituated)

Linguistics (Meta-Level)

CRITERIA			**VALUES**
Standards & Rules:	**Complex equivalents**	**Cause-effect statements**	Internal neuro-linguistic formats
Operationalize Meanings, Thinking Patterns— Meta-Programs	Nominalizations Identity statements	Beliefs about, How things work	

Neurology (Primary Level)

Experience:
Physiology, Behavior, Gestures, Breathing, and Naturally Occurring Anchors

Figure 4.10: Structural Relationship Between Meta-Model Distinctions
(Reformatted according to the Meta-States model)

Another way to hunt for the cause-effect involves continually asking:

"What came before that?"

"What has to exist for you in order for that to cause this?"

"What do you get out of it?" →●

From experience, and everything that follows as you go up the scale, you enter into the realm of Beliefs. We encounter beliefs about causation (how things work, what makes what happen) as well as beliefs about the rules that the person has constructed about the world. Inside these meta-beliefs we have the person's standards, values, beliefs about what should occur, what ought to happen, and so on. Also remember that beliefs function in a circular way. They exist at the beginning and at the end of mental constructions, and they have a self-fulfilling and self-validating nature. (This makes beliefs a product of a system, and hence a systemic phenomenon—something that emerges from the feedback system of thoughts and emotions reflecting back onto thoughts and emotions.)

Experience is the context in which we generate our beliefs, and this process does not stop with the generation of beliefs. When we take beliefs and go out in the world, we attempt to re-create and/or notice experiences which confirm our beliefs. With NLP it is possible for us to consciously and intentionally use new experiences (or contexts) in order to loosen up limiting beliefs. After all, if beliefs arise from experiences, then by generating new experiences we can create conflicting new beliefs. We can now create for ourselves and for others new situations where more enhancing beliefs can arise. Then we can compare those new beliefs with the old ones. This is a powerful tool for changing beliefs.

There are several levels of beliefs which function as generalizations about the way the world works and what things mean. Robert Dilts has identified six levels at which we have beliefs about ourselves (identity), our purpose (mission), our capabilities, our rules and values, our behavior, and about our context (environment) (Dilts, *Changing Beliefs With NLP,* 1990).

Generally speaking, with regard to beliefs, the more important the value the less conscious we will be of that belief. But when we learn to mind-read the structures of what has to exist in order for a belief or experience to operate, our mind-reading can become truly elegant and effective. This constitutes 'Master Practitioner mind-reading.'

To facilitate this level and kind of mind-reading, use the value exploration questions:

> "What is important about X?"
>
> "How is this important to you?"
>
> "What has to exist for you to experience this value?"
>
> "Do you always have to have that specific thing as part of the experience?"

An interesting thing happens whenever we use language, namely, with the words that we use, we always do or accomplish something. Our words, sentences, syntax, etc. always accomplish and achieve specific things. Therefore we need to constantly ask ourselves, "What specifically will these particular words accomplish?"

Using the Meta-Model understandings, modal operators provide us with a distinction that we can use to identify the rules or the criteria for values. Nominalizations provide us with the distinction that more often than not codes beliefs and values. On the other hand, specific sensory-based words and descriptions point us in the direction of experience.

Exploring the Experience—Values Connection

The following exercise offers more practice for exploring the connection between experience and values. Elicit some cause-effect relationships (bearing in mind that the person may hold some components of the structure in his or her unconscious mind). The following steps may make it easier to bring to the surface the hidden (unconscious) components of a belief structure:

1) A goes into a fully associated state with regard to the content of an experience.

2) B then assists A to amplify that state using submodalities, switching referential indices, or by using the frame, "If I were to take your place for a day, teach me how to 'be' you."

3) Track through and confirm verbally the cause-effect linkages in the belief/s.

This experiment provides practice in identifying the structure of values as the largest chunks when you hear nominalizations and complex equivalences. Practice identifying criteria as the next largest chunk in terms of rules and ways of operationalizing values. Identify sensory based experiences as the smallest chunk within the model.

Ask the person, "What is important about X?" Elicit information in a natural way to gather as much information as possible. Start at the largest chunk level and work down.

Linguistic Markers

The Cues of Semantic Reality

[Derived from Chris Hall]

Neuro-Linguistic Programming, by highlighting the language part of human experiencing, recognizes how language plays such a central role in the way each of us creates, represents, and transforms our experiences. It is therefore of great importance to be able to be access our languaging.

At Practitioner level, we learned about the importance of hearing predicates: visual, auditory, and kinesthetic. Why did we put such emphasis on them? Because these language forms mark out aspects of a person's ongoing experience. And, as we learned to do that, these distinctions enabled us to enter into the other person's world.

Now at Master Practitioner level, whenever we identify a language distinction that enables us to do this, we have a linguistic marker. Linguistic markers refer to the cues which mark how a person internally represents his or her experience. Recognizing these cues and learning what they mean gives us an insight into the model of the world in which that person (or even yourself) operates.

The NLP Meta-Programs provide additional ways by which we organize behavior and thought. We can think of them as referencing categories. Some refer to the Meta-Programs as sorting devices or even 'human software' which we use to run our content program.

Another part of becoming a Master Practitioner involves getting used to noticing people's dominant preferences for sorting and organizing information. This necessitates gaining proficiency in using the Meta-Program distinctions and recognising their linguistic markers. A good way is to start using them one at a time, so that you gradually develop your level of competence.

If you feel overwhelmed by the number of Meta-Programs, here is some good news. First, no one uses all of the Meta-Programs during a given experience at any one time. You certainly do not need to worry about that. Second, pay attention to those that stand out prominently. Using Meta-Programs as you communicate is more a matter of pacing anyway, which means asking ourselves,

> "Where is this person right now?"
>
> "What categories and concerns is this person sorting and paying attention to right now?
>
> "Which Meta-Programs most powerfully drive this person's attention at this moment?"

Once you discover a person's Meta-Programs, at least the ones specifically used for certain concerns—the driver Meta-Programs—then you can focus on packaging your communications in the most effective manner for that person by using the same programs. Meta-Programs operate in us all the time, in differing degrees and ways.

How would you describe the overall modeling skill in NLP? How would you summarize it? *Patterning!* Patterning refers to identifying, understanding, and using the patterns that govern how someone functions or 'works.' This means catching that person's strategies and noticing the distinctions s/he makes, or fails to make, as s/he moves through the world. Such detection enables you to become aware of the patterns that the person uses.

To do this we have to use the basic NLP communication frame as our beginning point. In this way we can treat all the information we receive from the person as both accurate and useful. No matter how 'dumb' or 'inaccurate' you perceive it, view it as accurate from the perspective of the communicator.

The question, as psychologist George Miller posited, becomes, "About what, and how, is this information accurate?" Suppose you hear someone say, "I'll be in and out in no time." What do you know from this statement? What linguistic markers have you heard? Does it not describe someone as an in time person? (Yes, there is no sequencing of 'time' in their statement.)

So the overall methodology in NLP involves first discovering what we find in someone's presentation—Meta-Model distinctions, Meta-Programs, etc.—then deciding how we may want to use these in accomplishing our desired outcome relative to that person. In this sense, NLP functions as a strategic way of thinking and functioning inasmuch as it enables us to move from present state to desired state with elegance. →●

Practicing Hearing Linguistic Markers

The following exercise will assist you in developing your ability to hear and handle linguistic markers. It gives you practice to detect linguistic markers in language patterns as well as identifying Meta-Programs.

1) In a group of four, B asks A, "What would you have absolutely no interest in buying?"

2) A identifies an item he or she has no interest in purchasing. After that, A remains silent for the rest of the exercise, or just continually says and signals "No."

3) B now attempts to convince A to buy the thing which A does not want to buy and continues trying to persuade A for five minutes. (Obviously, this exercise will evoke from B his or her own convincer strategies. B should just forge ahead regardless of A's non-persuasion and resistance.)

4) At the same time, C and D should simply listen to B, taking note of any linguistic markers they hear and observe. Begin with the following Meta-Programs and from them create a comprehensive list of the Meta-Programs that B manifests in this exercise. →●

- Orientation to Time (In Time/Through Time)
- Temporal Predicates (Verb tenses: Past, Present, Future)
- Representational Systems (VAK)

- Referencing: Self/Others (Internal/External)
- Matching Style: Similarity/Differences (Match/Mismatch)
- Motivation Direction: Moving Away From/Towards
- Modal Operators: Necessity/Possibility
- Chunk Size: Specific/General (Details/Global)

In this customer convincer exercise the person trying to convince A will in the process use and manifest his or her own Meta-Programs, and, by projecting them onto A, reveal how they convince him or herself. (After all, A has remained mostly a blank slate in this interchange—and this really invites projection!) In other words, this exercise generally gets the persuader to externalize his or her own Meta-Programs for the others. Feel free to use extreme examples. It will help to exaggerate the pattern as you learn it, e.g. "I would never buy an old rusted tin can."

Adding an After-Burner to the Persuasion

After you have completed the first game with each other and have a list of each person's Meta-Programs, this next exercise will enable you to add an 'after-burner' to your persuasion skills in handling and using linguistic markers and Meta-Programs.

1) B takes the Profile list of A's Meta-Programs, and uses it to package a communication to A that runs his or her Meta-Programs. Feel free to change the sequences on A's list if that helps.

2) Having run the persuasive communication to A, B now inquires, "What else could I do with this presentation in order to make it more compelling for you?" This will enable A and the other participants to identify missing ingredients (e.g. perceptual filters) that will make a communication to A more convincing, compelling, and influential.

3) B should now use whatever A says to then run a second, third, or fourth presentation and keep running the persuasion statement back in the sequence that A says feels more compelling, in order to check it out. B should continue until s/he paces A's Meta- Programs, values, beliefs, etc., and A wants to buy!

Installing Persistence Using Linguistic Markers

Let us now continue developing these skills in handling and using linguistic markers by applying them the theme of giving up and persistence. The next exercise will give you practice at using the linguistic markers of someone's Meta-Programs in order to install, covertly, a new enhancing strategy of persistence.

1) B starts by eliciting from A an experience (#1) where he or she speaks about having given up when things got tough. "Think of something you gave up on that you found hard or difficult. Think of something that you wanted to do, but you didn't." ●→

2) As B does this elicitation, s/he should identify as many of A's linguistic markers for Meta-Programs as possible. Then B should elicit from A an second experience (#2) that s/he also found difficult and challenging, but which s/he completed anyway (a persistence experience). "Now think of another experience where you did persist at something difficult. Recall a time when you kept at something even though you found it hard and then, through your perseverance, you finally accomplished some desired outcome, and felt great about it." Make sure that A picks an activity that was fun and enjoyable in spite of its difficulty. Here, again, note the linguistic markers. →●

3) At this point, B should confer with meta-persons C and D, so that together they identify all the linguistic markers and Meta-Programs.

4) With this list in hand, B should now take A's strategy for the 'persistence experience' (#2) and use its form and structure to map over the coding into A's 'giving up experience' (#1). B first runs an ecology check on a specific task to make sure that it will prove ecological for A to keep persisting with it. Once B has satisfied that requirement, s/he should keep shaping and refining A's thinking about the subject by having him or her use the Meta-Programs and strategies for persistence.

Debriefing

Identify the differences you experienced as you did this in terms of:

- The linguistic markers you found as most useful in providing clues to someone's values, standards, criteria, perceptual filters, etc.
- The linguistic markers that provide evidence of your own values, standards, etc.

And consider:

- How would you relate someone's Meta-Programs to their values and criteria?

At this point in the process, you should have developed the ability to identify the Meta-Programs you use which keep you from engaging in activities that you want to complete, but which you find difficult. So now:

- Describe your strategy for staying stuck, frustrated, limited, unresourceful.
- What linguistic markers indicate this?
- Which linguistic markers play a critical role in the strategy?

Consider:

- Do you want to change this strategy?

If you want to transform this, take the Meta-Programs that you found in your perseverance strategy experience (#2) and apply them to your stuck experience (#1). What happens when you do this? What insights and understandings can the others in your group provide regarding your adjectives, comparatives, nominalizations, modal operators, criteria, etc. that identify the critical Meta-Programs? →●

Several findings might arise from this exercise. In the "giving-up" strategy, we typically find several points of difficulty where people experience the feeling and decision of wanting to quit. Here people frequently fall into using a number of modal operators of impossibility, necessity, or dislike: "I can't stand…." "Why do I have to wait?" Or they might over-value some things so that even planning, scheduling, etc. now feel like violations of their values. Some people fail to create a long-term representation of how the immediate unpleasant steps would connect with their long-term values, and yet others frame their experience as difficult, a waste of time, intrusive, and so on.

On the other hand, when it comes to the persevering strategy, people frequently talk about how they become lost in time and totally absorbed in the activity—'in time.' Out of that experience they are able to transcend various immediate pains for the long-term gain of their goal(s). Sometimes when they frame a difficult activity with more enhancing values and words such as challenging, fun, opportunity, feedback, character building, and so on, they experience it as less painful and/or more acceptable.

In the state of perseverance, almost everyone adopts a 'through time' representation which takes into account the long-term benefit and pleasure of their direction. This actually enables them to make the difficulty pleasurable. "It gives me a warm feeling that spreads throughout my body." Reframing the difficulty in this way thereby enables them to experience it as 'a great time,' 'an accomplishment,' and so on. →●

Logical Levels

Throughout NLP, you will find constant reference to 'logical levels'; Dilts' levels, neurological levels, outcome levels, Korzybski's levels of abstraction, Bateson's levels of learning, etc. All these offer a very important set of distinctions for modeling, managing consciousness, communicating, and so on. Korzybski (1933/1994) paid much attention to this and devised a 'structural differential' in General Semantics to help people in the 1930s and 1940s to develop a 'consciousness of abstraction.' He argued that this played an absolutely essential role in both science and sanity (hence the title of his book, *Science & Sanity*). He sought to assist people in developing a neurological awareness that "whatever label we hang upon an experience, that label is not that thing." He talked about training in "a moment of silence" to drive in this distinction between map and territory.

Set Theory, or the Theory of Classes (from Russell & Whitehead, 1905) presents various levels of classes or categories and shows the crucial importance of the difference between levels and meta- levels. If we have a collection of ten groups, each of which contains ten things, what happens if we refer to this collection as a class called Groups of Ten? This class also has ten things in it, so can it now be put with the other ten groups and thus become the eleventh member of the class? Logically the answer has to be No, because the rule of meta-levels says that we cannot have a meta-level class as part of the class itself. No class can be a member of itself. In practical terms, the class of elephants is not an elephant. The illogic violates the logical system.

Gregory Bateson (1972) devoted much attention to sorting out classes of learning. In his classic work, *Steps Toward an Ecology of Mind*, he distinguishes Zero Learning, which involves no response to a stimulus. In Learning I, however, we have someone responding to a stimulus. The person has learned something. Perhaps someone has learned language, for example. This differs from Learning II where we learn about our learning. In Learning III we move up another logical level and learn about our learning of learning. This refers to changing our very paradigms and world views. Bateson also posited the possibility of Learning IV, but couldn't identify what that would entail, as it was beyond human comprehension. When asked about why he wanted to have a fourth level, he said he wanted to keep the possibilities of even higher levels open.

This model of the levels of learning or knowing means that knowledge operates at various levels, and therefore, that in becoming NLP Master Practitioners, we need to be able to discern at which level we, or others, operate. In terms of logical levels, both digital information (words, language, propositional statements, etc.) and analog information (non-verbal gestures, breathing, posture, etc.) can operate at higher or lower levels to each other. We can say words about a gesture; and we can gesture with our eyes, hands, tongue, or whatever, about a word. Both operate as para-messages although neither has a meta-position to the other.

Conclusion

Eric Robbie concluded one session about the Meta-Model by presenting the case of a man who would say about his life, "It's no use." Noting that this man's presupposition, by implication, suggested that he did not find life worth living, with this statement he essentially declared that he could find no reason to continue living. "At this point, I would question him, 'How then do you know to draw your next breath?' "

This Meta-Modeling response 'runs with the man's logic' by addressing the presupposition that Robbie heard in the man's words. He thereby addressed and challenged his model of the world, and, in doing so, invited him to do some re-mapping—an example of the power of the Meta-Model.

Becoming a master of the linguistics which run, drive, and effect neurology necessitates:

- considerable sensory awareness,
- considerable practice and experience in noticing words (linguistic markers), and the effects upon oneself and others,
- considerable practice at using the Meta-Model and the distinctions it provides,
- considerable appreciation for the meta-levels of consciousness that language initiates.

May you now give yourself lots of practice with these various aspects of Neuro-Linguistic Programming so that you can become truly masterful in your use of NLP.

Chapter Five

Master Level Persuasive Reframing

The Sleight of Mouth Patterns

[Derived from Chris Hall & Max Steinbach]

A card illusionist does a sleight of hand movement by performing a set of actions which distracts the viewers' attention from what s/he is doing. The viewers' attention is thereby drawn to one place, while the significant occurrences take place elsewhere. This 'mis-direction'—the sleight of hand—tricks the observer by creating an illusion which then results in a shock to consciousness. This process has been codified in the statement which encourages more illusion: "The hand is quicker than the eye."

The same kind of thing can, and does, occur with verbal behavior. It actually happens all the time in human interactions. Yet do such interactions occur just for fun and enjoyment, for a win/win situation for all involved, or to pull the wool over someone's eyes in order to take advantage of them? The ecology question addresses these concerns. For while manipulating someone to your sole advantage may work, it will only do so in the short term. In the long term, it will fail.

The NLP model assumes this ethical position because it operates within a systemic and long-term perspective. It also employs the presupposition that when people become resourceful, empowered, and at their best, they bring out their best, rather than their worst. This underscores the importance of the win/win perspective in personal relationships and communicating. It also eliminates any need to manipulate other people for negative ends, because doing so will only rebound on the manipulator. And since NLP grew out of a systemic paradigm which encourages systemic thinking, it therefore strongly disavows any behavior that creates long-term pain for others.

I would encourage you therefore to remember this with regard to the following about Sleight of Mouth patterns. Obviously, when we translate something as powerful as the Meta-Model into a conversational model we incorporate many powerful verbal forms which an unethical person could certainly misuse.

From a persuasion standpoint, we often find it easier and quicker to utilize a Sleight of Mouth pattern when communicating with a client, customer, loved one, or friend. We do so in order to redirect our listener's brain to the option of a new point of view. And we do this rather than go through all the trouble of Meta-Modeling. Instead, we reframe the person by using one of the Sleight of Mouth formats. And if the person buys it, then, presto! S/he will suddenly have a new perspective! We have provided a new and enhancing meaning to something that otherwise would have produced an unproductive state.

Conceptually, whenever we offer a different viewpoint, we essentially *frame* a piece of behavior (or understanding) in a way that transforms its meaning. The following Sleight of Mouth patterns offer ways for redirecting the brains of others as we attempt to expand their perspective, which then expands their model of the world which, in turn, makes their experiences bigger, broader, more expansive and more empowered. It truly offers them a positive gift.These patterns also grew out of another communication principle, namely, that people will fight you tooth and nail when they feel attacked. Induce someone into a state where s/he feels threatened, attacked, inadequate, or vulnerable, and you can count on all of his or her defence mechanisms going up. And that will further complicate communication clarity.

In view of that, these Sleight of Mouth patterns provide ways whereby we can track a person back to the experiences out of which the certain learnings (or beliefs) arose. In this way, we activate the central Meta-Model strategy. Then we can redirect the person's brain (e.g. the Swish pattern) to new and better understandings and perspectives (i.e. the reframing pattern) that offer more productive and useful ways of thinking about what s/he wants (i.e. the desired outcome pattern).

What problems do most of us have in life? Are they not about how easily we become entrenched and enmeshed in our maps, and how we so easily confuse our maps with reality? We forget that our perspectives, beliefs, understandings, 'drives', and so on, only exist as mental-neurological maps of reality, and are not the event itself. Korzybski described this as 'identifying' (identify map and territory). And yet reality involves far more than our mere maps of it. Our words and perceptions function inherently as fallible and limited constructions, so sometimes we really do need to have them shifted so that we can develop more enhancing maps.

Using the following Sleight of Mouth patterns we can engage in some extremely elegant 'map- shifting' with ourselves and others. As you practice them, notice if they shift you, or if you think they would create a shift for someone else. Some will elicit pleasant shifts. Some will evoke unpleasant shifts. Since we exist as "a semantic class of life" (Korzybski), whenever our internal representations shift, so does our experience, our neurology, our identity, etc. This is where 'the magic' occurs, so get out your wand, and let the magical times begin.

How to make these Verbal Transformations

1) Notice the Meta-Model distinctions that people offer you in their language. The Sleight of Mouth patterns arise from three Meta-Model distinctions (complex equivalence, mind reading, and cause-effect) which deal with larger level meanings.

Surface structures at this level frequently express beliefs. These may concern causation beliefs (C-E) which we can identify by listening for causative words (because, if, then, in order to, so that). Or they may concern meaning beliefs which we can hear in complex equivalences and universal quantifiers (all, always, never). As we listen for these words in the surface statements, we can then meta-model them.

2) Create an X = Y equation in your head, or cheat and do it on paper! Or, cheat in an even more creative way and write the equation on the blackboard in your mind. Formulate what the person says in such a way that you have some external

behaviour (EB, the X) equated to some internal representation (IR, the Y some internal understanding, state, significance etc.).The formal structure of this equation will look like this:

X = Y
E.B. = I.R.

Try your hand at the X = Y formula:

"She's angry or upset with me because she didn't smile at me as she usually does."

As you listen for the E.B. in the surface statements, representationally test them (track directly from the words offered to some sensory-based representation on the inner theater of your mind). You might want to think of this as 'video-thinking.' As you do so, notice or query what meaning (I.R.), the external behavior represents in the person's mental map.

Once you hear Complex Equivalence statements, turn them into the X = Y formal structure. For example, if you hear the statement,

"You made me forget the answer when you asked in that tone of voice,"

translate it into an equation:

'Your tone of voice' = 'my inability to remember.'

If someone says to you,

"I can't believe you're late again."

Respond with,

"Really? What does that mean to you then?"
"It means you don't care about me."

Now you have your formula:

'Being late' = 'not caring.'

3) Begin reframing the statement. When you have got the belief formulated to this stage, the time has come to use Sleight of Mouth patterns. And this is where the fun and magic begin! From here, you can try out all the shifts that the patterns offer.

As you do, always keep in mind that the heart of reframing involves the ability to distinguish between behavior and intent. This refers to distinguishing between what someone actually *does* (E.B.) and what that person *seeks to achieve* by doing it (his or her I.R. and the intentions that run them). In a sense, as Bandler and Grinder say in their book *Reframing*—all of us contain multiple personalities living in uneasy alliance in the same skin. Each part tries to fulfil its own outcome. The more aligned these parts become, the more they work together in harmony, and this allows us to experience a higher level of happiness.

The Art of Subtle Meta-Modeling

Once you have formulated the belief using the X = Y structure, you can begin reframing. To give some content to these patterns we will play around with the following statement beliefs:

A) "Saying mean things makes you a bad person."
B) "Cancer causes death."

1) **Reframe the E.B.—Content Reframe.** Here you create new meanings and frames about the behavior by redefining X in the equation.

    A) "Actually I do not say mean things; rather I'm attempting to express some truths and understandings I have."

    B) "Actually, cancer does not cause death, but a weakened immune system."

2) **Reframe the I.S.—Content Reframe.** Here you create new meanings and frames for the internal state by redefining Y in the equation.

A) "It is not the case that I'm bad, I just care enough about you to mention these things."

B) "What cancer really causes is fear and depression—two concerns that can provide much more danger to someone."

3) **Apply E.B. to the Speaker/Listener—Context Reframe.** With this pattern you essentially shift the referential index to the person making or hearing the statement:

A) "That's a mean thing to say to me."

B) "That belief has spread like cancer. I would find it interesting to see what would happen if the belief died out."

4) **Apply the I.S. to Speaker/Listener.** Another referential index shifts the context.

A) "Only a bad person could say a mean thing like that."

B) "That's a pretty deadly belief to hold onto. It can only lead to a dead-end street."

5) **Go to the Intent level to find the Positive Intention.** This move utilizes the basic process within the reframing models, namely, discovering the positive intent behind the belief or behavior. Here you guess the person's positive motive and attribute it to the person:

A) "You're trying to help people by having that belief."

B) "Aren't you trying to prevent a false hope with that idea and yet by believing it you are preventing any hope at all. Wouldn't it be better to try to look at it in some other way?"

6) **Go to the Consequences level.** In this move go to the outcome of the belief or behavior and explore its value. "Would you find this or that consequence desirable, useful, productive, enhancing, and so on?" Inquire about the consequences which

a belief or behavior would entail if followed to a conclusion. State the C–E prediction about where the belief will take the person:

A) "In the long run that belief will prevent people from speaking the truth to one another. How acceptable do you find that consequence for yourself and your relationships?"

B) "Beliefs like that tend to become self-fulfilling prophecies because people stop exploring their options. Does that sit well with you?"

7) **Go to another outcome, to a Meta-Outcome.** This move expands the time frame even further to discover additional outcomes that will result from the person's reality construct:

A) "Isn't the real issue a matter of how two people communicate and relate, not moralizing on how they express themselves verbally?"

B) "Isn't the real issue not what causes death, but what causes life and health? Why not explore that?"

8) **Chunk Up the X or Y**. In chunking up we identify higher level principles, understandings, and meanings that the belief or behavior may ultimately suggest. This move takes you to higher levels of abstraction and so expands the perspective.

A) "So one mean statement makes someone completely bad?"

B) "So one single mutation of a small part of a system will automatically cause destruction to ensue within the entire system?"

9) **Chunk Down the X or Y.** Here we test the reality of the belief by employing the basic meta-modeling process. We meta-model the language of the belief itself and index it to person, place, time, event, etc. Chunk down to the person's submodalities, criteria, and/or strategies:

A) "How specifically is that mean? What specifically do you mean by this term mean?"

B) "Which cancers specifically cause death? How specifically does cancer cause death?"

10) **Counter Example the Belief itself.** This reality testing move identifies and presents counter-examples which produce incontrovertible evidence to question the belief. The strategy here sometimes involves tracking the person backwards to the experience from which the learning arose. Behind counter-examples lies the presupposition that people always demonstrate the very thing they claim they cannot do:

A) "Could it ever be possible for someone to say a mean thing without being bad? This seems like a pretty mean thing to say to me."

B) "Have you ever heard of anyone who had cancer and lived?"

11) **Go to the level of the person's model of the world.** This chunking up move identifies the overall mental map that the person uses to negotiate the territory of the world. It helps them to dissociate from their map so that they may stop confusing their map with the territory.

A) "Where did you learn to think and judge statements in terms of meanness? Does that belief about meanness come from your model of the world? So who created that rule?" (Lost Performative)

B) "Are you aware that not all medical people hold that belief?"

12) **Go to the person's Reality Strategy.** This chunking down move focuses on the person's internal representations so that you can identify the pattern and strategy of their thinking. Challenge the data itself with, "How did you arrive at that understanding and conclusion?" Challenge the person's reality structure with, "How do you know?"

A) "When you think about that belief, how do you represent that in your mind?"

"Do you see, hear, or feel it?"

"How would you know if it was not true?"

"What, for you, would falsify this understanding?"

"What would you specifically see, hear or feel that would indicate that?"

B) "How do you see (or hear or feel) that so that it convinces you that it is true?"

13) **Change the Frame Size.** This move shifts the frame size by exaggerating the belief and by putting in some Universal Quantifiers:

A) "Since everyone has at some time said something mean, everyone must be bad."

B) "If all of the doctors and researchers working on cancer believed that, we'd never have any hope of finding a cure for cancer."

14) **Change the Temporal Frame.** This move shifts and expands the time frame. Here you go to the past or future to create a different frame-of-reference ('pseudo-orientation in time'):

A) "It may seem mean to you now, but in a year when you look back on how our relationship handles even these rough waters, I think you'll appreciate the feedback, especially if it helps you to become more effective."

15) **Go to a Meta-Frame.** This chunking up shift involves going to the largest conceptual levels and aims to get the person to temporarily step out of their frame altogether. Switch the referential index by asking, "How would it feel for you if others held this belief as well?"

A) "How enhancing do you think this idea about mean words creating bad people serves the human race? Would this encourage honesty, forthrightness, catharsis?"

B) "Would you recommend that everyone who gets any form of cancer should immediately think that it will cause them to die?"

16) **Access the Person's Hierarchy of Criteria.** This shift involves a move which appeals to the person's values. It enables the recipient to organize his or her thoughts and emotions according to priorities which s/he will find ecological. It enables him or her to gauge the relative importance of his/her own criteria. Inquire about the person's values and criteria that enables him or her to create understanding of the External Behavior and Internal State:

A) "Which do you value as really more important, how someone's voice sounds or what they actually do? Isn't it more important to be honest than patronizing or incongruent?"

B) "What is more important for you? To experience peace (like quietly giving in to fate) or fighting for options? Would you prefer to spend your energy hunting for options or use this to get people to feel sorry for you?"

17) **Create and develop a Metaphor or Story.** Here we tell a story that the person will find structurally isomorphic (has the same form) but uses different content and context, as a vehicle for embedding some of the previous patterns:

A) "When the fire broke out, Sam worked to get everyone out. One kid thought it would be unselfish if he waited to be the last one out. Sam yelled at him, 'Stupid, get off your butt and get out!'"

Sleight of Mouth Patterns as 'Brain Directionalizing' Tools

By now you have probably begun to appreciate why we call these language patterns "Sleight of Mouth". The original metaphor of the card illusionist demonstrating sleight of hand patterns gives us a powerful working metaphor for what we can now do with language. Using this technology enables us to shift the perceptual observations of the people with whom we work.

Behind the dynamic involved in these patterns of direction lies the ability to make certain distinctions and then use them creatively. The distinction we need to learn in order to make these directional shifts involve various conceptual components. Primarily these relate to how a person has organized and made distinctions in his or her mind with language. In other words, how they have semanticized (created meanings) about things. After all, ultimately, how and what meaning they have attributed to something always and inevitably becomes the controlling factor in perception.

We can now begin to use this principle in a way that empowers us to shift meanings. With these kind of Sleight of Mouth responses we can assist ourselves and others in deframing old perceptions and generating new ones. We can re-direct a human brain to go after more empowering meanings.

As an NLP Practitioner you will already know enough of the Meta-Model to comprehend the external/internal formula. When we make an external behavior (E.B.) equivalent to some internal state (I.S.) we call the resulting linguistic construction a complex equivalence (CEq).

Linguistically, this comes from the process of mind-reading (MR). We 'read', assume, and second-guess the meanings (values, intentions, decisions, standards, etc.) of the other person. What linguistic markers typically, or often, occur with complex equivalences? Words such as: equals, is, involves, means, etc. This highlights the importance of the *'is'* of identity, and the "is" if prediction. "When she looks at me with that frown (E.B.) I know she *is* angry (I.S.), because she *is* a hostile person"

Such talk indicates that the person operates from an internal organization which we call a 'meaning' or belief. The complex equivalence indicates that the speaker no longer makes certain distinctions that could probably be more useful. By reducing this conceptual and linguistic structure to a formula, we arrive at the equation E.B. = I.S.

Now whenever a human being operates from this kind of complex equivalence, operationally the person operates at the identity level, according to Dilts' model of the level of beliefs. In other words, this equation functions at a high level, a meta-level. The person assumes this equation represents *is* the person's nature, or even more abstract, human nature. (General Semantics describes this as the 'unsanity' of identification.) This belief then becomes the controlling influence over that person's consciousness. Yet from the Meta-Model we recognize several components within this structure as ill-formed. For one thing, we have not posited the locus of control within the person, but outside. ●→

Into the Fray…

With this understanding about the nature and construction of Sleight of Mouth patterns, we can now ask about the range of implications and usages for them. At NLP Master Practitioner level, in how many ways and in what areas of life can we use these patterns? How much more skilled with language and neurology do we become as we use these patterns in conversational swishing and conversational reframing with people?

Why do we include these patterns at Master Practitioner level? Primarily because, at this level, we presuppose an acquaintance of, and unconscious competence with, the Meta-Model. Using these patterns effectively and elegantly presupposes the ability to hear and detect cause-effect statements in everyday language and their associated linguistic markers that cue them (because, if, when, in order to, so that), and also the ability to recognize how such cause-effect relationships, over time, then give rise to various complex equivalences. Typically, complex equivalences lack any standard of comparison and therefore contain universal quantifiers (always, never). Consider the statement, "If you smile at me, I know you like me."

Using the equation formula, we have the external behavior (E.B. = smile) indicates, means, or relates to an internal state (I.S. = liking). The statement presupposes that:

- The second event causes the first event (liking causes smiling).
- This occurs in only one way. Liking has to equate to smiling, and only leads to smiling. It does not offer a choice for smiling without simultaneously positing that it causes or equals liking.

Probing and analyzing the sentence's structure in this way, of course, begins to make clear precisely how a meaning formula like this can become a problem for the person. It illustrates the structure of many of the problems that people have in life.

In a problem state, people often talk about the problem using cause-effect structures that then create complex equivalence structures (C-E → CEq). We learned this in the Meta-Model when we also learned the process for challenging these patterns. When we choose to question the linguistic patterning of something like this, and bring it to consciousness, we then have to decide: "Do I want to continue to format my thinking like this? Does this serve me well?"

When we use the Sleight of Mouth patterns, we challenge such structures subtly without bringing them into consciousness. We just do the shifting, swishing, and reframing without the other person realizing the transformations that they evoke at deeper (or higher) levels.

To train your intuitions about this, first identify the cause-effect linguistic pattern using the formula, "Some X makes Y." For example, consider the statement, "You make me frustrated."

Obviously, the ill-formedness of this structure clearly stands out. This statement gives the actor ('you') control and power over the subject's ('me') internal state ('frustrated'). This presupposes that the subject has no choice but to feel frustrated.

> "You made me forget because you asked that question in that tone of voice."

If you Meta-Model this, you ask, "*How* do you know that?" or "*What would happen* if you could remember?" From an ecology standpoint, this statement implies and suggests a victim position. It further internally organizes the person to take a passive position or role. And that presupposes an underlying limiting belief, "I'm powerless to do anything about it." Not a wise way to think.

So let us redirect the person. Let's send his or her mind into a more resourceful direction, this will assist the recipient of the communication to take control of his or her own responses, and doing this, will in turn prevent them from falling under the spell of the presuppositions which would otherwise slide in unnoticed.

So far we have been using language to get these kinds of sentences into a package or formula so that we can then use the Meta-Model. Further, we need to de-nominalize the words so that we stop dealing with purely 'trancy' words. Doing so will assist us to recover more sensory-specific words. The Meta-Model challenges provide us with a way to put heavy, vague nominalizations back into the form of actions which we can then see, hear, and feel.

Sleight of Mouth Pattern Exercise 1

1) In a group of four, A makes a statement of some belief along the lines of, "When you are late that means you are a bad person." Have them express it that bluntly using the X = Y structure. (Later they can practice this with more subtlety.) A may need to write out such generalizations in this E.B. = I.S. form.

2) B then generates four examples that redefine X (E.B.). For instance, to the E.B, 'You are late,' one reframe might be, "It's not that I'm late; I'm taking time to drive carefully."

3) C will then generates four examples that redefine Y (I.S.). So to the I.S. 'That makes you a bad person,' a reframe might be, "It's not that I'm bad; I'm just busy."

4) D then generates four different examples of that internal state, e.g. "What is really bad is not being late, but not coming home at all. Now I'd call that bad!"

More Examples

Consider the sentence, "When he doesn't smile at me, he thinks I'm stupid." By now you should have the ability to quickly and automatically hear this sentence in terms of the E.B. = I.S. formula. Look first for the E.B. Check your internal 'videotape' for what you would literally see, hear, or sense for 'not smiling.' Then the I.S. becomes obvious—'stupid.'

Another component of this ill-formed statement has to do with the identity word 'I' which the person has equated with a mental-emotional state and has labeled 'stupid.' Yet our 'self' does not consist merely of our behaviors, thoughts, thinking processes, etc. Our self—as a linguistic self-definition, and as an experiencing person who thinks, emotes, behaves, and so on—exists at a higher conceptual level. Behavior exists at lower logical level than does identity, so we must be beware of defining our self by using such adjectives.

Suppose someone says: "I can't learn." How do we respond to that?

- We could meta-model them, "How do you know that?"
- We could give them a counter-example, "What a learning! How did you ever learn that?"
- We could offer them a reframe, "Do you think you truly can't learn or that you just learn in a slower but surer way than others?"

As a Practitioner, you already know that beliefs inevitably set up post-hypnotic suggestions which then create expectations. And expectations, in turn, create mind-sets and perceptual sets which then begin to fulfil those very beliefs. It makes them real ('real-izes' them) as it causes the person to 'make real' the concept. When we use the basic Meta-Model strategy in responding to people, we essentially invite them to reconnect to their own experiences. Take the phrase, "I can't learn." This entire phrase functions as an 'extended nominalization,' so we ask for evidence, "What evidence do you have for this belief or for this 'state of being' belief?" Or, to put it another way, the person has nominalized him or herself. Think about that one!

Consider the impact and implications of a statement such as, "I am slow." Here the adjective 'slow' modifies 'I.' To challenge that we could say, "Oh, so you learn slowly?" That would, at least, start to de-nominalize that static representation. Doing this would recode 'slow' so that it would suddenly stop defining him or her as a person and as a self-definition, and we would see the statement as more relevant to a particular action, evaluation, response, etc.

'Am' functions as an associated language pattern derived from the verb 'to be,' but turned into and used as a noun or adjective. Accordingly, turning it back into a verb, or even an adverb, helps to enable us to dissociate with it at the belief level. This describes the difference between labeling oneself and labeling one's actions.

Chris Hall described a woman she once worked with who had a shoplifting problem. This woman turned to her and said, "I can't stop shoplifting." Chris gave her a quick Meta-Model response, "How do you know that?" The woman said, "Why, I get nervous and then I just have to shoplift."

To index when this feeling arose, and to break the unquestioned cause-effect presupposition within it, Chris followed up by asking, "When do you get nervous, before you go or after you have arrived there?" The woman said, "Well, before I go." To this Chris followed up with a validating summary of her strategy: "So you get nervous and then, to get rid of that feeling of nervousness, you go and shoplift. Does that describe it?" The woman affirmed it certainly did describe the process. Her shoplifting strategy therefore went:

K^-	$\rightarrow V^c$	$\rightarrow K^+$	$\rightarrow A_d$	$\rightarrow K^e$
Nervous feelings	Image of shopping	Feeling better Going shopping	"I think I'll go shopping."	Exit Going & stealing

Chris decided to leave this strategy intact and simply add a new line at the point of self-languaging (A_d), "Stop stealing." When

Chris installed this, she marked out the new line analogically, and then had the woman repeat it.

Using Counter-Examples

Counter-exampling offers a truly great and powerful Sleight of Mouth pattern because it redirects the brain and swishes it in an entirely new direction. Using the counter-exampling process essentially deframes the old generalizations and beliefs by offering a piece of reality for the mind that does not fit. One of my favorite counter-examples that challenges the statement, "I can't learn!" involves responding with, "How did you learn that?"!

We frequently encounter this paradox in ourselves as well as in other people. We find that the very thing we affirm and absolutely believe that we can't do, actually describes a trait or behavior that we demonstrate in our denials!

Do you remember the illustration given in one of the early NLP books involving Richard and John where a lady said she couldn't say "No!"? One of them invited her up to the front and told her to go around the audience and respond to any of their requests by saying"No!" This would prove that she could say "No." But she refused to participate in this exercise; she said "No" to Richard and John, arguing that she had to refuse this experiment or demonstration because she couldn't do that! In counter-exampling her, they set up a double-bind so that, either way, she had to manifest that skill.

The basic principle behind the power of counter-exampling is that people tend to demonstrate what they say they cannot do. So to, "I have no particular expectations…" we can respond, "How did you develop that expectation about yourself?" To, "I want to have more confidence because I don't have any confidence," we could respond, "My, you sound pretty confident about that!"

These examples of counter-exampling demonstrate the tendency this pattern has to create 'benevolent double-binds.' The reason for this arises from the fact that counter-exampling tends to bring up undeniable evidence to contradict their assertion and simultaneously gets a person to behaviorally do something that denies the generalization. In a sense, in counter-exampling we track the person back to experiences which prevent them from maintaining, or makes it hard for them to maintain, the old generalization. Counter-exampling questions provide a standard of comparison.

> "I don't think we have here a case of you learning slowly, but a case where you approach things methodically."

This reframe also dissociates the speaker from the behavior while simultaneously validating him or herself as a person.

> "Do you believe all learning has to occur in a fast way? Can someone learn in a slow way?"

Here we reframe an old belief that has not proved productive or enhancing for the person.

Now, how about:

> "I believe that there is no change."

Which Sleight of Mouth pattern comes to mind first? How would you counter-example this? How about:

> "Have you had that belief since birth, or has that understanding changed over the years?"

Remember, if you attack someone's belief, they will tend to defend it by fighting you tooth and nail. So avoid that. Rather, track them back to either the experience out of which the old learning came or to new experiences that can expand their maps:

> "How do you know that?"

> "What does believing that do for you?"

We can also use Sleight of Mouth patterns by using metaphors that begin with, "A friend of mine...."

Further, we can also use temporal presuppositions in such a way as to take a problem away from a person.

> "Now what *was* it that you *thought* at that time which *created* what at that time you *felt* was such a problem?"

Here four temporal terms (with all the presuppositions that they carry) create layer upon layer of distance from the problem and subtly suggest, by implication, that some change has already occurred. A person will feel the effect of this kind of response as very powerful.

Consider this statement,

> "Picking your nose in public means you're inconsiderate."

Did you notice first that it already has the E.B. = I.S. form? As a complex equivalence, it stands out. Now counter-example it:

> "I can think of a situation when, if a person didn't pick his nose, there might occur some consequences that would be worse than being merely inconsiderate, can you?"

Or, create a metaphor,

> "We were out on this camping trip and this mosquito flew up my nose...."

This piece of communication works indirectly.

As another counter-example to,

> "Blowing your nose in public means you are inconsiderate."

We could say,

> "Yes, that is inconsiderate... and so is snivelling your way through life and never blowing your nose."

Or we could reframe the act of 'blowing your nose' in such a way that it takes on some new meanings:

> "Blowing your nose is like clearing away the obstructions in life, so that you can breathe more fully."

Try the statement,

> "I am depressed."

What do we have here? 'Am,' as noted earlier, is a state-of-being statement and belief. Structurally, it has the form E.B. = Person/Self. This can become an especially dangerous and insidious kind of complex equivalence since identity exists at a higher logical level than a primary state.

With this we might want to begin with some Meta-Model questions: "How do you know this? Do you have these feelings all the time?" As the person has presented the statement, we see no movement in it at all. It stands as a solid, static, and unmoving kind of thing. So we could first de-nominalize it,

> "How do you right now experience this emotion of depressing?"

When we start with a global generalization that someone has condensed into a form like "I am depressed" we should first explore their evidence for the belief: "How do you know that?" "What lets you know that this means 'depression' and not 'patience' or 'boredom', or something else?" If they give you another vague generalization, "It feels that way," then we have to explore that. "How do you know that that feeling means you 'are' depressed? It might mean that you feel calm." And expect more vague fluff, "Because I lack energy." "Energy to do what? At what times? According to what standards?"

Questioning in this way looks for evidence, assists the speaker with indexing his or her generalizing, explores the structure of the experience, and seeks to move the person back to the experience out of which it came. And we do that in order that the person has a choice to re-map things in a more enhancing way. This Meta-Modeling process also induces a person to put the process back into a form which then provides inner movement. This reforms their internal mapping away from the static and permanent format of nominalizations.

Of course, such words and belief statements provide us with many indications as to the way the person has sorted him or herself out to inwardly code experiences. The word 'I' will help them to re-associate to the kinesthetics. Actually, the idea of getting a person back to experience and evidence lies at the very heart of NLP methodology. We might say that this represents a meta-paradigm within the model.

Aim to assist people to stop objectifying their self. Aim also to counteract any such self-defining in terms of victimization. That only indicates and reinforces the unenhancing beliefs of being a victim. Because, if someone believes that s/he will passively suffer being used and continue to assume that they can do nothing about it, they 'are' a victim. Conversely, when we de-nominalize the words and the 'I am' language, we powerfully assist people in building up an internal reference for thinking about life, reality, and experiences. And when they construct such maps, they will have many more choices.

Consider this toxic belief statement,

> "Being in control always gets results."

Stop and analyze that statement before reading on.

What do we have here, linguistically? Is there any complex equivalence in it? What, if anything, would fit the E.B. = I.S. formula? Actually, it fits more of an E.B. = E.B. form. And of course, 'always' marks out a universal quantifier. So, first we have to do some meta-modeling of the two External Behaviors:

> "What behaviors would I see if I saw you 'being in control'?"
>
> "What kind of results are you talking about here? Results in business, in your personal life?" etc.

Once we discover the person's meanings for the External Behaviors, we can then do a complex equivalence challenge:

> "Does not being in control ever not get results?"
>
> "How do you control being in control?" (This meta-question will take you to a meta level.)
>
> "Are you aware that being in control, in the way you have described, will not always get you the results you want?"

Of course, we always need to pace someone before we offer such reframes. We expand their model of the world by suggesting that different kinds of results can occur, and that some of these will be results that they want, while some will be results that they might not want.

Sometimes in working with people we find it highly valuable to delete any limiting or non-productive beliefs that get in the way. Generally, beliefs that limit set up expectations which in turn create perceptual filters cause the world to be viewed in ways that reinforce and support the limiting beliefs. ●→

When someone does that, they also begin to delete everything else that does not fit that perceptual filter. And, of course, in the long run this prevents or sabotages sensory awareness. At that point they need the ability to temporarily set aside the belief in order to see things anew, and to notice what they had not previously been aware of. →●

> "I am tired, but I want to go out tonight."

The structure of this statement creates such meaning that everything after the 'but' carries more importance than what goes before. 'But' typically functions as a form of negation. The person feels tired and wants to rest, yet *rest* does not hold as high a rank in the person's values as wanting to go out. This form operates in a manner opposite to the more common, "Yes, but…" format. Linguistically, 'and' functions as a connective, it links ideas together. 'But,' on the other hand, separates ideas at different logical levels. The second half of the sentence functions as the higher frame.

Counter-example this statement offered by one of the participants in the training,

> "Being knowledgeable means you will not be loved."

We have many responses within NLP whereby we could deframe and reframe this one. We could exaggerate each side of the E.B.= I.S. formula, first the E.B. then the I.S. Exaggeration, in fact, often assists the person receiving the Sleight of Mouth statement to find his or her own counter-example.

We could also identify the complex equivalence in this and challenge it by extending the frame.

> "Say, it seems to me that you yourself are using some very knowledgeable words as you tell me this!"

Or shift the referential index.

> "Have you ever spent time with someone whom you thought of as knowledgeable yet also lovable?"

Changing the Time Frame Pattern

As with other Sleight of Mouth patterns, when we reframe the 'time' structure or the relation of events to each we alter the meaning of the events. We often find and experience this as a very impactful response regarding some experiences, such as making decisions. Indecision indicates flipping back and forth between choices. As such, on the indecision threshold, it can amplify and push the indecision over the point of threshold.

I once heard Chris Hall describe a point in her life when she came to 'a point of indecision.' She explained how she resolved the indecision: "So, in my mind, I went out on my time-line and into my future, and then on to the end of my time-line. From there I turned around and looked back to the decision point on the day when I was attempting to make some decision. When I did this, the process brought about a dissociation for me. And the effect of that was that some new criteria began to come into play which provided me with the needed information and frame from which I could make a good decision. Now I could play each scenario out and more fully notice the values of risk, fear, hesitation, etc."

When we change the time frame of an event we often allow higher level values to come into play that will impact the decision. To the question "What do I fear?" and the state of fear itself, it often helps to gain a sense of the size of our fear's context. And we can do that simply by changing the time frame in our mind. We can this Sleight of Mouth pattern on ourselves to replace our repeating and looping auditory-digital worries when we get caught up in the state of indecision. Further, we can think of this technique as that of tracking people forward in time (or 'future pacing' them). → ●

Some of the other Sleight of Mouth patterns utilize the consequence frame. This move involves reframing the context by the use of exaggerating and asking a hypothetical question that has to do with the results or consequences of a belief or behavior:

> "What if you do get this or that, then what will happen?"

One man made the comment, "I want to feel calm so I can set her right." This Sleight of Mouth pattern involves four questions—the four questions associated with Cartesian Logic:

> "What would happen if you do?"
> "What would happen if you don't?"
> "What would *not* happen if you do?"
> "What would not happen if you don't?"

Notice the effect that responding to these four questions has on you. Does it not create a set of internal representations which then begin to generate both a *push* and a *pull* dynamic? Wouldn't you want that future *now* so that it becomes your present reality? ●→ ●

Yet other Sleight of Mouth patterns utilize various larger level *meta-frames*. These patterns chunk up to various levels.

> "What if everyone in the world took this position? How would you feel about that?"

"Obviously, this belief comes out of your model of the world; but now I wonder about where you got or created that model in the first place? And how productive do you find it?"

Just a word about 'just.' 'Just' often functions as a limiting and/or discounting representation:

"You are just (or only) doing this in order to help…."
"That's just a feeling…."
"That's just like a man/woman for you."

This first statement declares that I only have one motivation behind my behavior—a limiting and rather unrealistic idea. Besides mind-reading, it uses a universal quantifier and thereby creates a representation of a very simple, black-and-white world.

You can also use Sleight of Mouth patterns to undermine linguistic structures that you do not find enhancing for yourself. Suppose you wanted to say:

"Regarding the auditory-digital channel of words, we have understated its importance."

Now communicate this with a tonal emphasis on the last two words. What effect does that have when you emphasize, "its importance?"

Finally, recall the two kinds of word definitions. Sometimes we use words to equate with or stand for another word or words (i.e. a complex equivalence). At other times we use one word to point out to some experience or referent, and this is then a referencing word which indicates some empirical aspect of reality. In the first instance, we have a description, in the second we have an evaluation. And if we equate these (intensional definitions and extensional referencing), which actually function at different logical levels, we will surely confuse primary and meta-levels. Not a good thing. ●→

Conclusion

Now as you take these communication forms (the Sleight of Mouth patterns) and think about communicating with them as a dance (rather than a war), then you could freely use these rhythms of thought with elegance and grace as you conversationally reframe people. Imagine doing this. You now know many dance moves which you could make with people to move them into a more solution-focused orientation. And this knowledge provides you with ways of dancing at all kinds logical levels as well.

Your ongoing learning about the Sleight of Mouth patterns, as a way for using the Meta-Model, will probably move from the state of feeling unconvinced that you can do it, and that it is too complicated, to a point where you experience some doubt about it, which indicates a belief that you can't. Later you will begin to feel less unsure about it as you begin to wonder if it might become a possibility for you to learn and use it with elegance. Then later you will find yourself thinking, "Well, I see it as a possibility, although I don't believe it is very probable." Next will come the state of feeling motivated and wanting to learn and use the patterns. Then will come the setting down state of learning and putting the patterns into use in a way you find effective and elegant in your communications. Eventually, when you think about this ten years from now, looking back on when you first began to learn the Sleight of Mouth model, and from your wealth of experience and skill in it, begin to wonder, to really wonder, how there could have been a time when you didn't know it or use it in your everyday communications, because that seems so strange and unbelievable now… if you know what I mean. ●→●

Part Three

Neurology

Chapter Six

Mastering the Neurology of NLP

Neurology in NLP refers to anything and everything connected with the human nervous system as it engages in abstracting information from the world beyond our bodies. Within the domain of neurology are numerous sub-domains. One of these involves the sub-domain of the human sense receptors which allow us internally to abstract this information via neurotransmitters and bioelectrical impulses. Neurology also refers to the parts of the brain which process, code, transform, transduce, and output sensory-based information, i.e. our representational systems.

Our highest level of abstracting occurs when we get to our linguistic processing. This explains why lesions, drugs, and damage to the nervous system can so radically affect the way our mind works and thinks. Neurology also refers to the 'states' of consciousness that we enter in response to our abstractions, and the 'programming' of our thinking and responding, namely how we perceive (a neurological function) through our belief filters, understanding filters, Meta-Programs, values, etc.

In this chapter, as we delve into this subject, we should remember that we are not dealing with linear processes, but with systemic processes. The brain that produces consciousness functions as an system of interactions, with the result that language affects feelings, feelings affect language, and perception affects both. To map this out more accurately, and to incorporate it into our language behavior, Korzybski (1933/1994) suggests we use hyphens and hyphenated words. Hence we will talk and write about 'mind-body,' 'linguistic-neurology,' 'thought-emotion,' etc.

Advanced Representational Systems

One of the most basic assumptions in NLP comes from the realization that in our experiences and use of representational systems, we all differ. In spite of similarities in our nervous systems, we do not all see the same way. How we see differs between people. Our individual discrimination abilities and levels of acuity also differ. It is crucial for each of us to learn how to train our eyes, ears, and other sense organs, to make more and more discriminations in the qualities and distinctions of our sensory modalities.

How do we do this? Obviously we have to use and become conscious of using, our senses. We have to pay attention to 'seeing' and taking 'mental snapshots' of what we see. Do this now, and as you take such snapshots, close your eyes to see if you can reproduce (re-present) what you just saw. If you do not find the internal image really clear, snapshot it again and again. I use this procedure as homework with clients who have attention deficit, or difficulty with learning, remembering, etc. This exercise can also be carried out auditorally or kinesthetically.

One of the most important features of this process (if not *the* most important) concerns the process of receiving and using feedback. In fact, the process of using feedback to develop and train representational skills, according to Wyatt Woodsmall, highlights one of the central keys to genius itself, and thus in modeling genius. After all, one thing that sets a genius off from the rest of us involves how they make much finer discriminations using their representation systems than others normally do.

Expanding and Developing Images

Learning to See What You See and More

[Derived primarily from Wyatt Woodsmall]

With regard to vision, there are two different ways to see. We can see:

1) in *detail*—which we can call *'detail vision'*
2) in *context*—which we can call *'contextual vision'*

This distinction arises from the physiology of the eyes. For instance, if you defocus your eyes, notice how you then blur the details in your central vision and bring movement into focus in your peripheral vision. Try it. Scan first to get the gestalt of the situation and then scan a second time to get the details.

In the process of seeing we have a 'window of sharp focus' through which we view the world, and use to scan things. There are also times when our vision will 'splash,' so to speak, when a detail suddenly impacts our conscious awareness.

The principle of habituation lies at the heart of all of our patterns and habits. This 'perverse' tendency in our nature enables us to keep on doing whatever we have already started. Of course, this works well if what we are currently doing works, but it becomes a big problem when what we currently do does not work.

In childhood we begin to learn how to cope with situations using our representation systems and the discriminations we make inform us about the world around us. Subsequently, as we grow up, we tend to over-use the systems that provide us with the most useful information. Eventually we learn to make more and more discriminations. Yet this process can lead to creating imbalance.

We can become so used to and adept at using one sensory system that we might ignore the development of the other systems. Therefore to develop the other representation systems now, we have to put our usual patterns on hold… temporarily… and consciously focus on utilizing the under-developed ones.

We have two ways to use *the visual remembered* function of our visual system. When we access remembered images, we remember them in either in detail or in context, which is a digital either/or choice. So now we need to query how and in which system we have originally stored our memories and coded those pictures, images, internal sights in the first place?

Most people can remember photographs in detail better than something they have seen. The flat image of the picture aids the memory and refreshes it, making the memory clear, so *how* we stored the data determines to a great extent how much we can now retrieve. We might say, "As we store—so we retrieve"!

This has several implications in regard to the problem of forgetting. There are several possibilities regarding forgetting images, sounds, experiences, and so on, from childhood:

- We didn't record the memory in the first place. We blanked it out. We ignored it and didn't encode it at all. Somehow, we just didn't input it.

- We might currently experience a kind of 'pseudo-forgetting,' inasmuch as we have both short-term memory and long-term memory, and both weaken over time. We access things into our long-term memory via our short-term memory. Ultimately, we will only remember what we have 'processed' in the first place.

- We may have the ability to 'recall' a memory even though we can't 'remember' it. In psychological experiments about memory, two key ways are used to establish what a person remembers. First, we directly ask for the person to actively *remember*. Second, we have the person *recognize* previously learned information. People can always recognize far more than they can remember.

The images which we visually construct provide another central element of genius, and again, we have two ways to visually construct images. We can create visual pictures that have great detail and specificity, and we can create pictures that concentrate on the context. For example, consider the following strategy:

$$V^c \rightarrow V^e \rightarrow V^r/V^c$$

This ability involves making comparisons between visual images. To do this we could use a split-screen between what we remember and what we construct. We then alternate between them, making contrasts and running comparisons. We could then play two or four movies in our mind and pull out the similarities and the differences between them.

In effective reading, someone makes constructed pictures from the external visual words (V^e) on the paper or in the book. A skilled mathematician often has an internal constructed blackboard as part of his or her internal mental image, and uses it to do his or her calculations. What do all of these processes have in common? The translation of technical data or abstract data into internally constructed images or diagrams. This gives the expert the ability to 'see' abstractions, concepts, and other 'understandings'.

Expanding Auditory Representations

Hearing More Accurately & Constructing Auditory Images

While the visual system enables us to make spatial distinctions, the auditory system enables us to make time or *temporal distinctions.* We only hear because sound exists and varies over time. The auditory system, in fact, enables us to make temporal distinctions at a very fine level. Regarding tonal sounds, we have different abilities in hearing the higher and lower frequencies. We measure levels of sounds in decibels. On a continuum, they go from:

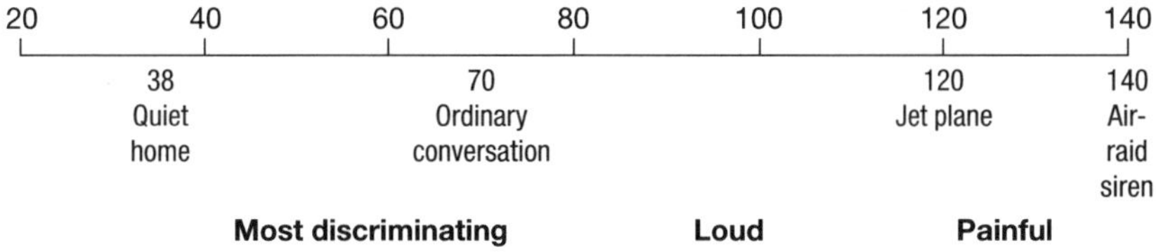

Figure 6.1: Decibel range

The factors that we recognize as the qualities of sounds include repetition rate, pitch, rhythm, etc. We recognize sound as 'noise' when we hear non-repetitive patterns. In order to develop your auditory skills, consider listening to sounds two or three times as loud/low as you do now; or develop the ability to hear and interpret far more expressiveness, inflection, and tone used in voices.

We also have two types of hearing just as we have two types of seeing. We can hear in *detail*—which enables us to repeat the words we have heard verbatim. People who can naturally do this will tend to become *sequential* in processing and thinking, i.e., they will focus on concentrating on one thing at a time. Such people tend to dislike interruptions, but once they do take a break they can switch attention easily.

We also may hear in a *contextual* way. This occurs when we get an overall impression from the sound and the words and then squeeze out, so to speak, the emotional impressions which the words leave with us. Such people will therefore pay little attention to content and so will lack specific awareness of what was said. Some people can handle chaotic situations and thrive on them, and can do several things at the same time. Such people usually need lots of contextual input.

With regard to *auditory tonal remembered* this gives us the ability to make distinctions that allow us to recognize voices on the phone and immediately tell one person's voice from that of several hundred others. This encoding of the remembered auditory provides us with a way of sorting which enables us to distinguish different voices.

We have two kinds of auditory tonal remembered,in detail or in context. Suppose we raise this query:

> "How can someone become, or be, a polyglot? What would enable a person to handle several languages with different sounds, words, phrases, etc., simultaneously without mixing up the different languages?"

Somehow, the polyglot must have a way of storing the different languages and their different tones and/or rhythms. S/he probably has not only developed a different set of auditory distinctions for each language, but also a different physiology (K) for each of them. And this seems to be the case. To train yourself to remember auditory tonal, expose yourself to more and more tones, rhythms, melodies, etc. As you do, pay particular attention to the different qualities within each so that you can make ever finer distinctions.

The representation system that comprises auditory construction refers to making up new and different sounds. In Western culture this has become a very weak sense. I believe that the dominant role of radio, TV, muzak, records, etc., has caused this degeneration. Today we depend too much on an external representation of the sensory data so that we end up coding and representing less and less of it in our heads. Consequently, many people have difficulty in coding such representations and this shows up in their inability to produce good representations of sounds. To develop this skill in yourself, practice adding some of the sounds, tones, voice qualities, etc. to your repertoire. Then start doing some auditory construction with those sounds. In the way that you creatively combine and mix pictures, do the same with sounds.

Part of the sensory stimulus overload involves leaving people with little or no time for *incorporation*. Instead, we suffer sensory stimulus overload. This reduces the impact of the sensory information we receive. It becomes diluted and mixed. You should, therefore, give yourself the gift of silence so that you can have time to meditate. Only then will you have the chance to code, process, play with, mix, and synergize the various pieces and components of your experiences.

Overload also creates a problem in terms of the 'structures of mental madness.' If someone inputs and inputs but never incorporates, never digests or integrates… but experiences all the data simultaneously, this causes confusion (literally, the fusing together of many disparate pieces). Such a person would suffer in the long term by ending up not knowing how to make necessary distinctions.

The Auditory Digital Representational System

In NLP what people generally describe in terms of self-talk, internal dialogue, language, thinking in words, etc., we designate as the auditory digital channel. And we symbolize this as A_d. The symbol A_t refers to the qualities and distinctions of auditory sounds and the symbol A_d refers to making sense or giving meaning in terms of words, language, and higher level symbolic systems. This moves us to a meta-level, where with language we develop this meta-sense by abstracting and attributing significance to the previous experiences encoded by the VAK. When we do this we truly enter into the semantic dimension.

This non-sensory channel for representation plays a central role to our humanity, the heart of our uniqueness—what Korzybski (1921) termed as 'time-binders.' This representation system provides us with the ability to give meaning to life, activities, actions, behaviors, experiences, and so on. It empowers us to engage in high-level cognitive thinking that makes up what we call logic, reason, and rationality.

Using Korzybski's 'Levels of Abstraction' we begin at the level of the sense receptors that abstract as they bring the energy manifestations from the outside world into our nervous system. After that comes the level of abstraction in our sensory system. These activate corresponding parts of the brain—visual cortex, auditory cortex, motor cortex, etc. Next comes another and even higher logical level of abstraction—language. Here we make sense of things by saying words and creating linguistic structures to represent the sensory level.

Let us think about the play on words involved in the phrase, 'to make sense.' This phrase describes how we use the auditory-digital sense to create, or make-up our map of reality. Note that we have no natural 'receptor' in our body for this auditory-digital sense in the same way that we have receptors for the other senses.

Where do we use our word, language, and symbolic thinking? We do it in our brain, within our left and right hemispheres, in the associated cortex, in the lower more primitive brain functions, and in the extensions of the nervous system, right out to the end receptors. Actually, we do it all over our bodies and it does not stop there. We even use extra-neural tools (books, computers, etc.) to continue the process. In all of these intra- and extra-neural processes we can make up or invent ideas, come to conclusions, make abstractions, generalizations, create concepts, and so on. Truly, this 'sense' comprises our human meaning-making sense and serves as the basis of our linguistic nature.

Further consideration reveals that this 'sense' seems to extend infinitely. In *Science & Sanity* (1933/1994) Alfred Korzybski said that, when it comes to words and language, we can always create more linguistic abstractions about our words and abstractions. We can always go meta yet another time to whatever we express and say something about that. In this sense, the language sense functions in an infinite and multi-layered way. This, by the way, supports our self-reflexive consciousness that leads to meta-cognition, meta-communication, meta-levels, and meta-states.

We call the language sense 'digital' in order to distinguish it from the language and sounds that we describe as 'analogical'. Accordingly, conversation involves both analog features (i.e. *how* we say something) as well as the words, and linguistic structures (the digital) which describe what we say. Together these two features of language can create powerful experiences.

For example, if we use some words and language forms to designate and reference something we evaluate as 'horrible, scary, terrible, frightening,' and use certain tones of voice, volume, breathing, etc., we can generate some very strong and powerfully negative emotions in ourselves and others. We can do this intentionally or unintentionally, to our benefit or to our detriment. ●→

Tones play an essential role in creating states and moods. Yet as Richard Bandler notes, in the West and especially in American culture, most people behave as if they are completely tone-deaf to auditory tonal information. Which sense most highly drives you? Does something have to *sound right* or *make sense* in order to convince you? Do you prefer one over the other?

When we remember words and events that create powerful feelings within us, we have a circuit that goes: $A_d \rightarrow Kr^{(remembered)}$. This describes the function of words in our nature and neurology that enable us to make sense and feel 'meaning', and 'meaningfulness.'

One way to code remembered words, and language itself, involves linking them to various kinesthetic sensations so that a word or a statement then carries a certain 'feeling' for us. Setting up an $A_d \rightarrow K^+$ circuit encodes our linguistic symbols and their referencing processes at a neurological level for quick access.

The auditory-digital system also codes and carries our words, language, statements, and therefore our beliefs, understandings, philosophies, and so on. Many people tend to over-identify with their A_d codings and even think of them as 'who they are.' When this happens, a person then confuses his or her map (at the linguistic level) with him or her 'self', and this has the effect of generating a notion, "I *am* what I say about myself"!

Have you ever fallen victim to that one—the 'is' of identity again? It seems a particular temptation to many of us. And yet this meta-level abstraction about our identity (in terms of our words) almost always creates more limitations than it creates resources.

We can question this. 'Who has got whom?' A basic principle governs human psychology and links control with identity. Briefly it goes as follows.

> We grant controlling power to whatever we identify with—in this case, our sense of 'self.' Conversely, once we dis-identify with an idea, event, person, etc., then we can take charge of ourselves in terms of controlling its influence over us. Let us make ideas, words, language, etc. our servants so that they will serve us well. Refuse to bow to them mindlessly.

Ironically and paradoxically, the ability to dissociate from our own processes begins to build within us the ability to master or control those very processes. If we identify with our emotions, then we essentially empower our emotions to control us. And they will! We become their slaves. We become emotional-dependents. The same applies to whatever we identify with.

We exist as much more than our A_d descriptions, definitions, and words! Our maps do not contain or encompass who we 'are.' "The map is not the territory." So we must not limit ourselves to merely the words in our head about anything, not even ourselves! Such 'word cages' will severely limit our possibilities. We must maintain an awareness that our language sense, like the other senses, merely operates as a representational function that we use, and is not 'us' in any existential or essential way.

Another important question regarding this language sense has arisen often in NLP and in other fields, namely:

> "How do we turn off our A_d channel and internal dialogue, especially when it goes on and on and on, looping and repeating? Can we turn it off?"

Since the auditory-digital function can create so much of our downtime processing, it can severely interfere with coming into uptime and maintaining an uptime state. So what can we do about it? How can we develop more control over our language representational functions? How can we develop an on/off switch for our auditory-digital sense? Here are some possible solutions:

1) **We can use the power of meditation.** Wyatt Woodsmall believes that completely stopping the auditory-digital sense takes about ten years of training using some form of focused meditation.

2) **We can use various interruptions to get it to stop.** Many people use a process whereby they jam their auditory-digital channel. They may use some form of meditative mantra to interrupt their internal languaging.

3) **We could re-language ourselves about our language sense.** We could substitute a new self-dialogue line—in the form of affirmations, permissions, suggestions, and so on. Or we could input new lists and procedures to use in directing our consciousness: "Stay in uptime." "Back to uptime." Or we could reframe the meaning of our internal chatter: "Ah, thoughtballs bouncing around upstairs again. How interesting."

4) **We could use a trance state.** We could go into a trance state and then regress to a time before we knew language, anchor that state, and then rehearse and refresh that anchor by future-pacing it to times and places where we need to stop the internal chatter from rattling away.

A major problem of intellectual and emotional growth, of learning, and even of NLP itself, arises when we try to learn all the right 'jive,' all the politically correct verbalizations, words, lines and so on, without ever changing. We typically get stuck at the auditory-digital level and disconnect the higher level learnings from their sensory-based levels.

When we experience and practice a technique, we learn it best and powerfully incorporate it into our neurology when we do it in an associated state. Only then does it become experiential learning for us. If we do not experience the reality (the neuro-linguistic reality), but just talk about it, we have moved to a dissociated state and have detached from it. These states occur at two different logical levels. So go experiential. Taking the languaged understandings of a process and translating them back to the VAK level provides us with a front door approach for directly incorporating, installing, and programming. This allows us to use, get, and access these powerful learnings.

This explains, in part, why we do the NLP exercises and practice drills the way we do and explains the importance and value of the basic induction line:

> "Think of a time when you really felt comfortable… when you felt very confident…"

True enough, we manage the files of our experiences using words and linguistic labels for such categories. This shows the value of the A_d remembered category. We can use it to assist us in retrieving information. The A_d construct category enables us to use words to map out new and different experiences, so that we can use them to program ourselves with much more empowering ways of responding.

Expanding our Sensations (The K System)

Feeling and Constructing More Feelings

How often do you think of calibration mainly as a visual external process? In Practitioner training we practice calibrating by having someone look for changes in the face, eyes, lips, skin coloration, blinking, and breathing (rate, location, depth). From a strategy standpoint, this process involves a V^r/V^e… over a period of time. We can also do this auditorily: A_d/A^r. How do we do this? By first noting the person's appearance in your mind, and then the changes.

What about kinesthetic construct (K^c) and kinesthetic remembered (K_r) representations? To chart these two systems involves charting the sensations that occur to and within the body.

Kinesthetic external refers to real time sensations. We have our skin sensors 'on' in the sense that we are taking in impressions. We are sorting for different qualities: texture, pressure, temperature (hot/cold), moisture and 'pain' (which also involves the brain's interpretation of 'something wrong'). How well do these sense qualities operate within our body and consciousness? 'Coming to our senses' entails noticing, paying attention, registering, and recording them so that we have good access to them and can thus utilize them to make clear distinctions.

Kinesthetic internal refers to our internal sensations within the body. These include our visceral feelings and those in our bones, muscles, and tendons. Our problem with this involves noticing and recording these sensations. The body state of equilibrium, which various mechanisms are continually creating means that as we achieve homeostasis we lose awareness of our sensations. The more balanced we are, the more difficult we find it to notice the sensations, but when our body gets out of balance we experience discomfort and become highly aware of our body's internal sensations.

The coordination of our system of muscles, which we refer to as movements, involves two kinds—gross and fine motor skills.

The digestive system with its sensations includes the mouth, throat, and stomach where we experience hunger, fullness, indigestion, etc. These sensations strongly and significantly affect our mood. Our urinary system also has sensations, as does the cardiovascular system of heart and lungs. How do you sense your internal organs when you feel relaxed? How do you experience the pulse waves in your body—in the finger tips, wrists and arms, and so on?

The respiratory system involves the process and function of breathing and describes one of the most powerful systems that we can pace in another person. The yogis use breathing to override their autonomic system. This makes perfect sense inasmuch as breathing is the only part of the autonomic nervous system that we can direct or manage with conscious awareness. It thus provides us with direct access to our autonomic nervous system.

The turbinals of the nose (the thin placated membrane-covered bony plates on the walls of the nasal chambers) provide a way for us to breathe through the nose. Some have described the sense of smell as 'the express-train to the brain.' Why? Because the smell receptors in the nose are connected directly to the frontal olfactory lobes of the brain and does not need to go through the cortex to register this information.

According to yogic principles, breathing through the mouth results in loss of energy and strength; a better choice involves breathing through the nose. Using the diaphragm to 'breathe from the stomach' gives us one of the most effective means for relaxing. The normal range for most people is 12 to 20 breaths per minute. Yet yogis believe that six breaths per minute is optimal.

Visual breathing is high up in the chest and in a relatively shallow manner.The most healthy way to breathe comes through using the diaphragm. Babies breathe in this way naturally. Kinesthetic breathing provides us with optimal oxidation. It also reduces stress if we breathe in a slow, rhythmic, and regular way. The rhythms of our breathing and of our heart are two basic rhythms of the body.

The human nervous system operates as a system of awareness. We have the voluntary nervous system—one which involves the major movements of the body. We also have the autonomic nervous system, which governs 'involuntary' actions such as secretion and peristalsis. Secretions from the glands and reproductive system greatly affect our sensations and our mental and emotional state.

The sympathetic nervous system speeds the body up, whereas the parasympathetic nervous system slows the body down. We can balance these two processes by using our breathing, by changing the rate at which we inhale and exhale. In a relaxed state, inhale and exhale slowly. The optimum ratio involves something like inhale for a count of five, hold your breath for a count of five, and then exhale for a count of ten.

In the kinesthetic system, the nostrils play a key role. We exhale differently at different times. No one side dominates; each dominates at different times. A change occurs every 90 minutes. When we breathe through the left nostril it indicates that we are operating more out of the right hemisphere of our brain, which has become more dominant. Right nostril breathing indicates we are operating more out of the left hemisphere of our brain. We can change this by simply lying down and putting our arm under our opposite shoulder. This will shift the circulation. We can shift hemisphere orientation also by putting our hand under the opposite armpit. Or close one nostril until the other takes over. At the point of switching one normally experiences a few minutes of euphoria.

Wyatt Woodsmall suggests that in the kinesthetic balance system most of us suffer due to having bodies that are twenty to forty pounds off-balance. We can try the scale test in order to check this out for ourselves. Stand with the left foot and then the right foot on a set of bathroom scales, and see if the same weight is indicated. Most people tend to put more weight on one side. Imbalance here can lead to developing emotional off-balance as well. By getting into kinesthetic balance we facilitate emotional balance. And given the importance that balance plays in so many skills, its importance becomes evident.

"Kinesthetic remembered (K^r) refers to remembering the feeling of a sensation. Kinesthetic memory plays an important role in keeping the body working in a good state and able to maintain balance. A muscle memory for movement leads to the often used strategy of a kinesthetic comparison by which we make the judgment that something 'feels right' ($K^e/K^r \rightarrow K^+$). Aim to encode the K^r into your nervous system as the baseline for the comparison.

How would you go about installing this? By making continual contrasts about what you evaluate as 'right' and what you consider 'wrong.' Use back and forth exercises to do this, for example, putting yourself in the right physiology for throwing a bowling ball. Do it,then break that state, shake off the sensations, and then test to see if you can return to that *kinesthetic remembered state.* You will also need to create a feedback mechanism which allows you to come up short, go long, and then start refining the 'sense' of distinctions.

The key to developing and refining these kinesthetic senses lies in getting immediate feedback to your actions, responses, postures, breathing, etc. Immediate feedback plays a crucial role in any kind of development and progress which depends on a refined kinesthetic awareness. Immediate feedback also works well for the unconscious mind. Delayed feedback works better for the conscious mind, although it has less impact on changing behavior. The effective use of immediate feedback is instrumental in creating lasting success patterns. →●

Another way to get the kind of feedback to mark and measure our responses involves using *biofeedback*. Using some biofeedback techniques even enables us to learn to control 'autonomic' functions. This demonstrates the importance of feedback in the process of skill development of any kind. Without the real-time information that immediate feedback provides, we end up just guessing whether our efforts have hit the target or not, and if so, to what extent, in what way, in what direction, etc. No wonder feedback plays so crucial a role in the learning of any skill. And the more immediate the feedback, the better and quicker the skill development.

We can also use our K^r representational system to recall the effects of a drug, and then use that remembered sense to activate the healing processes of the nervous system, even without taking the drug. Doing this then provides us with a way to obtain the benefit of a mood-altering chemical without suffering any side effects.

Kinesthetic construct (K^c) refers to the high level skill of constructing a kinesthetic sensation in our mind-body. As we develop this sense, it enables us to obtain various levels of physiological control: skin-temperature, blood-flow, heart-rate and so on; and also to achieve mental control of our brain-waves (beta, alpha, theta, delta). Mystic training develops this through the practice of relaxation and meditation.

Since the word 'sensations' may refer to either a feelings (K) or emotions (K^{meta}) in NLP, we need to distinguish carefully between these two phenomena. What we call 'emotions' properly emerge as a matrix of bodily sensations plus a mental interpretation of those sensations. Our auditory-digital labels provide us with code names for these complex phenomena—love, anger, hate, joy, jealousy.

In kinesthetically remembering (K^r) an emotion, we typically experience something similar to what we also call a state of consciousness. In working with states of consciousness, we need to remember that we can re-experience emotions in the here and now—any emotion that we have ever experienced. We don't have to wait for external circumstances or triggers.

We can simply remember what 'happiness', for example, felt like by recalling the unique personal codings for the sights, sounds, sensations, words, meanings, values, etc. that we used in the first place. When we do that, we induce a happy state in ourselves. This truly indicates the internal power we possess to run our own brain. We do not have to depend on external triggers or wait for ever-changing external events in order to become happy. Further, *remembering* plays a role in almost all of the emotions that we experience. So, wouldn't we be wasting a powerful resource if we chose not to recall positive emotional states most of the time. →●

To adopt a Master Practitioner attitude (the spirit of NLP), we aim to develop and maintain a healthy and joyous mind. How? We can do this simply by continually putting ourselves into a joyful state. If we wish to meditate, we can induce in ourselves a state of ecstasy so that it becomes a lot of fun. →●

We delude ourselves if we think that we have no control over our emotions. As we have just noted, we have tremendous power to run our own brain. To think otherwise represents one of the most dominant culturally conditioned programs that far too many people accept, to their detriment. With NLP, we can today take full 'response-ability' for our emotions and feelings precisely because we create them anyway. After all, they arise as products of our consciousness and nervous system. They occur *in* us.

Further, all our emotions have a temporal component. Notice how we have them represented and experienced in terms of time—past, present, and future. To experience guilt, grief, and sadness we have to adopt and code our internal representations with a past orientation. To experience 'boredom' we have to orient ourselves toward the eternal present. And when we feel 'anxiety,' we experience an emotion oriented towards the future. Atemporal emotions such as 'meaninglessness' involve a different way of structuring time.

To alter or transform any of these temporal emotions, we only have to recode the time-frames that we put around our representations. For example, try as hard as you can to experience worry, anxiety, or a similar fearful feeling as you think about it as in your past.

One structure for neurosis (meaning 'full of nerves') involves imagining the grief that you *will* experience, or *could* experience in the future, at the death of a loved one, and then beginning to feel it *now*. The strategy would go:

K^{c} (associated first-position, 3D image of loved one dying) $\rightarrow$ K^{-} (negative feelings)

What solution can we offer to a person operating with this limitation? We could invite him or her to rearrange the components, sensations and interpretations. We could recode 'the future' as 'not now,' and put it into black-and-white, out of focus, and so on.

Synesthesia

Creating Streamlined Neuro-Circuits Experiencing and Creating Wild and Wonderful Synergistic Patterns

At Master Practitioner level in the art of NLP, how do you define an analog response? When you think about a physical touch on another person, sometimes it is right to *pace* that person, but then again, sometimes it will *lead* them, and at other times it will *set* or *fire off* an anchor. It will depend on how that person associates the touch with a past similar experience. As any new experience becomes associated with another experience, we create an anchor.

Now the problem in some structures of confusion lies in how we present or structure an either/or pattern that does not fit the reality of that context. For instance, a digital either/or coding does not usually fit an analog situation. In a digital either/or choice, something simply cannot exist in two places at once. We either find the light switch in the on position or in the off position. We read the numeral on the watch as either signaling 5 or 6. In an analog situation, the 'something' under consideration may occur in any number of places along a continuum, located anywhere along an infinite range of possibilities.

Both digital and analog responses can become anchors. In one sense, we find digital anchors easier to deal with and manage inasmuch as we experience them as more definite, clear, and discrete. However, analog matching, repeated often enough, also becomes an anchor. And as it operates as such, we can more precisely describe what we mean by a 'sliding anchor.'

To set a sliding anchor, we may start at the top of someone's arm, anchor a response, and then slide our touch down the arm... just a bit. We could then have the person access the response state again but this time we would slide our touch down just a little further down the arm again. If we continue this same process, we would begin to teach the person's neurology to do more than just respond to the anchor. We would teach the person *to continue to respond* and *to increase that response.* In the end, that person would respond far more than they did in the first instance.

Let us apply this to the Meta-Program of options and procedures. At first these seem to be absolute digital choices. But then again, people who sort for procedures tend to also want procedures about their options. And people who sort for options in the way they orient themselves in adapting reality frequently want options in their procedures. So how do we describe this? Further, auditory-digital people often get stuck on specific levels of thinking until nudged to go elsewhere.

This means that beyond digital (either/or) and analog (a range along a continuum), we have other ways whereby we can describe and encode experiences. We can create a mixture of these forms, such as a sliding anchor, and we can create fused responses or synesthesias. *Synesthesia,* which refers to 'a bringing together' describes one such choice. Here an overlapping or cross-circuit occurs in the representation system. The effect of this shows up when we elicit one modality, and it automatically and immediately evokes a response and representation in another modality. In such cases, we cannot categorize the response as exclusively either digital or analog, but as a mixture.

In synesthesias, a neurological circuit has become 'hard-wired', so to speak, so that two representations seem to 'go off' simultaneously. An overlap of representations occurs, for instance, when someone:

- *sees* blood and *feels* terror (see-feel, V—K)
- *hears* a harsh tone of voice and *feels* fear (hear-feel, A—K)
- *hears* some soft music and *feels* relaxed (hears-feels, A—K)
- *smells* a scent and *sees* remembered pictures (smell-see, O—V^r)
- *sees* a frown and *hears* bad internal critical voice (see-hear, V—A_d)

and so on. These synesthesias may function as either resources or limitations.

> "As you continue to *hear* me talk about these words, you can *see* yourself using them to *improve* your *communications* on a day to day basis."

When a stimulus permeates experience in other representation system domains and evokes other sensory modalities, then we have a synesthesia occurring.

Notice what color comes to mind when you hear the number four (V—A)? How about seven? And a color for ten? And what sound does each number have? What smell? Taste?

What colors do you have associated with various tones:

A soft voice?
A tense voice?
A loud shriek?
A deep resonant voice?

Can you imagine a voice that feels as smooth as silk (A—K)?

What do you make of a loud jacket (A—V)?

What do you feel about the words and tones that you hear in ordinary conversation (A—K)?

Now to enhance your internal representational richness in these things, give yourself the opportunity to play around with synesthesias.

- Take colors and see how they connect up with sounds and smells.
- Take sensations in the body and see how they connect up with sounds and tastes.
- Look for and listen to all of the synesthesias that you can perceive in other people's language patterns.

Doing this will lead to more skill in managing these qualities in the way we encode our experience. It will enable us to use modalities and submodalities more consciously in our communicating with others, and that will, in turn, enrich those listening to us. For instance, we could use lower tones for communicating comfort and relaxation even if the information might otherwise arouse anxiety in the listener. We might use more rising tones and bright colors for generating movement and energy. We might use rhythm for flowing speech, and lack of rhythm to communicate what we would prefer to be disjointed, disconnected, and/or deframed. You already know from NLP hypnosis training that lowering your voice commands more attention from people.

Synesthesia Exercise

By design, this exercise will enable you to practice synesthesia patterns and obtain more control in eliciting change involving sensory system circuits and linkages in A—V and A—K representational systems:

1) A begins by saying the numbers 1 through 10 with a particular voice quality. B responds by saying whatever color (V) or feeling (K) that number brings to mind.

2) After B has identified specific images and sensations that they have linked to each number, A repeats the numbers using a different tonal quality. Notice what happens.

For this synesthesia exercise, do the following to practice eliciting synesthesias within the context of storytelling.

1) A tells B a short story using one representational system (V, A or K) and only varying the submodalities.

2) B then relates the story back to A with this difference: s/he shifts the submodalities. Notice how this invites a different pattern of responses from A. →●

Conclusion

We enter into the domain of neurology when we recognize and work with the fact that we represent information in our head—in our visual and auditory cortex centers, as well as in our motor cortex, associative cortex, and so on. These so-called 'mental' components of consciousness have a definite neurological basis. Such internal representations comprise part of a structure involving sensory-neurological and linguistic-neurological formats.

The NLP model offers the good and empowering news that we can develop and expand the way we code our internal representations, and the resources that result from doing so. Further, as we expand and develop our representational abilities for encoding information, constructing new codes, and altering old representations, we become empowered to make ever finer and more useful discriminations. This assists us in developing our personal genius.

Chapter Seven

The Wild and Wonderful World of Submodalities

[Most of the following came from a presentation by Eric Robbie.
He now disclaims this chapter. See his article on this in the
Journal of International NLP, 1987.]

In the process of becoming an NLP Practitioner, we learn that ultimately we experience our subjective sense of reality at the submodality level. We learn that it lies in not merely the images, sounds, or words that we have in our head which alone create our internal experience. Rather, we learn that the specific qualities of those sights, sounds, and sensations cue our brain-neurology about how to respond to and feel about our experience.

Therefore we do not begin to implement our goal, say of staying fit and trim, merely because we hold a picture of that goal in our mind. What activates our nervous system to exercise arises from the quality of that visual representation—perhaps seeing it in color and as a movie rather than as a black-and-white snapshot; perhaps seeing the picture as very sharp and close, rather than far away and fuzzy; or perhaps by seeing it from an associated position while hearing the words, "Just do it!" These submodality qualities and codings provide the brain-body with distinctions that make the goal uniquely motivating for us. A moving, colored, sharply-focused picture would create an entirely different experience for us inside than a far-away, black-and-white out-of-focus snapshot.

We can think about submodalities as functioning like on-off switches for consciousness, and therefore, for experience. In a computer, thousands of on-off switches direct electronic impulses down one decision path or another. Submodalities perform a similar function in our brains in that they cue finer distinctions. This explains, in part, the statement that we experience 'experience' at the submodality level.

Given this, what does it mean to master the field of submodalities? What qualifies us to become recognized as a master at this level of experience? How do we go about trying out our intuitions and cognitions of the functional role of submodalities?

Obviously, mastery begins with skill in *recognizing* submodalities. Next comes the art of recognizing which submodalities function as 'drivers'—in ourselves and in others. Only then will we develop skill in using the set of human technologies derived from submodalities. Ultimately, mastery lies in knowing the driver submodalities which run a given individual's consciousness and experiences. Shifting those drivers can bring about tremendous transformations.

After we have developed the recognition skills, we will need to develop submodality skills for eliciting, designing, installing, and interrupting patterns of behavior. In this way we become skilful in recognizing and creating synesthesias at the submodality level.

"Haven't I Met You Somewhere Before?"

Eliciting and Recognizing Submodalities

The following exercise provides practice in submodality elicitation by which you can attune yourself to recognizing submodalities, especially those which make all the difference in the world—your driver submodalities. You also discover the range of variation within your own submodalities. This will assist you in beginning to visually recognize submodality distinctions in others.

Visual	Auditory	Kinesthetic
Location	Location	Location
Distance	Distance	Intensity
Movement	Volume	Duration
Brightness	Pitch	Movement
Contrast	Tone	Temperature
Focus	Rhythm	Rhythm

Figure 7.1: Eliciting and recognizing submodalities

1) To start, both A and B put themselves into an intense as possible state of sensory awareness. B accesses and anchors an uptime state in A, as well as in him/herself.

2) B then elicits a positive experience from A. This experience provides the content for this submodality exploration.

3) Once A has this reference experience, B makes A become aware of its VAK analog distinctions. B uses the suggestions in Figure 7.1 using one distinction at a time, proceeding very slowly through the list and gradually varying each submodality (in both directions) in order to get a sense of what these variations do for A's inner experience.

   For example, B might begin by brightening the image to the point where the feeling begins to change (it reaches a threshold). At this point B stops and backs off slightly. B then varies the same submodality in the other direction (from brightness to dimness). Again, B stops and backs off slightly when it reaches a threshold. When B has finished exploring the range of each distinction, s/he restores the submodality coding back to the original setting, or the normal intensity that it had when s/he started.

4) Invite the person experiencing the positive state to notice his/her own submodality range, and to comment on it, in order that you can more accurately calibrate to his/her system.

   Note especially which of the variables you found the most effective in changing the intensity of the experience. As Person B you should continuously calibrate to the changes in Person A and ensure that s/he only change one variable at a time. When you switch roles and become Person A, alter each submodality across its range, notice the extent to which you can do this, and thus calibrate to your own system. Find the driver submodality (or submodalities) that has the greatest effect for you. They will involve the ones that affect a number of other submodalities as well.

5) Finally, take your three main drivers in each submodality and combine them. Then change them all at the same time and notice the effect this has. →●

With this learning process about how to drive your own submodalities, you can now consciously and intentionally intensify any experience you have, and do this by yourself. This ability to amplify (or diminish) your own inner states obviously provides you with the ability to create a propulsion system so that you can truly just *all-out Go For It!* →●

Reading Submodalities From The Outside

Advanced Calibration:

Questions:

> Do you think we could learn to read someone else's submodalities from the outside? To what extent do you think you could fine tune your calibration skills so that you could tell whether a person has an internal image in color or in black-and-white? A fuzzy picture or a clear one? Or whether they have an image which they code as close up as opposed to far away? Or a sound that they hear inside in a panoramic way versus one coming from a single location?

Eric Robbie believes in the possibility of such feats of calibration and 'mind-reading.' He accordingly designed much of the following training to accomplish just that. For a fuller description, see *The Journal of NLP International, Vol 1,* "Sub-Modality Eye Accessing Cues" (1987).

Achieving this depends, to a great extent, on your ability to access, cleanly and intensely, a strong uptime state. This will greatly assist you in calibrating at this level to the internal experiences of others. You need to fully and completely turn on all of your sensory awareness, or you will simply miss most of the cues of the other's experience. Further, it would be helpful to access a 'fast time' trance-state so that you begin to sense yourself as moving twice as fast as the world around you. In doing this, remember that you will need to learn to make some finer distinctions about people, their neurology, and their states—for which we have few, if any, words.

Begin by calibrating to people's internal dialogues. To do good calibration work with this evidence of internal experience, you need to train yourself to watch for the analogs of the auditory-digital representations. This means watching for movement(s) in the jaw and lower mouth as a person 'thinks.' Does s/he sub-vocalize? Can you see him/her mouthing words? What kind of a rhythm does s/he generate with the internal dialogue which may show up as muscle movements in the jaw and/or mouth?

What about detecting a person experiencing two dialogues going on in their mind simultaneously? To get some practice with this:

1) Get together with a partner and have your partner mentally debate a decision back and forth without talking aloud, while you just sit back (or forward!) and notice. What do you see? Hear? Sense? Does the person's head move back and forth? Do you discern any pattern to the internal experience of debating a decision? Do you detect that the person seems to have voices or representations stored in two different places to which they return to from time to time? It is not at all uncommon for someone to have the two internal voices sorted spatially in different locations.

2) Now, during this internal debate, invite your partner to drop the lower jaw so that his/her mouth is hanging open, and copy this yourself. Now notice the effect. It often cuts off the internal talk completely. With some people it will just reduce the amount or speed of the internal dialogue. What do you notice in yourself? In your partner? By changing the kinesthetics of your mouth and jaw, you can often interrupt those kinesthetic-auditory synesthesia patterns and/or powerfully affect the internal experience.

The auditory-digital representational system gives us a way of encoding our learnings, understandings, and memories, as well as a tracking system for recall and retrieval (now recognized as the field of Meta-Cognition). As such, it consolidates our highest abstractions by encoding complex and philosophical under- standings, which form some of the most important roles that language plays in our lives.

Further, the great majority of us grew up in an educational system that rewarded words and language by the giving of grades. From such experiences, many people may have come to over-value or over-trust words. We may have come to live too much of our lives in our auditory-digital channel. And when we do, we increasingly move away from the primary level of sensory experience. (In *General Semantics*, Korzybski described this as 'an intensional orientation' in contrast to 'an extensional orientation.') This over-reliance on words can have harmful effects upon us such as preventing us from truly encountering life at the sensory based level. Words can get in the way of experiencing things in new and different ways. As Fritz Perls said in his classic statement:

> "Lose your mind and come to your senses."

Reading Submodalities on the Outside Exercise

Being part of the following group exercise will allow you to play with your submodalities and to tune up your intuitions about them. This exercise will enable you to calibrate to others' internal experiences with more accuracy.

1) In a group of four, A goes inside and accesses a strong positive or negative memory experience.

2) B, C and D calibrate A, and should put themselves into a very intense uptime state so that they have all their sense receptors wide open to A, the experiencer. Now B, C and D watch and calibrate to A's breathing, movement, posture, eye movements, skin tone, etc. and listen as A tells them about that experience, meanwhile taking note of the submodalities that drive it. If necessary, B, C and D may ask questions about the submodalities of A's experience until they feel satisfied that they have begun to calibrate to A. Repeat this once or twice until B,C and D feel as though they have done it.

3) After B, C and D have calibrated to A, invite A to again access another strong experience without speaking about it. A should tell the story to him/herself in the same way that s/he would tell it to someone else and then silently experience those thoughts-and-feelings. Each observer, B, C and D can now begin to guess the submodalities of A's second experience. Each should write down on a sheet of paper a list of what they sense or guess about the submodalities. Our aim in this is to see how many of A's submodalities each person can get right.

In doing this process, speed counts. Go as fast as you can. When you guess—guess quickly. Typically, speed plays an important factor in this training. So look, calibrate, gauge, and guess. Do not spend time thinking about it. Just do it. And do it quickly! In fact, doing it quickly will assist you in turning off some of your own internal dialogue so that your own accessing at the words/language level will not get in the way. You will move into the 'unspeakable level' that Korzybski described. Begin by using the following list of submodalities. Later you can add more.

In the exercise, ask in this order:

Basic Submodalities

Color—Black/White
Bright—Dim
Focused—Defocused
Near—Far
Moving—Still
Big—Small
Border—Panoramic
Flat—3D

Other Submodalities you can play with:

Tilting
Shimmering
Sparkling
Spinning
Moving in unusual ways
Translucent pictures in front

Do you now feel skilled enough to begin reading submodality cues from the outside? How much more skilled have you become? What signs and signals of various submodalities cue you? Do you have any conscious awareness of what they are yet?

Can you tell the difference between when someone sees a big internal picture and when they see a very small one? Try having someone access each of these. What difference can you see on the outside that may register as an analog marker? Does the person lean back and look more upward when processing a really big picture, or lean forward and closer when thinking about some small particular detail of a picture? Similar actions occur when a person thinks about a picture as close or far away.

What would you guess constitute the submodalities of a trance state? Take a moment to see if you can identify them. Then, when you have a list of them, use your list to assist someone to go into that state. Use language which includes the submodalities that will lead them into that state.

A useful metaphor when thinking about this kind of calibration emerges from asking the following questions:

> "How do you describe the difference between a rifle and a shotgun?"
>
> "How do you calibrate to shooting a single shot at a single target when using a rifle?"
>
> "How does that differ when you have a shotgun in your hand?"
>
> "How do you calibrate to your target differently?"

With the rifle you focus in a narrow and highly concentrated way, and the fun lies in hitting a very specific target. When shooting with a shotgun, you use a larger pattern. The shot will disperse in a general pattern.

State Change Exercise

The following exercise will teach you how to move yourself from a state of frustration to a state of ecstasy. Step right up if you want this one! By design it will install an automatic direction for you to go in when you feel frustrated. The direction itself will aim you (your mind-emotions) so that you can end up at ecstasy. We use a threshold pattern to do this.

1) Anchor ecstasy in person A. As person B you begin by anchoring a high ecstasy state in A: "Think of an exquisite experience which you felt was absolutely ecstatic for you...."

2) Identify the submodalities of ecstasy. When A finds the reference experience, have him or her identify the submodalities that drive it. Calibrate as you do so.

3) Pick a new desired activity. Now invite A to choose something that he or she cannot do at the present time, but would like to do. Tell A to close his or her eyes and see a picture of him or herself doing that desired activity.

4) Once there, invite A to amplify all of the submodalities within these representations (including tastes, sounds, and smells) to the most amplified position possible.

5) Now invite A to white-out this picture. When the picture becomes completely white, you as person B should immediately fire off and amplify the ecstasy state, "And the more you feel the feelings of ecstacy, the more the picture of doing what you would like to do will come back." Use all the submodalities and analogs that match and increase A's ecstasy state. Have A do this process of whiting-out and letting the picture return three times, and very quickly. →●

6) Finally, break state and then test your work. In this process, keep calibrating yourself to seeing the submodalities from the outside. Keep using analogs that match and amplify the internal state so that you can keep learning to match the internal submodalities.

Conclusion

If you plan to completely master NLP devote yourself totally to developing expertise in the field of submodalities. Anything less will not bring about your mastery of this field.

What picture would you like to create for yourself that would represent this understanding of the crucial role of submodalities? And as you see that picture, feel totally free to use your submodality drivers to make it as real, present, compelling, and as attractive as it can feel in your neurology. Listen to the kind of internal dialogue of words that expresses that idea in the kind of sounds which really 'crank your case'. Notice how the voice that speaks imparting this information is so compelling, so strong, so 'right on'.

■ For the latest developments in Submodalities, see Hall, "The Secrets of Submodalities" *Anchor Point*, July 1998, and Hall & Bodenhamer, *The Distinctions of Genius* (1999).

Chapter Eight

Tracking Down Where Brains Go

The Art of Calibrating Strategies

[Derived in part from Tad James, and in part from Bob Klaus]

In Practitioner training, when you know the language of the representational systems, know how to detect representational system functioning (eye accessing cues, sensory predicates, sensory breathing patterns, etc.) you have all the tools to start engaging in the art of 'brain tracking,' better known as strategy work. Detecting the multitude of sequences that a brain and nervous system go through to produce a piece of behavior enables a competent NLPer to 'steal' pieces of excellence all day long (a favorite activity of people trained in NLP). And once stolen, they can also pass them around, thus making the world a better place.

As you begin this chapter, just how skilled do you feel at recognizing these sequences of representational steps? When you encounter another human being demonstrating a behavior—either expertise or pathology—can you recognize the sequence of representational steps? How often do you think strategically in terms of:

"What comprises the strategy of this person's behavior or skill?"
"How could I improve this strategy?"
"Where else could I put this strategy to good use?"

Thinking strategically in this way tunes our intuition to catch the internal structure of expertise, genius, and dysfunction. Dysfunction? Yes, of course. After all, viewed through the NLP presuppositions, every pathology has some value and usefulness somewhere. Of course, if you can detect the internal structure of any behavior, you can model it, interrupt it, improve it and, best of all, replicate it. Mastering strategies in NLP enables us to adopt the wide-eyed curiosity and wonderment of a child as we move into a world full of people who can do things we cannot do, knowing that we can, at least to some degree, model it for ourselves.

Strategy Elicitation & Usage

The key to strategy elicitation lies in the order and sequence of the strategy but a most important factor involves exhibiting great curiosity. Having the 'insatiable wonderment of a child' as we go about eliciting strategies endows the process with fun, excitement, and magic. →●

Do you know how to become more curious? How often do you adopt the state of (or experience) curiosity? Do you know anyone who maintains a strong sense of curiosity whom you could model? Or how about simply designing a strategy that would get you to that state?

For that matter, do you know when to stop eliciting the sequential elements of, say, a motivation strategy? How do you know you have the final K of the motivation strategy? Obviously, when a person feels motivated to buy or act. When a person reaches that point, he or she has reached the 'exit' part of the program. In the TOTE model, the desired behavior now occurs—the person feels like buying and so exits the motivation strategy to buy. They have arrived at the final K. (TOTE stands for Test Operate Test Exit, which comes from the model developed by the cognitive modelers, George Miller, Karl Pribram, and Eugene Galanter.)

Now if you work within the larger frame of eliciting a buying strategy, separate the motivation strategy from the decision strategy. The decision strategy begins with the person making a choice. Did you know where the motivation strategy ended when you decided?

How do you know when you have moved to the end of a decision strategy? The answer lies in the behavior that corresponds to that strategy and, in this case, to the behavior of deciding. You find the person in the process of actively making choices about something. By definition, this indicates that a TOTE process is underway, and that you have activated your decision strategy.

An NLP Practitioner elicits this strategy information about the flow of representational steps from the person using both words (linguistic markers and cues) and neurology (eye accessing, breathing patterns, etc.). This provides us with the ability to describe the structure of an experience. When we have the structure, we can then use it. Accordingly, for someone who makes decisions and who has a $V^r \rightarrow V^c \rightarrow K$ strategy, as a Practitioner of NLP, we would pace and utilize this structure by saying something like, "I wonder when you will have time to look (V) at our proposal and see that it meets your criteria (V) and feel good about it (K^{meta}). You can, can you not?"

Elicitation Practice

Take some time now to practice this skill of eliciting strategies. Suppose we want to elicit a buying strategy.

1) First, A accesses a buying state. B prompts A by saying something like, "Remember a time when you made a decision to buy something."

2) It has been found important that the person makes the decision alone, without anyone else's input. So check that. We want the reference experience to represent A's choice alone, rather than one influenced by others. B has A go through the process again, observing with care, and then estimating the structure of the person's strategy.

3) Next, elicit another decision strategy from A, but this time watch and listen for his or her convincer strategy. To do this, ask yourself, "What convinces this person to go ahead and buy? What evidence does s/he have to have to make that decision?" If you notice the person's 'loops' in the process, you will thereby begin to recognize some aspects of the person's convincer in the strategy.

4) After this, test the strategy that you have elicited. Do this by feeding it back to the person using his or her key words and noticing the responses this generates. If your elicitation has attained a level of precision, they should match.

A person's strategy for buying something might go as follows: First, the person might make a comparison between what s/he remembers seeing (in his or her mind or in a magazine) and what s/he now sees (V^r/V^c), with criteria judgments about such things as value, practicality, cost, etc. If or when the person feels s/he has met these criteria, then this will generate some good feelings inside (K^+) and this, in turn, could lead to him or her to say things like, "I think I will get this." (Ad and looping around with more words.) After doing this three times the person would feel convinced enough to exit and buy.

Honing Elicitation Skills

Question: When you are eliciting someone's more general buying strategy, how do you separate out the two sub-strategy routines—the motivation strategy from the decision strategy? Here we seek to understand two of the key components of buying behavior, feeling motivated to buy and then actually deciding to buy. Here we have a critical point. Not all motivated people actually buy. Why not? Because they do not actually go through the process of deciding to buy. Furthermore, some people may decide to buy, but have an ineffective motivation strategy and so they never get around to actually carrying it out.

The decision part of the buying strategy obviously begins with someone making a choice. Are you aware of the end of the motivation part of the buying strategy when you decide? How do you know that you have moved into the decision-making stage? The most obvious answer is that you will know when the person both actively makes a choice and acts on the decision.

In thinking about this, it has been realized that within the entire buying strategy there are actually four sub-strategies. These include:

- a strategy for feeling motivated
- a strategy for making a decision
- a strategy for feeling convinced
- a strategy for feeling assurance that you have made a good choice.

In other words, we have sub-strategies within a higher frame or higher strategy. Nor does it stop there.

Within the convincer strategy we may find several loops. So now we have to ascertain what causes the convincer strategy to fire in a person's processing, in terms of the submodalities by which he or she codes this.

There are many possible answers to this. For example:

- the strategy may work automatically
- the person may run the loop a certain number of times before feeling convinced
- the person may need a period of time to pass

or,

- the strategy may consistently never move to a place wherein the person feels convinced.

So in terms of convincer strategies, consider this question: Would you purchase a house sight unseen?

One man's decision-making/convincer strategy went as follows:

$$\begin{array}{lllllll} V^r & \rightarrow & A_d & \rightarrow & K^+ & & \\ V^r & \rightarrow & V^r & \rightarrow & A_d & \rightarrow & K^+ \\ V^r & \rightarrow & V^r & \rightarrow & A_d & \rightarrow & K^+ \\ V^r & \rightarrow & K^+ & \rightarrow & A_d \text{ ("Do it!")} & & \end{array}$$

Looking at the diagram, you can see that it takes four loops in which he accesses remembered images and says words to himself about those images in order to generate stronger and stronger kinesthetic sensations until his strategy exits with the decision to buy. The submodalities that he finds the most driving consist of images that he saw as very close and three-dimensional. He also codes his internal hearing with a voice that has a very quiet quality to it.

You can test a person's strategy by simply 'filling up' or 'running' his or her convincer strategy with the number of times required, or the period of time necessary, or the consistency which s/he requires. Also, you will probably find it valuable to access the person's strategy for change and learning if you are working with him or her in a context of personal development or therapy. We found one convincer strategy that goes as follows.

$$V^r/V^c \rightarrow A_d \rightarrow K$$
("It's okay.")

The man who used this strategy found himself feeling convinced about something if he did a visual comparison between the pictures that he ran—which he coded in color, close, dissociated, and 3D—and then made an evaluative judgment that resulted in a sense of, "Yes, I find this perfectly valid and okay." When he said that to himself, he would then feel "okay", which he coded as a calm feeling in his stomach.

When we use strategies in communicating, therapy, sales, and so on, we can close by using presuppositions to tie things up. We can say,

> "Would you like to try to recreate the panic or just find that you cannot?"

> "Let's say that if you tried to do it again and found that you couldn't do it, now that would be something to imagine, would it not, now, and how do you now feel?"

Moving from Elicitation to Utilization

We could use the following as a persuasion technique. We could elicit the learning strategy of someone who seems skilled at something by asking them,

> "Do you know how to do that?"

> "How do you know that you can do that?"

> "How do you know you feel convinced that you have learned something?"

Eliciting the strategies with such questions and gathering high quality information about the person's internal processes then enables us to feed back the same structure and submodality qualities we discover as impactful (the driving submodalities) for that person. For instance, for many people a soft tonality commonly operates as a convincer of 'niceness'.

The following illustrates a multi-layered learning strategy—a strategy of learning to learn—that we found in one participant. It ran as follows:

$$V^{c\ (\text{dissociated})} \rightarrow A_d^{\text{meta}} \rightarrow K \rightarrow A_d \rightarrow \text{Exit}$$

Meta-comments "That's it!"

This man would construct a dissociated movie of the information he wanted to learn while someone was presenting it to him. He would then say words about that internal movie on his representational screen. These words would comment on the contents of the image, what it meant to him, what he could use it for, and so on. When that felt good to him, he would then say to himself in an excited voice, "That's it!"

The learning strategy of another participant had this structure:

V–V–V →	Ke/Ki →	A_d →	V/K →	A_d	Loop
(synesthesia) Visual associated images	Rhythmic/ deepening trances	"That's it!" (Driver submodality)	Visuals creating a deeper trance	"Is it working?" "Try something else."	

This woman created numerous visual images on her mental screen. As she presented the first images of the ideas to be learned, she dissociated from them and put them at some distance. Finally, however, she would associate into them. As she viewed her internal pictures, she would increase the submodality qualities making the pictures bigger, brighter, closer, sharper, etc. She continued doing this until they became really intense, and then she would then fully associate into them. When this happened, she immediately sensed both external and internal kinesthetic sensations of rhythm and warmth. And then when she said to herself, "That's it!" all these pieces in her mind would start looping and growing stronger.

If at any point in this process she felt that a problem had emerged in how she imagined things might work out, she would use other words. She would say to herself in a calm and clear voice, "Try something else." Or she would run a reality check, "Is it working?" These would then signal her to begin shifting the images.

We can elicit a reassurance strategy in much the same way as we did the convincer strategy. We can ask such things as, "How easily can you remember a time now when you bought something with which you felt truly happy? What did that experience seem like or feel like for you?"

One man had a simple reassurance strategy, a basic $V \rightarrow K$ structure, in which the kinesthetic result would consist of a sense of flow, rhythm, and harmony. He felt assured of his knowledge and understanding when his visual representations of whatever he thought about would emerge as an internal movie. This would then generate a sensation of flow and rhythm and harmony in his midsection. The visual representations which cued this response were him seeing clearly associated (first position) pictures and images.

As you do these kinds of eliciting processes, keep yourself on track by asking:

> "What does this strategy need to consist of for this particular person to feel convinced?"
>
> "What has to exist for this person to feel reassured that s/he has made the right decision?"

If you want to assist someone in accessing his or her reassurance representations, you could use the following words:

> "I want you to imagine that you have taken this item home. Okay, good. Now as you consider this purchase from that future perspective, just notice if you find anything that might or could come up which you wouldn't feel totally reassured about?"
>
> "What would this experience feel like for you if you discovered yourself feeling totally satisfied with this?"

Modeling Using Strategies

A NLP refrain that goes back to Richard Bandler, and one that not only has been quoted in numerous books, but has become a mantra, goes as follows:

> **"NLP is an attitude, backed by a methodology which leaves behind it a trail of techniques."**

With regard to its 'technology,' NLP has a number of techniques that allow people to accomplish things. And as Practitioners of this art, we should always remember that this technology arises from, and centers in, the modeling process itself. By modeling, the co-developers created the current technology and, by modeling other experts and people excelling in various fields, they will continue to develop new and additional technologies in the coming years.

So let us now ask, "What questions can we use to fuel and empower the modeling process?" NLP modeling questions include:

> "What distinctions allow this person to create and experience this behavior as a possibility?"
>
> "What supporting beliefs enable him or her to do this?"
>
> "What linguistics make it possible to encode it?"
>
> "What other possibilities arise, given this behavior?"
>
> "What would happen if we combined that sequence of representational responses with this other piece?"

In modeling, Wyatt Woodsmall has relied on the following three aspects of human experiencing and used them to create a triangle of influences. We will encounter these three component pieces whenever we elicit strategies or create strategies. So even though we recognize the mind-body process as a holistic cybernetic system, for the sake of understanding, analysis, discussion, etc. we will separate the following pieces. I understand that David Gordon and Leslie Cameron-Bandler first elaborated these.

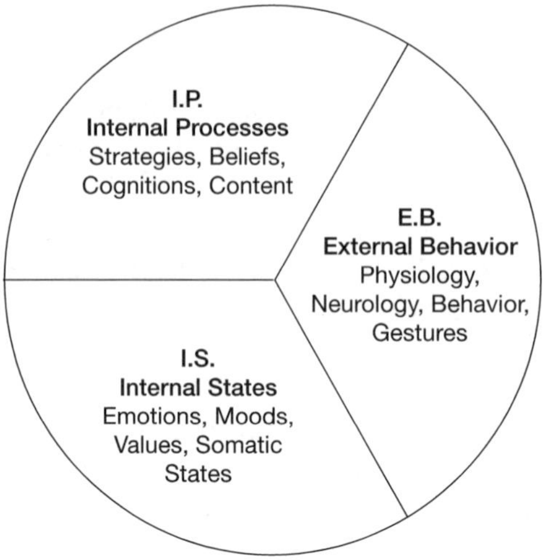

Figure 8.1: A triad of influences

From studies in the field of cybernetics, we know that effective change work involves integrating all three of these aspects of experience—external behavior, internal state, internal processes—which together make up the structure of subjective experience.

Now, if you believe you can or cannot do something, you almost always prove yourself right! How does this happen? What processes are operating to make that so? At the level of beliefs we have an internal program that runs our behavior. Our beliefs about the structure of the world undoubtedly operate as our most important beliefs because they set the frame on our entire orientation to reality and determine our higher states.

The Integration Process

How would you answer the following questions:

> "What integrates the internal processes, internal states, and external behavior."
> "Where does the actualization of these three parts of human experiencing occur?"
> "What unites and binds these three components together?"

Wyatt Woodsmall says that they come together in the NLP domain of submodalities. Why? Because if we can make distinctions between things, then we must have some way to make those distinctions. And making such distinctions inevitably occurs within the human nervous system, and possibly in consciousness. This brings up the role of submodalities in human experience, the distinctions that enable us to discern 'the difference that makes the difference.'

Regarding any behavior or experience, simply ask, "Just how do you do that?" The answer you receive will give you information about the person's internal processing from which the discernment of distinctions flows. This means that somehow the behavior or experience finds its source (how the person created it) via a distinguishing process. The person sorts and codes factors of the experience using different modality qualities. The person also represents beliefs about it, and not-beliefs as well, using different submodality patterns.

Strategy work (eliciting, identifying, mapping, redesigning, etc.) therefore involves tracking these finer distinctions. We also need to go inside and check the submodality patterns by which we know the difference between a belief and an unbelief. Doing this teaches us the submodality distinctions within and between these categories of external behavior, internal states, and internal processing.

Behind the entire framework of the art and skill of eliciting and utilizing strategies lies our ability, as NLP Practitioners, to detect and distinguish crucial differences. Practically, this refers to the ability to tell the difference between the crucial functions in a strategy from trivial or even accidental factors. When we elicit a strategy, we further need to distinguish between those things which the person has conscious awareness of and those outside of conscious awareness that may actually be driving the behavior. I mention these aspects of strategy elicitation in order to encourage you to aim to elicit this information in as clean and precise a manner as possible.

Revisiting the TOTE

The first step in eliciting a strategy involves task deconstruction. We deconstruct a task, or chunk a behavior down into smaller units: its skills, components, sub-tasks, modalities, Meta-Programs, etc. To do this, adopt a hungry and curious attitude as you go exploring: "What smaller, simpler, and more basic skills make up this skill?" When you ask this question in your exploration of a behavior or experience, you have begun to deconstruct the task.

If you have read Dilts *et al.*'s classic, *Neuro Linguistic Programming, Volume I: The Study of the Structure of Subjective Experience* (1980) then you will be familiar with Miller's TOTE model, which lies at the heart of NLP strategy work. I think we should more accurately call it a TOTE—O. This last O here stands for *Outcome,* which is a necessary ending to every TOTE, because every strategy leads to an outcome. And because every strategy takes us somewhere, we should notice those things which in the flow or process of the strategy do not play an equally important role.

The TOTE model essentially describes a flow chart of internal human processing. It tracks what a person *Tests* for, by comparing what the person wants (desired state) and what the person has (present state). It then identifies how the person *Operates* to change the present state to the desired state, and then runs a second *Testing* to check out the feedback from the operation. If the person has *not* congruently achieved the goal, s/he will Operate again. If the person *has* congruently achieved the goal or changed the criteria, s/he will finally *Exit*. This then brings the strategy to an end.

This refers to the elegance principle. The first Test in the TOTE model contains the trigger that begins the strategy. This trigger gets the person to begin to engage in the activity under consideration. It starts the strategy and moves the process into the Operation stage. A great many different things can trigger the strategy as many stimuli as can occur in the world The representation that we use of this trigger will be one of six things:

Visual
Auditory

Kinesthetic
Auditory-digital
Olfactory/Gustatory
Motor (6-tuple)

(See Dilts, *Roots of NLP*, 1983)

When we deal with a strategy at the operational stage, we deal with the activity, or a set of activities, that the person engages in while operating or functioning. This may involve the process of gathering data, remembering, some 6-tuple activity, a representational system or a certain sequence. But here comes the tricky part. Each step will not carry equal importance. Many times a strategy stage will loop around until some criteria meet the internal requirements of the person.

Whenever we deal with a strategy at the test stage, we should pay special attention to see if we can observe the occurrence of a comparison. The test will usually be a comparison between something in the external world and some internal criterion; although it could be a comparison of two internal criteria. Tests frequently come in the form of present state/desired state.

If we think in terms of the feedback from the outcome, then we can work backwards through the strategy steps and sequence in order to identify the person's specific criteria. These describe the criteria which someone has to have satisfied in order for the Test to receive a Go/No-Go decision. The Test in a strategy will usually involve noticing if some value has gone over a threshold. It is often the case that criteria have to be satisfied in more than one representational system.

The Testing Stage of the TOTE:

Visual	(looks right)
Auditory	(sounds right)
Kinesthetic	(feels right)
Auditory-digital	(makes sense)

Criteria test: 'right' test that fits the standards of what we consider important, essential and valuable.

When a person has moved into the Testing stage, his or her mind will operate in a special mode—in the match/mismatch comparison mode. Here the person may test for the difference between criteria/reality.

"What standard do I seek to obtain?"/"What actual results am I getting?"

There are numerous qualities we can use to do such testing. We can test by asking, "How much? How often? How intense?" etc.

When a strategy reaches the point of having passed a Test, it then moves to the Exit stage. This is another decision point in the strategy, and we typically find it coded with a kinesthetic signal (a positive or negative sensation). At this point, the person will ask, "Do I have a match?" "Does it reach the specified threshold?" "Can I ever get a match?" "Should I feel satisfied with it at this level?"

If the person does not experience a match in the comparison, then s/he has several options with regard to where to go next in the strategy:

- The person can engage in more operations and options by cycling back through and enriching the strategy.
- S/he can cycle back to the beginning and gather more data.
- The person can lower their standards, diminishing internally stored representations and/or threshold points.
- S/he can make the decision-point wider, thereby having a sense of more options.
- The person can simply Exit. S/he can forget that particular goal and simply choose another outcome entirely.

Now how can you use this information about strategies? How do you install a new strategy in yourself or another? How do you replicate a genius strategy?

Realize first of all that you will always be using your representational systems. Ultimately all experience, behavior, and skill occur at the sensory system level. Aim therefore to develop greater skill in using your sensory systems for representation, coding, discrimination, etc. Aim especially to develop a well-refined kinesthetic system.

As an example, consider the spelling strategy. You will not find it sufficient to merely make visual representations, or to construct new visuals for new words. You will also need a kinesthetic signal in the strategy which cues you for the sense of 'familiarity' and of 'being right.' This kinesthetic sense is, in fact, the Test or decision point for Spelled Right/Spelled Wrong. If you don't have this signal, or don't have it well-developed, you could look at misspelled words and then later reproduce them perfectly.

Working with strategies in this way will enable you to discover just how much we are constantly comparing things against our internal criteria. In this way, we are determining whether our decisions are good or bad. Genius primarily involves making highly refined distinctions in each of the representational systems. Transfer the bottom half of the comparison. The representational systems, and especially their submodality qualities, are ultimately the ABCs of behavior, and therefore of genius.

Modeling Patterns of Excellence by Increasing Familiarity with the Auditory-Digital System

In eliciting strategies of motivation and excellence, an NLP Practitioner will pay especial attention to the linguistic modality (auditory-digital—A_d). During Practitioner training, we learn the sensory predicates for the VAK modalities (see, hear, feel words), but do we also know the predicates for the auditory-digital modality? What kinds of words could you expect from someone who is in the A_d mode?

Bob Klaus has made the following list of the cues indicating the auditory-digital mode. Listen for, sort for, and pay special attention when people make frequent use of:

lists
labels
procedures
priority lists
meaning-making statements (complex equivalents)
criteria lists (of values, nominalizations)
metaphors
displays
details
classes, classifications, categories

Other more specific words that frequently function as linguistic markers for this modality include:

comprehensible, evaluation, reality, the facts, consideration, realization, knowledge, makes sense, ideas, logic, etc.

When a person moves to the auditory-digital mode, s/he begins to make abstractions, conclusions, generalizations, etc., about the sensory based information or other abstractions. And s/he does this for the purpose of 'making sense of things,' 'reasoning things out,' and so on. This moves the person to a higher logical level than the neurological level of sights, sounds, smells, and sensations (the VAK level). This represents another level in the abstracting process (a meta-state level).

Relying more and more on language and other symbolic systems describes a distinguishing factor of meta-states in contrast to meta-primary states.

An additional indicator of a person operating in the auditory-digital mode concerns the lack of obvious accessing cues. How will the person use his or her eyes when s/he is asked a downtime question? S/he may defocus his or her eyes, or move them slightly, and seem to stay present with you, or move to the auditory access positions. Because the person who favors the auditory-digital modality operates from, and lives in, a kind of secondary experience (abstracted from the sensory-based level), that person experiences more dissociation from sensory experience and lives more in a meta-position. (The Meta-States model modifies this statement considerably.)

The person in the auditory-digital mode also seeks information comprising facts and details, know-how, knowledge, understanding, and comprehension. In a word, such a person seeks things that 'make sense' and that organize his or her world using words.

The Values that Drive States of Excellence

Experiences of excellence start with a set of internal representations which evoke a corresponding state of excellence. Yet such experiences also operate as they do because of many supporting beliefs and values. To play with this, think about something to which you easily and without hesitation attribute the word 'excellence.' Now notice:

- What values do you presuppose in that state?
- What things of high importance have you inherently assumed occur in that state?

As we detect, find and identify the values that correspond to an experience or behavior of excellence, they then provide us with another path for moving toward that excellence. Typically the values that we need to install to empower us (or another) to move toward and install a state of excellence, are as follows:

courage	candor	commitment	loyalty
congruity	duty	integrity	selfless service
passion	gentleness	respect	care or love

Consider:

- What values would you like to add to this list?
- When you think about a skill, person, or experience of excellence, what other qualities and features stand out for you?
- What qualities endow it with that sense of excellence? →●

Now consider the structure of the nominalization 'values.' Values exist as ideas, thoughts, mental constructs. Yet we think many thoughts that we would not consider valuable. So what special kind of thought is a "value"?

Like all thoughts, thoughts about what we value have VAK sensory-based representations. We make pictures, hear sounds and words, feel sensations in our body. To have a value we have to move to a meta-level and *value* the referent of our representations. Mere representation alone does not create a value. Validation, confirmation, affirmation, etc., at a meta-level, sets a frame of higher thought about the referent, which enables us to think, "This is important." "I want and need this!"

Therefore, when we experience our values we experience them as strong and energized ideas. What energizes them? Where do such thoughts get their emotional intensity? From the higher frame-of-reference that confirms and validates them. This explains why values carry such strong emotions within them. Love, trust, achievement, connection, significantly contributing… we experience these kinds of ideas and feel them as energizing. No wonder they move us. No wonder they activate our motor programs.

Further, the emotional, somatic (bodily) energy of values contains both positive and negative energy. Our values as empowering ideas actually create both positive (+) and negative (–) psychic energy at the same time. These operate as the polar opposites of each other. If we feel positively motivated to learn and develop our intellectual powers and understandings, we simultaneously feel motivated to move away from ignorance, stupidity, stagnation, and so on. Therefore, inside every propulsion system we find strong and intense propelling (toward) values, and strong and intense aversion (away from) values. →●

No wonder then that our highest passions and energies, the ones that make up our states of commitment, passion, and excellence, correspond to the fulfilment or violation of our values. Because values activate our emotions, we inevitably act from our values and on behalf of our values. And conversely what we act out in terms of our behavior tends to reflect the deeper and/or older things that we actually value or have valued. This means that values operate as a meta-level frame that we need to consider and use in our modeling.

If our goals truly express our conscious values, then they will move us positively in the direction of fulfilling those highly valued experiences. The values associated with our desired states of excellence will generate strong positive feelings for what we want and strong aversion feelings that will move us away from de-valued experiences or negative evaluations.

We can make another important distinction with regard to our values. Namely, that they fall into two types: means values and end values. *End values* are those which express our objective, goal, or outcome. In contrast, *means values* concern our methods and processes for attaining the end values.

Accessing and Installing States of Excellence

In the following exercise, you have the opportunity to install some values of excellence in yourself. Use this exercise to practice installing and stacking anchors for the following kinds of states in yourself and those you work with: courage, candor, commitment, loyalty, selfless service, duty, integrity. Feel free to supplement this list with other values that you find and value and think of as values of excellence.

1) In pairs, B elicits from A a time when s/he felt very courageous.
2) Once A calls forth a specific referent for the value of excellence in courage, invite him or her to verbally generate a full sensory-based description of that experience.
3) B then calibrates and anchors that courage state for A. Do this with as many of the values of excellence as you desire to begin building for yourself.

Systems Theory helps us understand how these kinds of things fit together. Within a system, every dynamic component of the system performs certain functions. Hence we talk about the existence of the functions of parts, dynamics of parts, synesthesias, and so on. These functioning components relate to one another in a variety of ways. Each part exists and operates within an even larger system. Systems Theory also refers to the *'emergent properties'* of a system. An oft-repeated mantra-like principle asserts, "The whole of a system is greater than the sum of the parts." Korzybski, in developing his non-Aristotelian system way back in the 1930s, said that we do not merely add pieces together, but that a new quality, a non-additive element arises. In systems theory, we say that a new configuration or gestalt emerges.

Recognizing that human nature and human experiencing have these systemic qualities (non-additivity, emergence, feedback loops, etc.), enables us to discover how our representations, labels, strategies, values, beliefs, decisions, and so on, all fit together in the human mind-body system.

Furthermore, when it comes to companies of excellence, or environments that facilitate human excellence, researchers have identified that certain cultures function more productively than other cultures or contexts. In the business context, managers and consultants talk about the systemic environment as the group's culture. A culture describes the system of values, norms, acceptable behaviors, philosophy of presuppositions and beliefs about what that culture deems real, important, significant, and so on. In this sense, it sets the frame at a meta-level for what the people within that system experience as valuable and not-valuable. These component pieces create the cultural or organizational climate for those who live in it.

Explore the cultures that concern you by using the following questions:

- What values, norms, and philosophies within your cultures do you want to concern yourself with?
- Which ones significantly contribute to the development of excellence in the group?
- What kind of structure best enables you to build up that meta-context?

As you identify each and every value, norm, and philosophy that enhances and builds excellence in yourself and others, use your NLP distinctions to make them specific. By doing so, you will access the strategy that runs it and which you can use to induce the corresponding state of excellence into yourself. →●

Finally, when you have all of the specific steps that build up the strategy of a particular excellence in a particular environment, create a stacked anchor, and then fire and hold all of these anchors simultaneously.

The Art of Modeling—Momentarily Becoming Someone Else

The Ultimate in Strategy Work

[Derived from both Bandler and Robbie]

In NLP we explore modeling at several levels. We talk about linguistic modeling when we model beliefs, values, understandings, etc. We talk about neurological modeling when we model posture, tone, gesture, movement, etc. At Master Practitioner level, the heart of effectively using non-verbal qualities of another's communication provides us with an important piece of information about how to model another person's area of expertise.

This form of modeling means adopting, as completely as possible, the non-verbal attitude of the other person. To do that you need to access the experience of the other person. One way to do this involves posturing your body in precisely the same position (or attitude) as the other person and ask yourself the following types of questions:

> "If I always had to live and orient myself this way as I move through the world, what would be true for me?"

> "What would be true for me emotionally, cognitively, interpersonally, somatically, and so on?"

> "What am I aware of? What ideas, intuitions and feelings come to me as I stand, move, posture, gesture, and so on, in this way?"

This exercise, of course, underscores the importance of posture and position in taking on and learning about another's reality. By doing it, you will discover how posture cannot but help reflect and access values as well as representations, understandings etc. Simply by adopting another person's posture, you will often create a pathway to access that person's inner world of representations, values, beliefs, intuitions, etc. You may even begin to sense the experiences which have contributed to that person's view of the world.

How or why does this process work? Probably because we all live within our values and express those values in physical/neurological ways by means of our body. And since we share a similar kind of nervous system, neurology, etc., and relate to the same environmental forces (gravity, movement, culture, etc.), taking on another's physiology expands our awareness of the other person's experience.

Modeling Exercise 1

1) Get with a partner, or several people and begin by observing how a particular person stands, moves, breathes, and gestures. Think about these observations in terms of what you would need to do to match and/or mirror this person.

2) After you have observed these non-verbal aspects of communication, adopt all of them yourself. Step inside those same physiologies, behaviors, movements, etc.

3) After you have done that as thoroughly as you can, begin to notice the qualities, thoughts, awarenesses, and so on, that these postures and movements evoke in you. As you do, keep asking yourself, "What does this trigger in me?" Take a moment or two 'to become someone else'.

Human bodies inevitably communicate values. In saying this, we refer to the neurological aspect of NLP that utilizes the communication of rhythm, posture, breathing, muscle tension, eye scanning, etc. Here you need to search for the bodily correlates of a person's values and Meta-Programs. For instance, people doing small chunking often lean forward as though moving in to get closer to seeing the details. Contrast this to how most people do large chunking. In handling larger pieces of information, they will typically lean back as if by doing so they can see the big picture. This forward or backward movement then acts as a non-verbal signal of the chunking pattern (Meta-Program) of specific/gestalt. In this way you can begin to learn to read submodalities and Meta-Programs from the outside. (See Hall & Bodenhamer, *Figuring Out People*, 1997, Chapter 11.)

Modeling Exercise 2

To gain more practice, use the following exercise modeling to provide yourself with some training in the art of momentarily becoming someone else. This will give you practice in aligning your physiology to match another's, to use your sensory acuity and flexibility as you gather information about another's beliefs, values and experience.

1) In a group of four people, designate A as the Model and B as the one to model A. B studies A and then stands next to A and adopts a similar posture.

2) C and D now observe A, and assist B in getting the best possible match. C, the Shaper, gathers information by feeling the state of A's muscle groups, and provides this information to B verbally, and also adjusts B's physiology to make it identical to the way A organizes his or her physiology. D (meta-person observer) will also able to provide information about the focus of attention, energy, and so on. C continues to mold B to get as good as possible representation of A's physiology. The more detail you attend to, the better the modeling.

3) When the molding and shaping has been done to the satisfaction of B, C, and D, then B should go inside and silently ask him or herself, "If I always had to move through life like this, what would have to be true for me?"

Conclusion

NLP arose from one level of modeling and continues to grow and develop through the modeling process. We have moved to modeling not only what an expert *does* excellently, but also *how* s/he does it. Even so, the modeling aspect of NLP is extremely complex since it includes numerous pieces of a systemic nature. Consequently, mastery of this art will need much time and practice. Doing so involves mastering the process of thinking strategically, sorting and unpacking strategies, listening for linguistic markers in a person's language that indicate different aspects of his or her strategy, developing the personal flexibility of trying on various pieces of another's strategy, etc.

From this chapter, you can see that NL predominantly involves and thrives on modeling. The first thing that NLP modeled was the verbal language behavior of three expert therapists and their non-verbal communication behavior. Out of that modeling came the seminal books *Structure of Magic, Volumes I & II* (1975, 1976). And because NLP continues to grow and develop through the modeling process, this is an area of expertise of the utmost importance to all Master Practitioners.

Chapter Nine

Visiting More Exotic and Empowering States

[Derived primarily from Richard Bandler]

In NLP, we use 'state' as a shorthand term for a total mind-body, linguistic-semantic-neurological phenomenon. The state you experience at any given moment (and you always experience some state) will have components of thought, internal representation, neurology, physiology, emotion, beliefs, values, etc. These function in a way that can be resourceful or limiting, productive or sabotaging, positive or negative, pleasant or painful, empowering or disempowering.

Learning about states in order to manage them more effectively, is part and parcel of Practitioner training. In mastering this training, you will want to gain a firm grasp of the skills and principles of state management. Then you will no longer stand at the mercy of every stimulus, mood, event or person that happens to come your way. You will have developed the ability to sustain the spirit of NLP, know how to interrupt non-productive states, and access those states which keep you resilient, learning, highly motivated, and at your best.

Chaining States of Consciousness

Once you know about how states work in terms of their component parts (sensory based information, language, physiology), how to interrupt a state, how to access and transform a state, you will then have all the pieces that make you ready to develop the higher level skill of chaining states together. Chaining states creates a process whereby you (or anyone else for that matter) can move away from a state that you find limiting and unresourceful, to one that allows you to be more resourceful.

Check this out. Think of a time or a situation where you would find this ability to change your state particularly useful. Does a time come to mind? For example, you may have experienced a time when what you wanted was to shift from a depressed state to a totally joyful state—but that involved too much of a jump to make. Some people have drawn erroneous conclusions from their understanding of NLP that a person can go from feeling totally down and defeated, to feeling totally excited by just anchoring. It simply does not work that way! And even if it did, who wants the manic-depressive strategy for living day by day?

Sometimes we simply have to first move to a less unresourceful state, then to another one which gives us less problems, then to a more neutral state. From there we can steer ourselves to a mildly resourceful state; then to a more powerful resourceful state; and finally to an intensely ferocious resourceful state. Sometimes a person has to gently nudge him or herself from state to state so that s/he experiences the state shifts as more ecological and respectful.

The wonderful thing about this chaining states procedure is that you do not need to create any new neurological equipment inside yourself in order to achieve it. You already have all the necessary equipment. In fact, you already do this every day anyway, do you not? After all, when you wake up in the morning, you wake up in some state. But you don't stay there all day. Something happens in the external world, or in your mind, and lo and behold, you shift states; you get into another state. Nor do you then stay in that one all day. You are continually shifting out of one state into another. And so on.

Suppose now that you kept a journal of all the states you went in and out of during the day? You would probably find that you go in and out of half a dozen to perhaps two dozen states over the course of a day. If you continued to journal over weeks and months, you would probably discover that you have your favorites—states of choice. You have your habitual up states and your habitual down ones. In other words, you naturally veer from state to state.

You might also discover that sometimes you get into a state and you stay there for a long time, perhaps for hours. And that you have your own little rituals (environmental and internal anchors) that can put you back into that state at the snap of a finger. Many people I know can fly into a rage at a moment's notice. They usually practice this when driving! Others have a 'telephone voice' and can switch to a calm, centered, adult-sounding voice in a millisecond.

Chaining States Exercise

Let us start this state-chaining process by building a chain of states that can move someone from the state of hesitation to the state of 'Going For It!' As we do, imagine how useful you might find having a strategy like this at your fingertips. Our intention in using this next exercise is to simply practice using presuppositional sentences whereby you can chain a sequence of states together. Utilizing the following list of states, link and anchor them together:

1. Hesitation
2. Frustration
3. Impatience
4. Wanton Desire
5. Total Go For It

Hesitation → Frustration → Impatience → Wanton Desire → Total Go For It!

1) In a group of five, have A slow down his or her external world as s/he gets into a nicely relaxed and calm state.

2) B, C, D, and E each choose one of the above five states to elicit. Each person should write out six sentences which they will read to A as a state induction. These statements should presuppose the state which they want to evoke in A.

3) Let each person then practice with A, testing to see if his or her statements fit A's reality.

4) When each person and A feel fully prepared, B, C, D and E in turn read two of his or her sentences to A using all the appropriate intonation patterns. By each person having a different

location with respect to A, this will also set up some spatial anchoring and linkage.

The process of reading the presuppositional statements should occur while A feels comfortable and receptive. The rest of the group read their statements and cycle through this process three or four times. In doing so, they will set up various tonal and visual anchors. When they have finished, test the anchors by going around the group using only the spatial (visual) anchors.

5) Test the work. Does A now go from hesitation to 'Total Go For It'? Test the anchors by cycling using only the spatial anchors. ●→●

I have included some examples of the kind of statements to use on A. Remember to pace A non-verbally when running the pattern with him or her. After reading the following statements, create five more statements that would really fit your beliefs, values, understandings, and submodalities.

HESITATION

"As you think about what you want, a little doubt comes into your mind."

"The picture forms and then blurs, only for a moment."

"While the thought attracts you, other thoughts keep intruding into your mind and turning you off."

FRUSTRATION

"You want it, but something arises to block you. You can't have it!"

"You say to yourself at the point of being blocked, 'Why can't it leave me alone?'"

"In your frustration you shout, 'Get out of here, will you!'"

IMPATIENCE

You say to yourself, "Now, why not now?"

"Let me at it! It's mine; it's just a matter of time. I want it now, there's no good reason in the world not to have it now."

WANTON DESIRE

"This desire stands before you so clear and bright that its attractiveness multiplies three-fold."

"You have no doubt that you want this, and you want it now."

"Your desire grows. You hear a voice within telling you, 'Reach out and savor this delicious attraction right now!'"

GO FOR IT!

"Every fiber of your being now strains forward, every part of your mind and heart yearns passionately for this. Your breathing even now speeds up as if motivating you to reach out and make it yours."

Setting Sliding Anchors

You can further extend this work and practice amplifying the resourceful states by using everything you know about submodalities and sliding anchors. To do this,

1) Set a kinesthetic anchor for each of the five states (from hesitation to Go for it!).

2) Now utilizing the driver submodalities of the subject, amplify each of the states until the person seems to rise to a pitch of intensity in terms of the feelings of that state.

3) Next, anchor each of the amplified states with a sliding anchor starting perhaps at the top of the shoulder on the right arm. Each time you reaccess that state move the anchor a little

further down the arm. Doing this sets up an analog anchor which communicates metaphorically: 'keep increasing the intensity of this feeling.' It sets up a direction.

4) Afterwards, test the anchors and the chain by firing off the anchor for frustration and see what happens. If you have established the process thoroughly, the anchor should lead the person almost immediately into the state of Going for it! →●

Creating States of Excellence

When you observe those people whom you recognize as functioning at a level of excellence at some skill, task, or activity, you quickly discover that these individuals think and feel in highly motivated ways and that they have effective strategies for accomplishing things in their area of expertise. This combination makes them highly effective in their domain of excellence. And they have something else going for them.

They have an easy access to the altered states in which they do their best work (competence, excitement, passion, calmness, commitment, and so on). If this partly describes the strategy of expertise, suppose you too could quickly, systematically, and regularly develop an easy access to your own best states? That would turbocharge your efforts, would it not? So let us do it! →●

As we think about modeling such excellence and installing such strategies in ourselves, we can use the following exercise to assist ourselves in this process.

1) First access an altered state in Person A, one that the person recognizes as a state of excellence.

2) Next amplify that state by using presuppositions and Person A's own driver submodalities to crank this state up.

3) Now loop Person A through the chain that you created earlier. This will take him or her from the state of holding on to mediocrity to letting go of all hesitation to fully 'Go for it'.

Use the following states as you link them into a chain:

1. Holding on
2. Fear
3. Anticipation
4. Confidence/Belief
5. Letting go

In modeling, we use one key question to cycle through in probing to the essence of the strategy, namely, "What must logically be available to a person in order for this behavior, response, choice, etc. to occur?" Asking this question gets us involved in the kind of presuppositional thinking about experiences of excellence that will help us to stay focused and distinguish between crucial and trivial factors. We can also use it as a form of backtracking which then allows us to get to the underlying (or over-arching) structures of experience, namely, to the beliefs, interpretations, model of the world, decisions, values, etc. which make the behavior possible at meta-levels.

Richard Bandler illustrated this principle with his story about working with a baseball player. He had been hired to model a particular ballplayer's strategy for effectiveness when batting. He first got the fellow into state. "Then I kept asking, 'What are you doing? What are you experiencing that allows you to be really 'on'? He commented simply and shortly, 'I just really see the ball.'"

What does that mean? True to form, Richard kept meta-modeling him about precisely what he meant. "And what I discovered was that truly excellent ballplayers know how to experience quick trance states, so that they can alter their internal reality to deal with their external world. This is one of those times when there's no right or wrong, but many choices."

"As I continued to work with the player, I asked him to make a particular car big in his mind. Then I used some amplification language: 'Now even bigger.' I experimented with his consciousness to see if he could make the car he was observing go at only two miles per hour. And sure enough, this was one of the skills that enabled him to do what he could do."

Here we can see that the ballplayer's ability to manifest excellence depended upon a particular altered state of mind. He had to get into the state where he could 'really see the ball.' And so he did. He quickly and unconsciously just did that and this had become so streamlined over the years that he no longer even knew how he did it. He had easy access to this resource state of making the world go into slow motion, the ball become bigger, and himself totally confident and focused on it.

When it comes to applying the process of chaining states together, we need to make our desired outcome to be able to go from a state in which we feel ourselves holding back to one where we begin to steer ourselves into another state—initially perhaps into a state of hesitation—and from there, to one where we think and feel highly motivated. In so doing we first need to (consciously) create each intermediate state, amplify it, shape it, anchor it, and so on. Then we run through the process until we also have easy access to the resourceful states that truly enhance our performance.

If you think of the state of 'Letting Go' as a state of mind where the conscious mind gets excited and goes, 'Aauugh!' and a voice turns on, 'You're losing control!' then, obviously, this will prevent you from letting go. It would be too much of a jump. It would interrupt your state. And that happens with many people. They begin to access a state, but, when they start to experience it more fully, their mind jumps to a higher logical level, they become self-conscious, and that, in effect, breaks state.

Making too big a jump between states cannot only create a pattern interrupt (a standard NLP technique in its own right), but also create amnesia. Think back to a time when you focused your attention completely on something, when you became totally absorbed in a project, or when you accessed a strong, productive state involving something of immense importance... and then the phone rang, someone knocked on the door, or a bell went off. You got up. You handled the interruption and then you found yourself wondering, "Now where was I? I can't remember what I was doing." Amnesia.

This highlights the importance of questioning and exploring the intermediate states.

"What states could lie between those two extreme states?"

"What other state could someone induce that would provide a smaller jump?"

"What about the state of anticipation—would it lead to holding on by going through fear?"

"Could you evoke the state of letting go by leading through excitement, relaxation, trust, belief, confidence?"

Use the following exercise to eliminate getting stuck in the state of frustration. Use it to custom-make some useful designer states. Then we can use the extra energy that we would otherwise waste in experiencing frustration for hours on end more productively. You can now attend to your outcomes and invent new ways of achieving them.

As you access three or four intermediate states between frustration and motivation, anchor each state onto the back of the experiencer's hand. Set an anchor on and between each knuckle. Once you have that in place, use the sequence of your designed chain to begin training them to move sequentially through these states. Begin with the frustration anchor and state. Hold it while you simultaneously fire off and hold the next anchor. As the person moves into the next state, hold that anchor and fire off the next, and then hold that until you have fully accessed the next state, and so on. Continue this until you have fired all of the knuckle anchors. Finally, test your work. → ●

Designer Human Experiences

On Richard Bandler's training in 1989, he decided to call this process 'Designer Human Experiences.' He was talking about engineering designer states, and he presented this process as a way for us to tailor-fit our mind and our experiences to what we want which truly fits for us. It empowers us to identify the states and internal experiences that we want to have, build them, install them, and practice them until they become habitual.

Experiment with the tonality that an auditory-digital person (A_d) uses. While you have him/her accessing auditorily, introduce some new self-talk lines for the person, but do this using his/her tonality. This can work in a very sneaky way. Because when you use that person's tonality, s/he may very well fail to recognize that it isn't his or her voice! The person might even assume the words as his/her own since s/he hears them in his/her own voice.

Actually, this particular use of someone's own driver submodalities is nothing new in NLP. But for the one who has mastered adopting another person's submodalities in his or her own communication, this will certainly increase the power of the process and move that person to a new level of application elegance.

If you now feel ready to do some Designer Human Engineering, then you can use this next exercise to begin to design for yourself five absolutely exquisite chains of states.

1) Begin by picking two polarities that tend to torment you on a regular basis. For instance, you could pick:

   insecure—confident; stuck—resourceful; stressed-out—calm; bitter and hateful—loving and concerned; etc. Any pair of polarity states will do.

2) Next, identify one of these states as your stuck point (i.e. insecurity, stressed-out, depressed, lonely, fearful, worried, etc.) with the other polarity as your desired outcome. Make your desired state a particularly resourceful one that you would like to access. Now think of these polarities as being on a continuum.

3) Identify three to five states which lie in between these two polarities. During the process, these function as pivot points which you will use to steer yourself off and away from the stuck point, into the new direction toward a new desired state. Keep asking yourself, "What lies in between these two states?"

4) You need to do some preparatory work in building up the presuppositions, suggestions, beliefs, and values that correspond

to those states and which elicit them for you. When you have done this, go ahead and set up a chain that incorporates all these polar and intermediate states.

5) Invite a partner to use your suggestions and language expressions to elicit each state in you and to amplify them. Then have the person link each of those states to the next one. Remember, as you do this, that this functions as a directionalizing pattern similar to the Swish Pattern. By design we want the anchors to send you into a new direction. As these states become chained in a sequence, the experience of going into a state at the negative end will send you towards the positive.

6) Once you have well anchored the states in the experiencer, invite a programmer to stand on either side and to begin to use some presuppositional statements to induce a nice trance state. When in trance, invite the person to cycle through the chain, beginning with the unresourceful polarity. Ensure that you always guide him or her gradually into increasingly resourceful states until the person reaches the other polarity. Do this repeatedly until the process becomes streamlined.

When you are doing the programming, use your best hypnotic tonality by lowering your voice and dropping the tone at the end of a sentence. The person's unconscious mind will take that communication as a command. This happens because usually the voice and tone go up at the end of a statement which activates the conscious mind, and in this experience, we need to avoid doing this.

This way of understanding that behaviors and states lie on a continuum goes back to Aristotle. In his book, *Nicomachean Ethics*, Aristotle wrote chapter after chapter about the importance of 'the middle.' Vice, he argued, always involved the lack of balance. It involves some virtue that someone had taken to the point of excess or defect, the person has overdone or underdone some virtue. Too much anger leads to rage, violence, and uncontrollable domination. But too little does not work well either. It makes someone unable to stand up for or against things.

Aristotle, as an 'almost early-NLPer,' knew about the states in the middle, but little about veering from one to the other, or chaining states together in order to move a person from a place of limitation and stuckness to accessing his/her highest resources. But now, with this process, you do!

Inducing More Fun, Flirting and Friendliness

One high level state inherent in the NLP model, and one especially modeled by Richard Bandler, is the one he calls 'the state of sizzle.' He just loved to induce Practitioners on his workshops into a flirtatious state. In his trainings, he ran what he called his 'Flirting Class.' He always seemed to have a lot to say about it.

Let me begin with a disclaimer. Flirting here does not mean lustful. The state of feeling and acting flirtatiously involves more the behaviors of smiling, acting in a friendly manner, treating people respectfully, letting people know you like them, having some music in your soul (or at least in your head), looking approachable, and other such things.

Given this definition, how well do you flirt at work, at home, on the bus, with kids, with seniors, with strangers? What, for you, operates as the key to the strategy of successful flirting? Bandler describes some things that you especially need to avoid, such as 'putting on a face and tonality of negativity', 'talking about your problems—especially the problems of your last partner!'

The first thing that will enhance your success in accessing an intense flirtatious state involves getting a nice tune in your head. Have a tune in there that gives you some internal rhythm. Make it strong enough and intense enough so that you can feel it, and you can move to it. Do you have one? As you become a Master Practitioner, you know that you need to go beyond merely reading this material; you need to experience it neurologically. And you can. Now. → ●

As you now induce in yourself a positive state of mind and emotion, one where you feel that you live in a friendly universe, look out into the world with eyes that can see the value of people and respect them. Look beyond their faces and clothes and skin color and shapes. Look into them as a wonderful mystery, as people from a wild and wonderful reality with their dreams and hopes and passions.

The flirting state begins here. It starts as a gentle and thoughtful state of appreciation. Now, what would intensify this experience for you? Would looking out onto the world through a golden filter help? What if you projected a rainbow of colors out into the world and onto people? Since you can do anything in your brain that will help you get into a good state, do whatever works for you.

When you flirt with someone of the opposite sex, you need to do some slight mismatching. If you want to flirt successfully, do not sit or stand in a direct line with the other person. Do not sit straight across the table. When you do that it typically represents a kind of confrontational position. Rather, cross over the boundaries between you and the other person. As you do this, you will begin to discover the structure of seductiveness. Most people find it more seductive to cross the boundaries, which allow them to behave with an air of mystery, a bit of unknown.

The strategy of relating and feeling seductive also involves a voice characterized by a quieter, softer, and less direct tone. This state communicates two things simultaneously. Essentially it says, 'Go away closer!'

Of course, as you intensify the flirting with a mate or partner, so will your state. And we call such a state a state of 'sizzle.' So now just allow yourself to recall from your memories what it is like to feel absolutely sizzling for someone you care for very much. And when you get there, turn to a partner and communicate this sizzle to him or her non-verbally. Give yourself a minute to practice communicating it with your eyes, your body, and your energy. When you have this state fully accessed, then let your partner set an anchor for it.

For married couples or couples in a committed relationship, what better way to rekindle the flame than to practice accessing this seduction anchor again and again. Don't you find it that way, now? So just have your partner recall a time when s/he operated from such an optimal state and when that special person felt magical, glowing, and sparkling. Or simply invite him or her to fully imagine what that would feel like. Or you could even invite your partner to model someone they have seen in real life or in the movies, someone who was being magical and sparkling. As the person accesses the state, set a sliding anchor on the upper arm. Ask them to then close his or her eyes and to keep them closed. As you slide the anchor downward, re-access the state again and again, this will amplify the state and its submodalities. Continue to do this until the person simply glows. Do not quit until you hear the person sizzling.

The person assisting in setting the anchor for the state should concentrate on building it both consciously and unconsciously by installing a set of post-hypnotic suggestions. These should be directed at getting the person to automatically touch the anchor whenever s/he wants to feel good. You could even continue to stack the person's states with other resourceful states that will become important to him/her for protection and strength.

Feel free to use the word 'sizzle' in the process of anchoring, or any other word that might anchor this state such as 'Yum!' Afterwards, have the person open his or her eyes and look around the room. Then test your work. Combine submodalities and unconscious chaining by finding an experience when s/he felt absolute wanton ecstasy. →●

The following exercise offers some practice in using post-hypnotic suggestions in accessing and working with states. It also provides more practice in eliciting and installing post-hypnotic suggestions.

1) B should perform a rapid trance induction with A and then establish a Yes/No signal system.

2) B can then ask A's unconscious mind to respond with a Yes if it would like to intensify pleasurable responses toward smiles and other positive behaviors from someone A likes, during the next 24 hours, and to intensify those responses whenever desired in the future.

3) After obtaining a Yes response, have A open his or her eyes. B winks slowly at A and blows a kiss.

Conclusion

How masterful do you now feel with regard to this relevant and personal art of accessing and managing your states? Obviously, the art and technology of doing this play a central role, not only to the informational side of NLP, but in the actual practice. So give yourself plenty of experience with the state development and management exercises included in these chapters. Set out on an exploratory journey for new, exquisite and wonderful states to visit, model, and install.

Meta-states: Self-Reflexive Consciousness in Human States

When the first edition of this book went to print, Meta-States was a new development in NLP which utilized Korzybski's and Bateson's models concerning logical levels. Meta-States also provides a tracking language for use when we experience states-about-states, as we do when we become afraid of our fear (paranoid), or angry for feeling afraid (a self-conflicting state), or guilty about feeling angry about feeling afraid (higher level self-torturing pattern). Self-esteem operates as a Meta-State, in which someone has thoughts-and-feelings of esteem (value, appraisal) about an abstraction (one's self) based upon some event, action, feelings, and so on. When we experience a Meta-State (and we experience many of them every day), we enter the realm of semantic reality in which we create and experience Meta-Level experiences, beliefs, values, etc.

Chapter Ten
NLP Meta-Programs

[Derived partially from Bandler, Robbie, Hall, Woodsmall and repackaged in this format shortly after the training. More recently, with Bob Bodenhamer, I have taken this formatting of the Meta-Programs, and have authored *Figuring Out People: Design Engineering Using Meta-Programs, 1997*]

The NLP Meta-Programs refer to some very basic organizing principles in the way we perceive, behave, and think. These Meta-Programs operate in a more fundamental way than any specific learned program such as those for bicycle riding, doing algebra, baking a cake, driving a car, running a computer program, and so on. Instead, these programs exist and operate at a meta-level, and so they do not deal with content, rather they address structure, context, and process. They address the subject of how we sort and attend to information, and hence to our 'perceptual grids.'

The term 'Meta-Programs' refers to those programs *meta* to (above, beyond, about) awareness. Consequently Meta-Programs describe how our perceptual filters have become programmed to notice, attend to, sort for, and process certain kinds of information. They deal with our patterns of sorting information about the world.

For instance, with reading, such as the reading you are now doing, some people read the words (visual external stimuli) and *hear* those words in their head. They make sense of the marks on the page by representing the information using an internal auditory voice. Others *see* images of the words (or what those words refer to) on the internal screen of their consciousness, so to speak. They use the visual modality. Still others have *sensations* about the words or their referents; they sense movement, texture, warmth, rhythm, and so on. They code the information using various kinesthetic representations within their mind-body in terms of sensations, movements, breathing, tension, and so on. Each Meta-Program distinction has its own way of representing VAK choices.

Further, when some people read, they look for things that match what they already know and have already learned. As matchers, they sort for information that fits with their previous knowledge. Others look for things that they do not know, which they find unfamiliar. As mismatchers, they look for differences, being interested in detecting things that differ. Yet another Meta-Program distinction.

Now, if regular *content* programs (typing, playing ball, driving a car, tasting wine, being friendly, etc.) tend to become unconscious over time, this applies much more to Meta-Programs. The Meta-Programs of awareness and perception function in a habitual way, outside our awareness. Although outside of awareness, they nonetheless continue to operate. They operate very systematically which makes them so powerful.

As you get to know more about the Meta-Programs, you will discover and experience that in a way they are very close to your temperament (a nominalization for your 'temper' of mind-emotion) and constitutional nature (two more nominalizations). At times you may think, "This is the way I am!" But beware of that kind of thinking.

It usually serves us well to avoid identifying our self (our concept of our existential being) with how we have learned to run our brain. Meta-Programs only describe how we have learned to use our consciousness up until now. They can change, they do change, and they will continue to change. Further, we are much more than just our Meta-Programs of perception. So while we have a tendency to identify with our unconscious sorting style, it also helps our sanity to avoid doing this. (Korzybski said that all forms of identifying constitute a form of 'unsanity.')

As sorting devices (or perceptual filters), our Meta-Programs operate at a level between sensory based experience and our beliefs. This explains why we typically experience them as almost the same as our inherent temperament and nature: they seem solidly consistent with the way we behave perceptually.

Further, when we detect and specify those Meta-Programs that functions as our driver Meta-Programs, we will have discovered those programs we tend to use to process information, and consequently, which programs greatly influence our reality strategy. Meta-Programs accordingly provide us with information as to how we experience our 'self,' and about the basic components of what we call our 'personality.' We can therefore use them to identify basic personality profiles. Precisely because these programs lie so close to home, they enable us to track how a person thinks, perceives, and experiences. (See *Personality Ordering and Disordering Using NLP and Neuro-Semantics,* 2000)

The value in knowing and recognizing someone's Meta-Programs lies in the fact that once we know how someone organizes their 'self' and their 'reality,' we can then pace (match) those Meta-Programs (or our own) in order to gain immediate and deep rapport. This benefits us by allowing us to communicate optimally by matching the way the other person naturally processes information. This, in turn, will give maximum impact to our message for that person, and this will enhance our ability to influence, persuade and motivate.

Exploring Another's Subjective Reality to Notice Processing Styles

The saying "the map is not the territory" (Korzybski 1933/1994) enables us to distinguish the two levels of reality which we all navigate daily. We refer to this distinction every time we say, "The difference is just semantics." The world of semantics (meaning, significance, frame) exists solely within consciousness. It does not exist in the external world. Semantic reality (and hence Korzybski's term 'neuro-semantics') reflects our abstracting, thinking, evaluating, and so on.

When we confuse the territory (basic reality) with our map of it (subjective reality) we also fail to recognize how different processing styles (the various ways people think) influence what we experience and feel. In this regard the NLP paradigm operates as a form of cognitive psychology, and reflects the kind of wisdom that we find in the old Hebrew proverb, "As a man thinks in his heart, so he is" (*Proverbs 23:7*).

It is also found in the modern-day REBT model (Rational-Emotive Behavioral Therapy). Rational-Emotive's 'ABCs of Emotions' asserts the same neurological fact.

> Activating events (A) can only trigger Consequences (C) of emotion and behavior in someone as those events get processed through the person's Belief system (B) (understandings, interpretations, meanings, appraisals, perspectives).

We all live our lives in this realm of personal subjective reality and understand (or fail to understand) each other. So if we work from the assumption that others process information, emote, respond, and experience reality in the same way that we do, we thereby fail to realize the wonderful uniqueness of others. We also tend to project our own model of the world onto other people, and in so doing this blinds us to the multitude of ways in which people think and experience. This constitutes one of the primary ways in which we misread others; we are reading them through the filter of our own patterns.

Learning To See Patterns of Perception

The Patterned Ways for Coding and Sorting Data

If the Meta-Programs operate so much out of consciousness, then how do we bring these programs into awareness? What allows us to become more aware of them and of the effect they have on the way we process information and communicate interactively with others? First we *go meta* to these processes so that we may become aware of them and notice how they work. Until we do that, we will have little choice with regard to our perceptions, and thus little control over our communication.

This process provides an experiental exercise for becoming aware of the Meta-Programs.

1) Assist a person to fully experience a state. Once in that state, amplify it. Do not try to elicit the operating Meta-Programs of an experience before you have elicited the state with which you want to work because you will not get 'clean' information.

2) Switch referential indices. You can frame this, "Suppose I became you for the day. How would I do that?"

Asking such a question communicates many presuppositions. It presupposes that the person has:

- awareness,
- the capacity for becoming aware and communicating it,
- that their 'way of being' in the world represents a learning or skill,
- that we can model this by making explicit the pieces about what one has to do inside one's head, body, and so on.

3) Anchor this experience. If you need to amplify it even more, you could build a sliding anchor.

4) Slow the experience down and keep recycling. Most subjective experiences go by too fast to catch all the patterns and programs within them the first time through. And just as you can see and hear so much more of a fast-paced movie during the second and third viewings, so recycling through the experience with the person will enable you to gather more information.

5) Invite the person to go back and forth between associated and dissociated states as they experience that reference experience. Then have them talk about it.

With regard to the way that we code information, pay attention to sensory data and process thoughts. The NLP cognitive-behavioral model both describes our unique models of the world and creates them. The powerful and surprising thing lies in how we can find predictable patterns in the way people do this. For example, we all have regular patterns for how we delete, generalize, and distort our models of the world. These habitual sorting patterns typically operate outside of our awareness, which makes them both unconscious and difficult to detect. Yet we can identify these patterns (the Meta-Programs) by observing the structures of our internal mapping which generate our skills, abilities, and experiences.

Given this, playfully imagine for just a moment that you had a way to detect, sort out, and pay attention to these meta-level patterns. Just suppose.... If you could consciously detect and track how any one person pays attention to the world, then you would have a more effective way of understanding and even predicting that person's style of hearing and responding to things. This would also give you some awareness of what that person holds true in his or her model of reality. Now wouldn't you find that extremely valuable? Wouldn't that make people and their responses seem less confusing, and more systematic and understandable?

Knowing someone's model of the world, as well as having the flexibility to alter your own communication so that you could meet him or her in it, would give you the ability to connect with people where you find them. Matching someone's Meta-Programs describes another aspect of rapport. When we create this quality of relating, we get less resistance, less conflict, and less misunderstandings.

At first glance, other people's ways of thinking, sorting, processing, emoting, communicating and behaving may seem rather chaotic and random. People often say, "You can't figure people out." "People are completely unpredictable!" Yet at the same time people also behave systematically enough so that we can get a general sense of what seems in character and what does not. After all, we are creatures of habit. Most of us keep experiencing the same kinds of problems over and over, do we not?

So, for all the bad press that habits receive, our habits do keep us consistent and regular. Without habits we would 'bounce off the walls' even more than we do already! Habit keeps depressed people depressed. They do not wake up schizophrenic one day, phobic the next, and with an anti-social personality the next, and so on. They present themselves habitually as depressed. They run that program regularly, systematically, and predictably. And as long as their model of reality remains consistent, that describes how they will function. In fact, they cannot change until their model of the world changes.

Also, we all follow patterns for how and what we pay attention to, process, code, emote, speak, and so on. In this sense, habits are a form of patterning. And because we work in patterns, the following Meta-Patterns identify the kinds of patterning that govern how we perceive, process information, emote, and so on. These things inform our sense of reality, and thereby determine the world in which we live.

Recognizing the patterns by which people think, decide, act, buy, and respond enables us to identify the predictable patterns that we regularly use and rely upon. We can use them to provide a way to detect someone's processing style in their everyday communication. This presents us with another wonder-filled aspect of the Meta-Programs, because people forever manifest them in their communication and behavior.

Utilization

Learning to Use the Meta-Programs

As a practical learning procedure, take each of the Meta-Programs individually and practice until you develop some proficiency in recognizing and using it in speaking. Taking them one at a time will prevent you from feeling overwhelmed by them. Some people will need to give themselves permission to start hearing how others mentally sort and process information. Going meta and listening for these processing patterns may evoke a sense of self-consciousness for a while.

When you are able to recognize these mental sorting patterns, you will have an understanding of the steps which someone goes through in order to arrive at a decision. Using that information, you can create greater rapport and understanding as you communicate.

Generally speaking, open-ended questions are more likely to elicit Meta-Program information:

> "Would you tell me about one of your favorite holiday experiences?"

> "What do you think about developing more effectiveness in communication skills?"

Even a classic closed question such as "Do you see this glass as half empty or half full?" can work well. In order to respond to this question, the person will indicate his/her typical way of perceiving. Which aspect does s/he first develop awareness of: fullness or emptiness? The person's response will tell you if s/he tends towards optimism or pessimism. Typically, the way a person perceives that proverbial glass will give an indication as to how s/he experiences and responds to other values as well.

You could also use 'downtime' questions to elicit Meta-Programs. These questions require the person to go inside to access the information s/he needs in order to respond. Because s/he does not have the information at his or her fingertips, s/he will typically begin to *demonstrate* his or her Meta-Program, and act it out in various ways. So to elicit Meta-Programs simply ask someone to fully and completely recall some experience and then have him or her step into that experience and feel it as fully as though s/he were there.

Not all Meta-Programs are of the same importance. Each differs according to how someone uses and values it in a particular task or situation. Therefore we not only need to identify which Meta-Programs someone uses in a task, but also to prioritize them in terms of importance to that person. Have these questions in mind as you interact with the person:

> "Which of the Meta-Programs are the most important and impactful for this person?"

> "What Meta-Program seems to exercise the most significance within this person's experience?"

You can then respond to the person in an everyday conversational way that will naturally motivate and influence him/her. Although the full list of Meta-Programs may appear overwhelming upon first encounter, you can make them more manageable by using the Sorting Grid, Figure 10.1 on page 272 to keep track. The Sorting Grid will help you organize them in your own thinking and memory. You can also use it as a tool to make a psychological profile of yourself and others whom you know well. It will assist you in thinking about these processing patterns.

When you feel ready to use this Meta-Program information which you have gathered about someone, practice writing some pacing (matching) statements. This will do more to increase your communication skills than any other exercise.

For example, if someone operates as a strong Self sorter (Self Referencing) who mismatches with counter-examples (or with polarity responses), s/he will tend to challenge people with "Prove it to me!" statements. And then, if you don't watch out, this can spiral into a pointless matching of wits. Knowing this, you can now counter this with a pacing statement such as:

> "You seem so good at knowing your needs that only you can decide what you consider as ultimately right. No question about that. And I don't know if what I have to say will make any difference, but anyway here it is."

Such a communication will pace the person's Meta-Programs, by matching the way they structure his/her thinking and emoting. It will also validate his/her processing style and model of the world. Instead of fighting that style of being, you will be able to utilize it.

With a general or global sorter who uses the visual mode, you will undoubtedly want to keep your details to a minimum and describe his/her future possibilities vaguely. In that way the person can shape these into his/her own images.

> "And with your clear eye, I'm sure you can see just how you could use this in your business to improve production in several ways."

Given that person's Meta-Programs, s/he can! The person will also feel respected because you did not bore him/her with details.

As you learn to match a person's sorting patterns, you will have no need to swim against the tidal current of that person's basic inclinations. And so in this way you will add a turbo charge to your high powered communication skills.

So, how do you proceed? First, become fully acquainted with your own Meta-Programs. This will deepen your own understanding of how you operate at these psychological levels. It will also deepen your appreciation of the value of these Meta-Programs. Then you will know just the right way to sell yourself on something you want. It will provide you with a custom-made self-motivation program to perfectly fit your own personality. And, you would find that useful, would you not?

The overall pattern for utilizing Meta-Programs in communication involves aiming to match your communications with the other person's Meta-Programs. In this way you will be pacing his or her model of the world, and this will make your communications maximally effective. In business you will find this process invaluable for getting people matched to the jobs best suited to their Meta-Program preferences.

Liking and Disliking and the Meta-Programs

How do these Meta-Programs relate to personal liking and/or disliking? It is often frequently the case that the basis for liking someone lies at the Meta-Program level. We tend to like people who think, act and value like us. So the natural state of feeling 'in sync' with someone usually means that both people operate 'on the same wavelength' in how they sort, attend to, and communicate information. Ultimately, liking also involves a sharing of values and a similar orientation toward reality. When we operate in a similar way to the other person, it feels as though we 'know' them and their world.

Conversely, disliking typically involves seeing, hearing, and feeling in a way that feels at odds with the other person. It involves taking a basically very different approach to people, information, events, and having a different orientation to reality. Check this out.

Use the following Meta-Program elicitation exercise to explore patterns of liking and disliking. You need to use body rapport, Meta-Model questions and Meta-Program questions. By design this will give you practice in eliciting Meta-Programs and recognizing their influence on our experiences.

1) B elicits from A a time when s/he liked someone upon the first meeting.

2) Once A has a reference experience, B asks "How did you decide that you liked that person?"

3) Then, using the Meta-Program list, elicit as much information as possible about A's processing and sorting.

4) Repeat this same process for a time when A disliked a stranger upon first meeting. "How did you decide that you disliked that person?"

5) When you have completed this exercise, invite C (meta-person) to feed back the information s/he saw and heard in A's response in terms of Meta-Programs. If you have a fourth person in the group, let him/her also feed back to B (the coach) the information that D has gathered about B's Meta-Programs.

In the final analysis, the states of liking and disliking ultimately break down to a matter of values and Meta-Program styles. Generally speaking, people share the same values and/or qualities in their Meta-Programs with the people they like (friends) and do not share these values and/or qualities with people they dislike (enemies). In the latter situation the values and orientation styles conflict. This may make it difficult for these individuals to pace the other because there is little rapport at a deep level.

People-Reading Tools

In order to develop people-reading literacy skills you need to have several NLP tools. The following include the main ones:

First and foremost, *turned-on sensory awareness*. Open your eyes, ears and other senses to the information that others continuously offer you. Move into uptime, put all of your downtime thoughts, emotions, and filters on hold, so that you become aware only of the stimuli before you.

Your skill in *listening attentively* enhances your reading of Meta-Programs. Learn to distinguish between descriptive and evaluative terms. This helps you avoid reading others through using your own patterns and filters, and enables you to distinguish between what you actually see, hear, sense in sensory awareness (descriptive) and between the values and meanings which come from memories, values, traumas, beliefs (evaluative).

When you ask yourself, "What does this descriptive element (language, gesture, behavior, emotion, and so on) mean to me?" you are accessing your meaning systems. Because all evaluative words and processing occur within our own model of the world. In order to get into uptime, we have to shift, to go meta, and get out of content.

As you hear the person's words listen out for the linguistic markers that mark out the person's representations of experience, and then use them to gain insights into that person's model of the world. Each driver Meta-Program provides significant information about the kind and quality of world that the person lives in. The Meta-Programs detected through words provide us with information about the ways people organize their behavior and thoughts. You could think of these as referencing categories.

Second, *develop comprehensive awareness of the patterns*. This provides you with an important people-reading tool. This awareness enables you to organize and sort the input offered you and gives you ways of using your senses to make more sophisticated distinctions. Learn these patterns, drill them in, memorize them, utilize and practice them every chance you get and do so until they become second nature to you. They will then become so much a part of your own processing that they will drop into your subconscious and become automatic.

In the same way that we learn how to make auditory discriminations in order to appreciate music, and visual discriminations in order to appreciate art, so training our senses to note subtle and discrete differences gives us a more accurate way of perceiving other people's communication patterns. This means that we must go meta to content so that we can hear the structure of the patterns presented.

Third, *develop clean kinesthetic awareness.* One of our greatest tools for reading people involves noticing our own feelings and responses. This necessitates being calm in ourselves and cleanly noting the feelings, sensations, impressions, and emotions within us. Just being kinesthetically aware of another is not sufficient. We must have kinesthetic channels uncontaminated by our own emotional filters and predispositions. This describes where most people who have learned how to feel and respond in a sensitive way to their feelings tend to fail. The emotions they think they hear, see and feel in others are actually their own feelings that they have projected onto the other.

This ability to distinguish between what we receive as input from the outside, and what we generate within ourselves, separates proficient communicators from mind-readers. Together with the other tools, the sorting grid provides a way of keeping tabs on ourselves or any given individual.

Fourth, *go meta to the meta-levels* of the person's temperament, mental, emotional, relational, self-image, value, time, and communication processing. Program yourself to ask the questions;

> "What is this person telling me about his or her Meta-Programs?"
>
> "What does this reveal about me, and about the other person?"

Fifth, *keep all your reading tentative.* Test your reading of the other person by inviting more information from the other person, and by testing it against the person's overall configuration of traits. Keeping readings tentative and constantly gathering more up-to-date information enables us to calibrate to the ever- changing experiences of the person before us. By doing this, we respect his or her uniqueness.

The Effect that Reading Meta-Programs will have on you

Sometimes people express the fear that: "This will make them more manipulative with people." This depends, of course, on what you mean by 'manipulative.' It will certainly give you greater skill in handling people effectively—which strikes me as a very positive form of influencing. Whether or not you use these skills to treat people with less respect as you try to 'wrap them around your little finger' so that you can get something from them without giving something in return, ultimately depends on your own personal ethics and morality.

Typically, understanding ourselves and others psychologically helps us become more real and more authentic. Since such understanding takes us beyond someone's masks and roles, it enables us to identify the patterns and values behind and below the cover-ups. Rollo May has written,

> "The more penetrating your insights into the workings of the human personality, the more you will be convinced of the uselessness of trying to fool others."

Deception seldom works in the long run.

Changing Meta-Programs

As most people begin to work with the Meta-Programs, they observe that some of the programs tend to function more productively and beneficially than others. This then raises the question about changing Meta-Programs: "Can I change my Meta-Programs, or are they genetically wired in?" Actually, changing Meta-Programs involves a fairly simple procedure. We can do so simply by giving ourselves permission to adopt a particular Meta-Program for running our perceptions and sorting information so that it will enhance our life. Then we only have to attend to the distinction (global rather than specific, for example) until we develop enough flexibility of consciousness for being able to choose which to use.

Sometimes simply trying on another sorting pattern for running our own brain sufficiently enables us to run our brain in that way. In fact, the process of reading, understanding, noticing, pacing, and working with Meta-Programs itself functions as a way of developing a flexibility of consciousness and allows us to give our brain other Meta-Programs options at will. After all, the Meta-Programs themselves are neither static nor hard-wired in our neurology. They function as perceptual behaviors. So as we program ourselves to focus on details or to chunk up to the big picture, we thereby train our consciousness to become more flexible.

The more we use the Meta-Program distinctions the more we train our brain to make additional and finer sensory discriminations. This then expands our model of the world and removes many limitations that have been holding us back… until now.

The Meta-Programs

I. Temperamental Sorting Factors

#1. Emotional Coping Sorting
PASSIVE/AGGRESSIVE
To identify this pattern begin by asking:

> "When you feel threatened, or challenged, by some stress, what immediate emotional response arises? Do you want to get away from the stress or to go toward it?"

Invite the person to tell you about an instance when s/he faced a high stress situation, and notice if they describe a 'go toward' or 'go away from' response.

Aggressive people go toward their stressors. More often than not, they actually like challenges, stress, pressure and adventure.

Passive people, on the other hand, forever try to get away from stress and strain. They want more than anything to make peace, to create harmony, and to make things pleasant and nice for everyone. These toward and away from emotional responses arise from our built-in fight/flight syndrome.

The tempering quality of assertive responding (thinking, feeling, and speaking) copes with these energies so that we do not automatically fight or flee. The fight or flight feeling will still exist as part of the assertive response, but it is under the person's control.

This enables him/her to maintain enough presence of mind so that s/he can think and talk out the stresses, rather than act them out.

To communicate with an aggressive person, pace them by taking their idea and wrestling with it. Explore it, question the person about it, have them future-pace it. An aggressive person will want you to confront it, deal with it, and grapple with the ideas and responses, so respond in a direct and forthright way, thus affirming these qualities in him or her.

To pace and communicate with a passive person, hear his/her ideas and emotions out. Give verbal and non-verbal pacing signs that essentially say, "Tell me more. I find this interesting, and I want to understand you and what you think and feel about this." Do not confront or disagree directly. Talk about the importance of finding harmony, peace, staying pleasant and nice.

Aggressive people tend to use the modal operators of possibility, while passive people use those of necessity. Those with an Approach style of going at things think and talk in terms of possibilities, ideals, and hopes. They focus on what they want. Avoidance people with the away from style tend to think and talk more in terms of what they avoid and about pressures of laws, rules, protocols, and necessities they feel upon them (shoulds, musts, and have tos).

The fight/flight stress response also affects whether we use an associated or dissociated approach. When you see someone experience the fight/flight responses who is emotionally associated (seeing, hearing, and feeling from first perceptual position), you will see obvious changes in breathing, skin color, pupil dilation, etc. When you get a dissociated fight/flight response to high stress, the person will seem cold and unfeeling, unemotional, unaffected and not accessing their kinesthetics. The person seems to be operating from the third perceptual position. and tends to adopt the Satir 'computer mode.' If the person has become stuck in that mode, s/he will then probably 'stuff' the emotions in an unhealthy way.

An assertive person may also choose to go into computer mode and dissociate. The difference, however, lies in the fact that the person will do so by choice. When you ask about the stress state, the person may first access some of the kinesthetics of stress and then choose to dissociate and cope with his or her thinking and speaking rather than acting out the evoked survival emotions.

#2. *Temperament*

STRONG-WILLED/COMPLIANT

A strong-willed person by definition, has a very hard time being told anything. When you attempt to tell such a person something, you get an automatic and immediate response of resistance. At the other end of the continuum, the compliant person operates temperamentally in a flexible, receptive, open and sensitive way.

To identify these patterns, notice whether a person 'bristles' when told, ordered, demanded, forced or is dealt with in a direct way. As with other temperament factors, people vary along a continuum between extremely compliant to extremely strong-willed, with the majority falling somewhere in the middle. People who have developed a strong will through experiencing trauma, or otherwise creating strong beliefs through their life learning, will usually demonstrate more control over their will.

To pace and communicate with a strong-willed person, avoid all direct frontal telling styles. Rather than telling the person anything, suggest, hint, prod, plant idea seeds, playfully tease, and so on. Use any and all of the indirect communication skills in your toolbox. When you seed to pace and communicate with a compliant person, you will find this both easy and enjoyable—just express your thoughts.

II. Self-Modality Factors

#3. *Self-Image*

SELF-ESTEEM/SELF-CONFIDENCE

One of the most basic aspects of awareness involves our sense of self: the images, concepts, ideas and verbalizations we use to conceptualize our 'self.' Because these images (visual, auditory, languaged) usually lie outside our level of awareness, we might think of them as meta-images, a meta-level of beliefs about identity or self-definition.

We can also break our over-all self-image down into two major aspects: our sense of value or worth regarding our dignity and being-ness; and our sense of competence and capability regarding our skills, abilities, and actions. Because most people have these two aspects fused (confused), mixed, and intertwined, this creates additional problems in separating person and behavior, being and doing, esteem and confidence.

Our sense of worth (esteem and appraisal of value) can fall along a continuum between extreme worthlessness—'being a rotten person' (low self-esteem) to being highly valued (high self-esteem). We may base this sense on temporal (conditional) factors or upon unconditional factors. We may believe that our value as a human being exists as a given, as our inheritance as a human being.

Our sense of competence (self-confidence), on the other hand, refers to those feelings of pride, capacity, and experience that we can do certain things, pull off various tasks, achieve and accomplish various goals. We may base this on experiences (positive and negative), training, beliefs, relationships, etc.

If we suffer from low self-esteem and then try to build it upon the foundation of our competences, we forever put ourselves on a treadmill of trying to become okay as a person by means of achievement. However, this generally works in a self-defeating way, as we have put ourselves on a useless and senseless course forever attempting to become 'good enough' and 'okay enough' to value ourselves. In the long run, conditional self-esteeming just does not work. In fact, it actually makes for self-contempt and/or egotism. Conversely, thinking of our self-value as a given we can become self-forgetful and unpretentious inasmuch as we operate from an unconditional appraisal of value and dignity.

III. Mental Processing Factors

#4. Chunk Size

GENERAL OR GLOBAL/SPECIFIC OR DETAILED

With regard to the size of the chunks of information with which people prefer to think, communicate and learn, people tend to fall into two main categories. Some prefer specific information (the smaller chunks) and so go for the details. They understand and feel comfortable with smaller, more detailed pieces of information. Typically, they also prefer to arrange them in sequences so they can induce upward. We describe people with this sorting style, inductive thinkers. "Give me the details and let me see what it means to me."

Those who prefer the big picture have a more global outlook. They tend to first make sense of the world in terms of an overall frame. They first go for a picture of the forest; later they chunk down to the trees. They want a gestalt. Afterwards they can deduce downward to the smaller chunks. We described these folks as deductive thinkers. "Give me your general concept or idea and let me see what that rationally implies."

We have two primary formats for thinking and reasoning which are defined by the ability to move between greater specificity and greater abstraction. We call it inductive reasoning when we move from specific to abstract (chunking up). We call it deductive reasoning when we move from abstract to specific (chunking down). Chunking up also enables someone to train his or her intuition and to make intuitive jumps. Such a person needs a huge amount of information in order to chunk up to the larger levels. Conversely, deductive reasoning, the ability to chunk down to specifics, enables someone to find concrete examples and practical ways of applying abstract concepts.

The person who sorts in generalities or globally, can easily recall times s/he felt bored to a high level of frustration by someone who felt compelled to feed him or her detail upon detail that s/he really didn't want. The person who sorts specifically and in details can recall the frustration of dealing with someone who seemed willing to give them only the big picture, and left out the important details. Specific sorters tend to believe that if you keep your eye on the pennies, the dollars will take care of themselves. General sorters believe that if you keep your eye on the dollars, the pennies will take care of themselves.

To detect this pattern ask a question such as:

> "What do you want first when you hear about something new—the big picture or the details?"

Someone who gives you many specific details and sequences, operates as a specific sorter. On the contrary, if someone talks in terms of overviews, principles, and concepts, then this person operates as a general sorter. Knowing which style someone prefers to use gives you some important information about how to package your communication to that person in an effective sequence.

To pace and communicate with a detail person, give lots of specific details, break things down into small details. Use many modifiers and proper nouns. Conversely, to communicate with a gestalt thinker, talk in concepts, principles, and the larger ideas. Skip the details—use generalities.

If you approach a gestalt person with specifics, you will most likely bore and/or frustrate that person into dropping out of the communication interchange. If you approach a detail person with generalities, you will most likely create distrust and confusion because by talking in such a vague way you will not be supplying enough details for that person to feel comfortable. Top-notch communicators develop the ability and flexibility to move in either direction and to handle either chunk size of information depending on the level that the other person uses.

#5. *Match/Mismatch Sort*

SAMENESS/DIFFERENCE, AGREE/DISAGREE

People fall into two general categories based on how they make comparisons when they first encounter information. Some people focus their attention on the similarity between things and how they match their previous experiences. Such individuals will typically also value security and stability. They will usually want their world to stay the same; they do not particularly like change. Other people will typically notice differences—the things that are not the same as before, that stand out, that do not fit. Those who mismatch tend to value change, variety, and newness. They usually do not like static situations. Extreme mismatchers may even get excited about revolutionary change.

The pattern of Matching with Exception means that someone first notices similarities and then notices differences. These people like things to remain relatively the same, but allow for and enjoy gradual change. The pattern of Mismatching with Exception conversely involves someone first noticing differences and then similarities. These people like change and variety, but not revolutionary change. To discover this pattern ask any relational question:

> "What relationship do you see between what you do now on a daily basis and what you did last year?"

Arrange three coins on a table with two heads and one tail, and ask:

> "What is the relationship between these three objects?"

Generally speaking, those who match will tell you how things relate to each other in terms of similarity. They focus on the stability of the things. Conversely, mismatchers will talk about how things differ. They will talk about what is new, what has changed, what is now different—evolutionary and revolutionary changes. The patterns of Matching with Exception and Mismatching with Exception will involve a discussion of how things have gradually changed over time. Listen for comparatives: more, less, better, worse, cheaper, dearer, and so on.

To communicate with matchers, stress areas of mutual agreement, security, what we both want, and we will ignore differences. With mismatchers, stress how things differ, stand out, change, the new features about them, and so on. Talk about adventure and development. With those people who use the exception pattern, continually alternate your conversation between matching and mismatching.

We may often experience mismatchers as 'difficult' people. Mismatchers consistently go for counter-examples when presented with ideas or suggestions. They will give a list of "Yes, buts" to demonstrate why your idea will not work. We can play with this. Present your idea as something that probably will not work, and the mismatcher will mismatch this and give you a list of reasons why it will! "I have some serious reservations about whether we can get this project out on time...."

Polarity Sorters operate as extreme mismatchers who will respond automatically with the opposite response from the one we want or expect. Here again, we probably need to play the polarity. In Uncle Remus, Brer Rabbit did this by begging Brer Fox not to throw him into the briar patch—the very response he really wanted.

When you offer matchers something new, expect them to first respond, "It seems to me that this is just like..." as they start by processing for similarities. Matchers generally feel quite comfortable in perceiving similarities more than differences. When persuading them, play to their comfort zones by stressing the similarities between your proposal and what they already have familiarity with. More people use a matching sort than a mismatching, which explains the success of standardized franchises across the country, across the world.

#6. Representation System

VISUAL/AUDITORY/KINESTHETIC/AUDITORY-DIGITAL

We think by 're-presenting' sensory data on the inside which we have processed using our external senses. Most people typically develop a most highly favored representational system, and this leads to this particular Meta-Program distinction: People can function primarily as visual, auditory, auditory-digital, or kinesthetic in their thinking, learning, and remembering. The sensory channel that someone primarily relies on indicates that person's most favored representation system. In NLP, we call the one they use to access stored data the lead system.

To discover this pattern of human processing, simply listen for the predicates (verbs, adverbs, adjectives) in someone's language. Specifically listen for visual, auditory, kinesthetic, and/or language predicates. Also, watch for the person's eye scanning movements. The general pattern is as follows:

- eyes moving up or defocusing straight ahead for visual accessing,
- eyes moving down to the right indicate kinesthetic accessing,
- eyes moving laterally on the level way indicate auditory accessing,
- and eyes moving down to the left indicate auditory-digital.

Once you identify the pattern, pace the person's preferred system in your language and gestures by using the specific predicates and directions.

#7. *Information Gathering Style*

UPTIME/DOWNTIME

When we are processing data, we can pay attention to our internal subjective world (what we call Downtime, and what Bateson termed *Creatura*), or our external world (what we call Uptime; Bateson's world of *Plethora*).

Uptime refers to a state of sensory awareness in which we are paying attention to the stimuli that we are receiving from the outside. When communicating, we filter according to the other person's responses (posture, eye contact, gestures, etc), rather than by our own assumptions (our model of the world) about those actions. In uptime we generate little information from our own internal stimuli.

Downtime refers to the state of consciousness in which we primarily pay attention to internal things… our thoughts, ideas, memories, beliefs, emotions, and so on. While doing this, of course, we become blind and deaf to the external world, and in a trance state of internal awareness in which our own images, sounds, words, sensations, and so on, provide the most compelling data. In downtime, the other person does not seem to be present because s/he makes minimum eye contact with us. The person may be defocusing his or her eyes and staring off into space.

With most people, expect these uptime and downtime patterns to be alternating. If you try to listen while mostly in downtime, you will end up making assumptions based on your internal thinking and feeling rather than on the person before you. You will be hearing what you expect to hear, mind-reading, projecting, and so on, which is a fantastically poor listening strategy!

#8. Direction Filter

TOWARD/AWAY FROM, PAST ASSURANCE/FUTURE POSSIBILITIES, APPROACH/AVOIDANCE

Two general tendencies govern how someone moves in respect to their goals and objectives. We can move toward or away from various objectives, goals, and values. With the moving toward style the person moves toward what s/he wants to achieve. Their desired outcomes or goals pull them into the future. Such people become oriented with a 'go toward' response style; they feel motivated to achieve, attain, and obtain. They set priorities, but may have difficulty in recognizing what they should perhaps avoid. And they operate best when motivated by 'carrots' (incentives, targets).

With the moving Away From style the person moves away from the things s/he does not want. These people concentrate on what they want to avoid or get away from. They orient themselves in the world with an away from response style. They feel motivated primarily to move away from, avoid, and get rid of threats, dangers, problems, and so on. These people may also have trouble with goal-setting and managing priorities; they become easily distracted by negative situations. They feel best motivated by 'the stick' (threats, negative consequences, pressure).

What we move toward or away from lies bound up with our values. We all have both toward values and away from values. What do you value? What do you not value? Which orientational style predominates in your life and sets the primary directional force? Or do you find them pretty well balanced?

We can discover this pattern by simply asking someone:

> "What do you want?"
> "What do you want from a relationship?"
> "What do you want from a job?"

"What will having this do for you?"
"What is important about X?"

From those with the toward pattern we will hear their goals and specific wants. From those with the away from pattern we will hear their avoidances, fears, problems, and so on. We usually state these values as nominalizations because we typically encode values in this way.

To pace and communicate (or negotiate, manage or relate) with a toward person, talk about what you can do that will help the person to achieve his or her outcomes. Mention the carrots, bonuses, and incentives inherent in your plan or idea. With away from people, talk about what you can help them avoid, the problems that they can minimize or put off, and the things that will not go wrong. Stress how easy your idea or plan will make life.

Away from people also tend to sort for past assurances, so provide them with a history of evidence. They want to rest assured that their choice represents one already proven over time. Toward people will tend to sort for future possibilities, and they will have a brighter, 'blue-sky' orientation. They enjoy the possibilities that come with open-ended opportunities. They feel attracted to bigger risks for greater potential payoffs.

This approach/avoidance sorting category often shows up when someone is about to buy something: avoidance responders want to know what problems they can take care of by using your product; goal-oriented people will find the problem-avoidance approach too negative.

#9. Sorting Style

OPTIONS/PROCEDURES

Two primary responding styles govern when people deal with the world, either adapting to it or making it adapt to them. This will show up in how people respond to instructions, and how they get things done. We refer to these two styles as procedures and options.

People who prefer the procedures approach like following procedures, and they may not even know how to generate them if not given. They seem to thrive on doing tasks 'the right way,' and feel more motivated when following the procedure. Sometimes they will have an almost compulsive need to complete the procedure—closure they treat as highly important.

People who prefer the options approach seem better at developing new procedures and at figuring out alternatives to a procedure. They do not thrive so well when they have to follow strict guidelines. If something works, they prefer to improve it or alter it. What they find most valuable is using and acting on their creativity, ability to innovate, and on improving traditional ways of doing things.

In order to discover this pattern, simply ask why questions: "Why did you choose your car (job, town, or whatever)?" Then listen to the reasons people give you. If they talk about choosing and expanding their options, they probably prefer the options style. If they tell you a story and/or give you lots of facts, but don't talk about choosing, they probably sort by procedures. They answer a why question as if they had been asked a how question.

To pace and communicate with people who prefer options, talk about possibilities, options, and innovations. Allow them to violate procedures: "We'll bend the rules for you!" Don't give them fixed procedures, but play it by ear, stress the alternatives. Listen for possibilities, choices, reasons, other ways, alternatives.

Pacing and communicating with those who prefer the procedures approach means laying out a procedure for them that clearly takes them from their present state to their desired state. Give them ways of dealing with procedural break downs. Listen for the right way, proven techniques, correct procedures, and how to…

#10. Perception

SENSORS/INTUITORS

Two contrasting ways govern how we gather information. We can use our senses or we can intuit. Sensors gather information about the world through their empirical senses—the sensory modalities.

They use their capacities for seeing, hearing, feeling, smelling, and tasting to deal with concrete and factual experiences. And because they tend to rely upon accessing an uptime state, this generally makes them empiricists and pragmatists.

Intuitors, on the other hand, gather information through non-sensory means. They intuit things using their internal knowings of experience, feelings, knowledge, and so on. They look for possibilities, make assumptions about what things mean, look for relationships, and appraise the larger significance of things. And because they approach things abstractly and holistically, this tends to make them rationalists and visionaries. They tend to do more downtime work.

To discover this pattern ask:

> "When you listen to a speech or conversation, do you tend to hear the specific data given or do you intuit what the speaker must mean and/or intend?"
>
> "Do you want to hear proof and evidence or do you seem to jump to that conclusion and find it obvious?"
>
> "Do you tend to take more interest in your intuition about it? Which do you find most important, the actual or the possible?"
>
> "What basis do you use for making the most of your decisions; the practical or abstract possibilities?"

Listen for sensory based words in the sensor style; and for intuition, possibilities, and concepts in the intuitor style. With sensors, aim to communicate by using the sensory modalities, by talking in specific details that you make explicit. With intuitors, feel free to speak in abstract terms, about your intuition, and talk about possibilities as well as your overall frame.

#11. Perception

BLACK-AND-WHITE CONTINUUM

Some minds seem highly skilled in discerning broad categories, while others seem more skilled in engaging in sophisticated discernments that take the gray areas into account. Black-and-white thinking enables people to make clear and definite distinctions, motivates them to make more judgments. They tend to make quick decisions. Continuum thinking enables people to discriminate at much finer levels, motivates them to make fewer judgments. They tend to respond indecisively.

Continuum thinkers talk about the gray areas, use numerous qualifiers and conditionals in their language, and continually correct themselves about other possibilities. When over-done, they can even 'yes, but' themselves, and then end up in more indecision. Black-and-white thinkers will express themselves in a far more definite and less tolerant way. Typically they will feel tempted to be dogmatic, and may even talk in perfectionist terms.

We all tend to use black-and-white thinking when we get into states of stress, danger, or overload. When we hit our stress threshold, physiologically our autonomic nervous system withdraws blood from the brain and stomach in order to send blood to our larger muscle groups, and this activates our fight/flight response. This subsequently seems to evoke an all-or-nothing (survivalist) thinking pattern. So watch for and take stress into account when discriminating between these sorting styles.

#12. *Adaptation*

JUDGERS/PERCEIVERS, CONTROLLERS/FLOATERS

Two principle styles govern how we adapt ourselves to life, to external reality, to events, and to information. Moving through the world judging and evaluating things puts us into the judging style. Judgers desire (and attempt) to make life adapt to them. They live life according to a plan. They want things neat and orderly, they like closure, definite boundaries (or laws), clear cut categories, and rules.

An alternative to that involves moving through the world just perceiving and noticing. Perceivers adapt to life by perceiving, observing, noting, witnessing, and accepting. They flow through life more easily and with fewer judgments about right and wrong. They do what they feel like in the moment; they rely on their intuitions, feelings, or spirit telling them how to respond. They want to keep their options open and so they typically avoid closure. They will have more difficulty deciding, evaluating, and taking a moral stand.

Discover this pattern by simply asking:

> "Do you like to live life spontaneously as the spirit moves you or according to a plan?"

> "Do you find it easy or difficult to make up your mind?"

Listen for lists and schedules in Judgers. They will tend to organize their sense of time in the through time mode. Nor do they tend to change their minds easily. New data must warrant and demand change. In Perceivers listen for spontaneity, freedom, and understanding.

To pace and communicate with a Judger, present yourself as prompt, organized, decisive, and focused on your outcome. Talk about order, becoming organized, acting in a definite way, with resolution, structure, and commitment. With a Perceiver, behave spontaneously. Don't insist on schedules. Frame decisions as keeping our options open, and avoid wrapping things up too quickly. Talk with them about living in a free, open, and flexible way. Talk about 'waiting and seeing,' open-endedness and tentativeness.

#13. *Perception*

ACTIVE/REFLECTIVE/INACTIVE

Ask the question:

> "When you find yourself in a new situation, do you usually act quickly after sizing it up or do you do a detailed study of all the consequences before acting?"

Active people take the typical 'doers' approach to life. They make things happen. Often they act first, and think later! As entrepreneurs and go-getters, they shape the world. And while they make more mistakes, they also get more things done!

Reflective people tend to study and ponder rather than act. This makes them more passive as they sit back to contemplate before acting. This belief motivates them to say, "Don't do anything rash!" Those with a mixture of both undoubtedly have a style that more often than not provides a more balanced and healthy approach. Those who behave in an inactive way neither study nor act—they ignore. Pace each type in your communication by appealing to the appropriate values.

IV. Reference Factors/Emotional Programs

#14. Frame of Reference

AUTHORITY SORT, INTERNAL/EXTERNAL, SELF-REFERENT/ OTHER-REFERENT

Two fundamental ways govern how we evaluate someone, situation, experience, or idea. We can use an internal frame of reference or an external frame of reference. This filter is concerned with our locus of judgment, which describes where we locate the judgment or authority for our actions: Do we put it inside or outside of ourselves? Who (or what) do we use as a reference?

Those who operate in Internal Mode evaluate things on the basis of what they think appropriate. They motivate themselves and make their own decisions. They choose and validate what they do, how they do it, and the choices they make. They gather information from others, but decide about it on their own. So we say that they 'live from within.' Such people have a self referencing style which enables them to decide within themselves and to know for themselves what they want, need, believe, feel, and value.

Those who operate in the External Mode evaluate things on the basis of what others think, or utilizing some other external reference. They look to others for guidance, information, motivation, and decisions. Typically, they have a greater need for feedback about how others think about their actions. They can even get lost without guidance or feedback from others. We say that they 'live primarily from without' and so there is the danger that they may become 'people pleasers.' Some can become so dependent on others that they get caught up in the 'Being Nice' syndrome.

These other referencing people need so much feedback and information from others about what they know, understand, want, believe, feel, and value that they frequently do not listen to their own voice or develop their own mind. A linguistic cue for this occurs in the use of the word 'you' when someone is talking about themselves.

Discover this pattern by asking:

> "How do you know when your actions, words, thoughts, etc., hit the mark of being right or correct?"
>
> "How do you know that you've done a good job?"
>
> "How do you know that you chose the right bank (car, house, etc.)?"

Then listen for whether the person tells you whether they decided themselves or whether they got the information from some outside source.

Internals will say, "I just know. I feel it. It feels right." They will speak of their own values, beliefs and understandings, and they will speak assertively and forthrightly.

Externals will say things like, "My boss tells me. I look at the figures...." They will speak of placating and pleasing others precisely because they care so much about approval.

> "When it comes to decision making, how do you generally go about it?"
>
> "What kind of information do you consider important to you when making decisions?"

In pacing and communicating with Internals emphasize that they will know from inside.

> "So having thought about this, what do you think?"

"Only you can make this decision, and having this information, I trust you'll give me a call at your convenience."

Help the person to clarify their thinking. With Externals, emphasize what others think. Give statistics, data, and testimonials from significant others.

"Let me offer you some feedback that you might find interesting."

For example, people who do internal referencing would decide which stereo to buy by identifying their own personal values, interests, inclinations, situations, and so on. Those who do external referencing would care about the inclinations, thoughts, opinions, and feelings of other people and about information from other sources (mass media, consumer reports, advertising). It is more difficult to notice the pattern with those people who do internal referencing and then run an external check, or those who do external referencing and then do an internal check. Both will offer a difficult to discern pattern. In that case seek to determine which part of the pattern comes first.

#15. Reason Filter

MODAL OPERATORS, NECESSITY/POSSIBILITY/DESIRE

Modal operators describe those words that linguists use to indicate the mode from which we operate (our modus operandi). NLP adopted this term from Transformational Grammar. These auxiliary verbs indicate our operational mode in moving through the world or in handling certain events, and reflect on relationships and orientations. These words also suggest the reasons we act as we do. Such words function as the auditory-digital component of our motivation strategy—the words we use to get ourselves moving.

Necessity words (must, have to, should) indicate that we operate from a model of law, rule, or obligation. *Impossibility* words (can't, shouldn't, must not) indicate a taboo law that prevents, inhibits, and forbids certain actions. *Possibility* words (can, will, may, would, could) reflect a more optimistic model of the world, one where we can think of things as possible. *Desire* words (want to, love to, get to) arise from a model of the world that runs on and from personal desires. *Choice* words (choose to, want to, opt for) indicate a world model of will, choice, freedom, and so on.

As you ask questions that presuppose motivation, listen for the Modal Operator words in the language that you hear:

> "Why did you choose your present job?"
> "Why have you chosen this school, (schedule, course)?"

Notice whether the person gives you a reason. If you hear no reasons, the person probably operates from a mode of necessity—they have to! If you get a reason, it will relate to possibilities, obligations, or desires.

These words arise within different models of the world. They also create differing emotional and behavioral responses. In the Possibility Mode people do what they want to do, and so they will have or develop reasons to explain (or justify) why they get to do what they want to do. These people will be constantly looking for new opportunities for expanding their options. Possibility people generally believe they have some degree of control over life and so they feel motivated to make choices and to take action. In the Necessity Mode people look upon life as an obligation, a matter of submission, a routine, or burden. Accordingly, they feel they have little to no choice. They often believe they live in a world of stuckness, and given their model of limitation, that is how they experience their world.

Those who use both necessity and possibility words, and operate from both models, will feel motivated by using both options and obligations to different degrees for different situations. Impossibility words (can't, shouldn't) create personal limitations and a passive style of coping—which severely limits a person's responsiveness. Such words indicate taboos. Desire words lead to more motivation and drive, unless they become wild, uncontrolled, and unrealistic, in which case, this will typically lead to disappointment, disillusionment, and frustration.

When packaging your communication, aim to match the other person's Modal Operators, or to subtly provide the person with reframes by using other modes of operating in the world. "I wonder what it would feel like to really get into the attitude that 'I get to go to work'."

#16. *Experience of Emotion*
ASSOCIATED/DISSOCIATED

We process data in either an associated or in a dissociated manner. In dissociation mode we think and relate to the information, event, person, etc., with a sense of psychological distance from the emotional impact of the item. By creating a dissociated representation, I will see my 'self' in the picture—perhaps my younger self. I will not see the world through my own eyes; I will hear, smell, and feel things as if they occurred 'over there.' In doing this, I will have 'stepped back from' and 'out of' the images, sounds, and sensations on my mental screen. Dissociated thoughts think about things.

In the associated mode someone experiences the full impact of an event, person, and/or information emotionally. When I have an associated representation I see what I see when in that situation, looking out through my own eyes. I hear what I would hear when there. I smell, taste, and feel the event as if immediately present. Even if the event occurred half-a-century ago, I cue my nervous system with associated thoughts, think of the thing, and so my whole neurology responds as if I were really there.

To identify the dissociation mode, note the emotional affect of the person. It will seem mild, dull, bland, or in some other way as if at a distance. The Satir category of 'computer mode' describes this style of communication. A person will talk *about* things rather than *of* things. Associated representations, conversely, will involve a full body response as if re-experiencing the VAK, and as if 'in state' again. In this case look for full body kinesthetic and motor responses.

#17. *Convincer Sort*
BELIEVABILITY/REPRESENTATIONAL SYSTEMS

As we grow in experience, we learn to value different qualities which enable us to believe in people, products, and events and to feel convinced. Some people believe things, make decisions, and act because it looks right (V); others need something to sound right (A^t); others believe when it makes sense (A_d); and yet others when it feels right (K^+). What makes something believable to you? What convinces you?

We can identify this pattern in someone by asking questions which presuppose making a decision:

> "Why did you decide on your present car?"

> "What helps you decide where to go on vacation? As you make a decision about where to go on vacation, how do you think? Do you see it? Hear it? Feel it?"

Two factors in this sorting pattern play a crucial role: which mode the person sorts for (V, A, K, A_d), and the number of times it takes to become believable. Listen for the sensory-system predicates and qualities.

Those who operate primarily in the visual mode do things because something looks right—they see data. When the picture strikes them as compelling, they act.

Those who operate primarily in the auditory mode need to have a representation that sounds right. They hear it 'clear as a bell' and so it 'rings their bell.'

People who make their decisions using language need to have just the right words or self-talk that produces convincing feelings that meet their criteria. Such individuals like data, facts, and reasons. If something is logical and reasonable, it is the rational thing to choose.

Those who operate in the kinesthetic mode use a visceral representation of their choice which triggers the right tactile or internal sensations—it has to feel right.

To discover this pattern ask:

> "What tells you that you have found the right product for you?"

When communicating, present your information in the corresponding sensory channel that convinces the other person. Use appropriate predicates to juice up your descriptions and then match their convincer strategy.

Remember to identify what demonstrates believability: "How often does someone have to demonstrate competence to you before you feel convinced?" Determine whether the convincer (or believability) occurs:

1. *Automatically*: They begin from the state of feeling convinced.
2. *Over a number of times*: Find out how many times it takes.
3. *Over a period of time*: Find out how long a time period.
4. *Consistently*: They never get into a state of feeling convinced.

You will find someone with an automatic convincer an easy sell. Such a person will start out believing in what you are offering unless shown otherwise. Most people, however, have to go through the decision process a number of times in order to feel convinced about something. Such people will not feel persuaded until they have heard a number of presentations. You need to find out from them, "How many times?" Use repetition with these people and speak to them the number of times required by their strategy.

Others need a certain period of time to pass before they will feel convinced. For them, the crucial element involves time in their convincer. Will that person, event, product hold up over time? Or does a certain amount of time have to pass and then they will believe? Tad James suggests that we wait 10% of their time (6 days if 60 days represents their period of time), and then contact them: "You know, I've been so busy since the last time we talked, it seems like it's been two months."

People who have a consistent convincer never give anyone the benefit of the doubt. They never feel convinced. Nothing ever persuades them. We have to prove ourselves, our product, our serves, etc., to them every single time! Therefore just use pacing language to match that: "I know you'll never be convinced that this is the right time for you to do this, so the only way for you to really know is the right time is to get started in order to find out."

#18. Preference Filter

PRIMARY INTEREST, PEOPLE/PLACE/THINGS/ACTIVITY/INFORMATION

When we ask about someone's favorite way to take a vacation, his or her most preferred mode of working, or one of the top ten experiences in life, we thereby elicit his or her Preference Filter. Primary interests typically fall into the following categories:

- people (who)
- place (where)
- things (what)
- activity (how)
- information (why, what information)
- time (when).

This means that people will vary in what they most care about: who they spend time with (people); where they go (location), what is involved (objects or things); the kinds of behaviors and activities they engage in (activity); or the kind of data obtained or understanding gained (information). Obviously, an individual's sorting style will speak volumes about a person's basic values.

To discover this pattern, we need only ask about preferences:

> "What would be really important for you in choosing how to spend your next two week vacation?"
>
> "What factors—things, people, activities, etc.—would you consider essential for experiencing a really great holiday?"

This filter identifies the person's crucial and important values. And these will give you information about the specific motivators which will probably draw that person out.

#19. Values

EMOTIONAL NEEDS AND BELIEF SYSTEMS ABOUT IMPORTANCE

The word 'value,' as a nominalization, refers to a thought or an idea about what we treat as important in our model of the world. Values indicate those things which we have chosen to think of as significant and meaningful. We code such ideas in the same way that we code any other thought, namely, using VAK representations and language. The process of valuing—investing mental-and-emotional energy into our values—gives them emotional juice or power. Our values describe those things which we appreciate, enjoy, care about, love, and desire. We also believe in them. At a meta-level to our representations, we validate and confirm their significance to us.

Abraham Maslow created a hierarchy of needs, or emotional values. In that list he included:

- *Physiological needs*: survival, food, water, sunlight.
- *Safety needs*: freedom from threat , security, predictability.
- *Love needs*: relationships and affection, belonging.
- *Esteem needs*: achievement, recognition, self-esteem, and respect from others.
- *Self-actualisation needs*: development of capability to the fullest potential.

He saw all of these as of central importance in human experience. Obviously these do not represent the only motivating values. We can easily extend the list to include: power, control, achievement, affiliation, transcendence, ease, pleasure, romance, sex, knowledge, religion, harmony, challenge, and so on.

When we listen carefully to other people we will hear them indicate their motivating values in their languaging. We only need to tune our ears and notice the value-laden words that refer to those concepts, states, experiences, and so on, that someone values and treats as highly important—their values.

> "What values does this person express and talk about?"
>
> "What values seem implied and presupposed by what this person devotes his or her time, energy, thought, emotion, and actions to?"
>
> "What do I sense that this person thinks of as important, valuable, and meaningful?"
>
> "What values govern this person's way of being in the world?"

"What values does this person go toward?"

"What values does s/he move away from?"

Notice also to what extent his or her values match the passive/aggressive values.

Every driver Meta-Program indicates a value. Does the person use the Visual system as his or her most highly used system? Look to see if that person also values pictures, sights, colors, etc. Does the person talk about details? When you feel ready to communicate, influence, or persuade, use and appeal to the person's values. People cannot help but respond to their own values.

#20. Goal or Value Sort

DISENGAGERS/OPTIMIZERS/PERFECTIONISTS

People differ in how they pursue or go for goals. When some people engage in goal-setting they strive for perfection. Others merely seek optimal achievement. Others refuse to consciously engage in the goal-setting process at all.

Going for perfection creates perfectionists. These people never feel satisfied with their performance (or yours!). "I could have done it better." "It wasn't good enough." They will typically set unrealistically high goals which will set them up for disappointment and frustration. They use the end product of their goal as their criterion for moving forward, and thereby discount the process of getting there as being part of the goal.

Those who engage in goal-setting by optimizing behave more pragmatically. They simply do the best with what they have, and then leave it at that. They set goals using small steps so that they can appreciate little stages of success along the way. This makes the process fun in and of itself.

The disengagers altogether refuse to go after goals. They have usually become demoralized after bad goal-setting experiences. Many get that way through the frustration of having sought perfectionist goals and finding that that kind of goal-setting did not work.

Many have suffered trauma about competition or goal seeking, and consequently have developed negative beliefs about this.

This perceptual filter about goals and striving for objectives helps us predict:

- when a person will stop in his or her efforts of persevering toward a goal;
- the manner in which s/he will set goals and strive for them;
- and recognize these goals have been met.

Invite someone to talk about a goal by saying:

> "Tell me about a goal that you have recently set for yourself."
>
> "Tell me about an instance when you motivated yourself by setting a goal."
>
> "If we took on a project together, would you become more interested in getting started, maintaining the process during the middle, or wrapping it up at the end?"

Perfectionists begin projects well, but typically get bogged down in details or caught up in negative emotional states (disappointment, frustration, judgment). They talk a great deal about the end product, but block themselves from getting there. They tend to evaluate the end product as 'never good enough.'

Optimizers seem to flow along a lot better and, ironically, produce higher levels of excellence because they aim at getting it 'good enough,' rather than insisting on perfection. They focus on the process of getting there and enjoying that process.

#21. Value Buying Sort

COST/QUALITY/TIME

In purchasing and deciding, we generally take three sorting values into consideration These include cost, quality, and time. This means that some people will mainly concern themselves about the price; others will focus on the quality of the product or service; and others will care more about the time constraints involved.

In terms of actually purchasing something, these values may conflict with each other. So while people often mention cost as the chief purchase decision factor, they may actually care more about the factors of quality, convenience, or time depending on other considerations around the decision to purchase. A list of quality and comfort features can quickly override the first-mentioned cost factor.

When a person is struggling with prioritizing these values, ask him or her to imagine a triangle with the sides labeled:

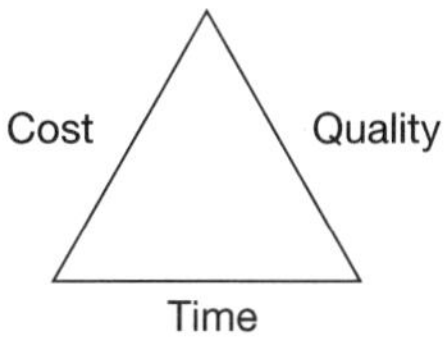

You can have any two of these, but not all three. Use this to help yourself, or someone else, decide about how you or the other person will prioritize these factors for a given purchase. "Put a dot at the place that represents where you feel yourself at in your choices inside the triangle." "Choose which two you are going for." This technique can help him or her to see the tradeoffs between the choice between cost, quality, and time. It can also help the person avoid feeling victimized if s/he whimsically changes his or her mind later.

V. Time Factors

#22. Time-Tenses

PAST/PRESENT/FUTURE

How we process time determines how we understand time as a concept and how we experience and respond to time as we move through the world. Time does not exist as a sensory-based phenomenon. Time operates as a mental construct we have about the relationship between events. We develop an understanding of time that relates to how we perceive events happening 'out there,' as a way of making sense of sequence, cause and effect, 'before' and 'after' and so on. Our sense of time is built around our understanding and comprehension of events, causality, evolution, change, memory, and so on.

The characteristics of time include direction, duration, orientation, and continuity. What we call time orientation refers to the way we sort out the tenses of time: past, present, future, and atemporal.

People who 'spend' a great deal of time in the past think about where they have lived and what it means to them. They use many past references and past tenses in their language.

Those who live in the now (the present) have a much more present-tense orientation in their language and references. If overdone the person may live so much in the now that they no longer think consequentially.

Those who live in the future will use future tenses and references. If overdone they can be so oriented in the future that they fail to make plans today for that future. Atemporal refers to thinking, feeling, acting, and living as if 'out of time,' where time has no meaning or relevance.

#23. *Time Experience*

IN TIME/THROUGH TIME, SEQUENTIAL/RANDOM SORTING

We sort time's duration based on our own point of reference to it. If someone perceives time from an associated position of living in it—as ever present, and themselves as participants within it—then this Meta-Program calls them an *In Time* person. If someone sorts time from a distant perspective, as living outside of it, we call this sorting style *Through Time.* These aspects of our processing also relate to the way that we store our memories.

Use the basic Time-Line elicitation to identify how someone experiences time—in either an In Time or a Through Time way:

> "As you take a moment to relax and to feel calm… allow yourself to recall a memory from the past, something simple like brushing your teeth or going to work. Think about it last week… last month, last year…, five years ago…. Now think about that event tomorrow…, next week…, next month…,

next year..., five years from now.... Now point to the direction in which you seem to have located your past..., and the direction in which you locate your future."

People who use the *Through Time* way of sorting time usually store their memories from left to right, or from down to up. They experience time as a continuous flow. This flow of time may seem long or short, but primarily they experience it as sequential and continuous. They also have an awareness of time's duration. And their memories are usually dissociated.

In Time people typically store the past behind them and the future in front of them. Their time-line runs from back to front or in some other direction that goes through their body. In other words, they experience themselves as living in time, inside the time-line. Accordingly, they will remember their memories in an associated form and will have less awareness of time's duration. *In Time* people may tend to get 'lost in time,' in the eternal now.

Through-Time people will tend to sort time, life, events, tasks, and so on, sequentially. They find that they can go by the book, following rules, protocols, procedures. They also approach thinking, deciding, buying, etc, in a more systematic manner. They typically operate in highly sequential ways and tend to like well-established procedures and structured events.

In-Time people tend to sort more randomly. They go off on tangents, think laterally, and seem to have less regard for time constraints than their sequentially sorting counterparts. Random sorters especially enjoy bouncing creative ideas around, making new connections and insights. A random sorter may seem to be all over the place, interrupting and asking off-the-wall, out-of-sequence questions.

VI. Relational Factors

#24. Socializing Filter

EXTROVERT/INTROVERT/AMBIVERT

This perceptual filter relates to how we choose to relate and spend time socializing with other people, and how we deal with recharging our motivational batteries. When some people feel down, they turn outward to others for encouragement, support, and personal renewal. We call this pattern the extrovert pattern. Others turn inward and go off by themselves in order to deal with down feelings, stress, demotivation, and so on. We call this the introvert pattern.

Extroversion and introversion, as used here, refer to our desire, need, and enjoyment in spending time with others as opposed to experiencing solitude when they feel drained, discouraged, or worn out. This refers to the feeling of needing to recharge or revitalize our emotional batteries.

To discover this pattern, we need only to ask:

> "When you need your emotional batteries to be recharged, do you prefer to be with others or to get away by yourself?"

Those who talk about sometimes wanting to get away from people and sometimes wanting to socialize demonstrate the ambivert pattern. This indicates a flexibility that can access and use either pattern.

#25. Affiliation Filter

INDEPENDENT/TEAM, PLAYER/MANAGER

This filter refers to how we process our time with people in the context of working on a task. How do you experience yourself vis-a-vis a group engaged in some project? You can identify this pattern by asking three questions:

> "Do you know what you need in order to become more successful at work?"

> "Do you know what someone else needs to become more successful?"

> "Do you find it easy or not to tell that person?"

Managers will answer Yes, Yes, and Yes to these questions.

The Independents will answer Yes and No, or Yes, Yes, and No. This latter response indicates that the person has the capacity for management, but doesn't want it.

A Bureaucrat will answer No, Yes, and Yes.

To discover a person's need for affiliation or for independence, ask the following open-ended question and let the person remember or imagine a situation:

> "Tell me about a work situation in which you felt the happiest—or describe what you imagine would be a really happy one."

Independent people like to do things on their own and to take responsibility for their own motivation and management. They score highly on self-control and discipline.

Team players prefer the comradeship involved in participating as part of a team. They like togetherness, family, and being around people united on a common project.

Management players prefer the supervisory role of directing and guiding people.

Pace your communication according to the particular style of task interaction you identify.

VII. Communication Factors

#26. Satir Categories

PLACATING/BLAMING/COMPUTING/DISTRACTING/LEVELING

THE BASIC COMMUNICATION MODES

Communication involves both content and style—what and how we communicate. Virginia Satir organized the following basic communication styles into five modes which are called the Satir Categories. The first four of these stances indicate ineffective and non-productive styles that we will only occasionally find useful. Noticing these communication styles in others (and in oneself) develops our ability to read someone's style of thinking and communicating more accurately, and therefore pace him or her more effectively.

Placating refers to 'soothing, pleasing, pacifying, and making concessions.' When someone feels that they ought to please others, they have become addicted to other people's approval. Placaters typically fear that others will become angry, go away, or reject them. Therefore placaters talk in an ingratiating way, trying always to please, apologizing, and never disagreeing. Verbally we find their words very agreeable. The placating posture seems to say, "I'm helpless and worthless." Placaters wiggle, fidget, lean. Like cocker spaniel puppies, they come across as desperate to please.

You can try on the placating style by thinking and feeling like 'a worthless nothing,' and by playing the role of the 'Yes man.' Talk as though you can do nothing for yourself and as if you must always get approval. Tell yourself that you feel lucky that others allow you to eat, breathe, and live. Adopt a position as though you owe everyone gratitude, that you will be held responsible for everything that goes wrong in the world, that you could have stopped the rain "if you used your brains—but you don't have any." Agree with any criticism made about you. Adopt the style of the most syrupy, martyrish, bootlicking person you can imagine.

Satir says that you should imagine being down on one knee, wobbling a bit, putting out your hand in a begging fashion, with head up so that your neck hurts and your eyes begin to strain. Then, in no time at all, you'll probably get a headache. Talking from this position your voice will become whiny and squeaky since you will not have enough air to speak with a rich, full voice. Next, use placating statements, "Oh, you know me, I don't mind. Whatever anybody else wants is fine with me. What do I want to do? I don't know. What would you like to do?"

Blaming refers to "finding fault, dictating, and bossing." The blamer acts in a superior manner and sends out the message, "If it weren't for you, everything would be all right." Blamers feel that nobody cares about them. Internally blamers feel tightness in muscles and organs which indicate rising blood pressure. A blamer's voice sounds hard, tight, shrill and loud. To try on the blamer mode by becoming loud and tyrannical in your talk, and cutting everything and everyone down to size. Be sure to point your finger accusingly. Start sentences with, "You never do this," "You always...," "Why don't you...?" Don't bother about an answer. Focus your interest on throwing your weight around rather than finding things out.

Blamers breathe in spurts, often holding their breath. This makes their throat muscles tight. A first-rate blamer has bulging eyes, taut neck muscles, and flaring nostrils. They get red in the face as their voice becomes hoarse. To do this, stand with one hand on your hip and the other arm extended with index finger pointing straight out. Now screw up your face, curl your lip, flare your nostrils, call names, and criticize. "You never consider my feelings." "Nobody around here ever pays any attention to me!" "Do you always have to put yourself first? Why can't you think about anybody but yourself?" Blamers use many universal quantifiers (never, nothing, nobody, everything, none).

Computing describes a style of detachment from a person's emotions. Computers respond in a very correct and reasonable way. Generally speaking, s/he shows no semblance of feelings, but remains calm, cool, and collected. Star Trek's Mr. Spock offers an ideal model of computing. The computer's body will feel dry and cool, the voice becomes monotone, while verbal utterances take on an abstract quality. Typically people adopt this stance out of fear of their feelings or having modeled this mode from some figure of authority.

To try on the computing mode, use the longest words possible. (After one paragraph no one be listening anyway!) Imagine your spine as a long heavy steel rod that does not bend. Keep everything as motionless as possible. Let your voice go dead, have no feeling from the cranium down. Use impersonal statements as you talk. "There is undoubtedly a simple solution to this problem." "It has become obvious that the current situation has been grossly exaggerated." "Clearly the considerable advantages of this activity have been made manifest." "Preferences of this kind are statistically rather prevalent in this domain."

Sometimes the dissociation that the computer mode offers provides a valuable resource when we want to defuse a hot-head or critic, or whenever we want our emotions out of the way. The computer mode easily allows us to 'play anthropologist/scientist' when gathering information. Of course, if we constantly use big, vague words that do not communicate much, we can also prevent personal communication. To an indirect criticism such as, "Some people really don't know when to stop talking," you could respond in full computer mode: "That is undoubtedly an interesting idea and certainly true of some people."

Distracting refers to a communication behavioral style based on unpredictability. Distracters always alter and interrupt others and themselves by cycling rapidly through the other patterns and constantly shifting modes. The distracter alternates between blaming, placating, and leveling, and then moves into irrelevance, with no focus. Whatever the distracter says or does represents an irrelevant response to what anyone else says or does. The internal feelings that go along with distracting are dizziness and panic. The voice often becomes singsong, or out of tune with the words, and it will go up and down without reason. This pattern makes for a style of communication that we call crazymaking.

To try on this distraction mode, think of yourself as a kind of lopsided top that constantly spins, but goes nowhere. Keep busily moving your mouth, body, arms, and legs. Start picking lint off the other's garment. Press your knees together in an exaggerated, knock-kneed fashion so that this pushes your buttocks out which in turn causes you hunch your shoulders. Ignore questions, or come back on a different subject.

Leveling refers to responding in an assertive, balanced and even way. The leveling response enables us to speak in a straightforward, direct, forthright, and honest manner. When we are genuinely leveling, we express our messages congruently so that our words match our facial expressions, body posture, and voice tone. This makes relationships non-threatening, more caring, and capable of creating true intimacy.

With the exception of leveling, these patterns reveal a mismatch between the way a person feels on the inside and the way s/he expresses feelings in language and behavior. As a guideline, two people using the same Satir mode (apart from the leveling mode) will go nowhere in their communication. So, apart from the leveling mode, do not try to match the Satir mode that you perceive in another as this tends to intensify it.

#27. *Response Style*

CONGRUENT/INCONGRUENT/POLARITY/COMPETITIVE/META

We can respond to things in a number of ways. We can talk about information, people, events, experiences, feelings, and so on. We can respond:

- Congruently or incongruently
- By polarizing to the opposite end of the continuum
- Competitively
- By going meta to the experience, and thinking or commenting about it.

A congruent response describes one that fits and feels aligned with the content. For example, a congruent response to a serene nature scene such as a quiet place of green grass and a babbling brook would be to feel relaxed and calm. Responding incongruently would be thinking-and-feeling something that was inappropriate or 'out- of-sync' with the peaceful scene, such as thinking about an attacking bear. Another incongruous response would involve feeling angry or depressed.

A polarity response flips to the opposite pole. So in the serene context, one might begin to feel stressed and uptight; the mind might start entertaining thoughts of danger, how the peace will not last, how calmness represents a false reality, and so on. A polarity response represents an opposing view. Since polarity sorters typically come back automatically with the opposite response from the one we wish to generate, we can use the Brer Rabbit's 'Briar Patch' approach with them by playing the polarity and inviting them to think of the opposite in the first place.

A competitive response describes one that views things in terms of win/lose. The mind runs comparisons between who is judged the best, first, fastest, strongest, etc. A competitive responder might get excited, "I bet I can relax faster or more completely than you!" A meta response refers to moving to a level above the immediate content and thinking about it. "I find it interesting to know whether you have the images of that calm scene coded as fuzzy or crystal clear. If you made your internal images sharper and more focused, would that increase your feelings of serenity?" This way of witnessing the structure of the representations indicates a meta response.

The more flexibility we develop in the way we respond, the better we will be able to deal with wide variability in communication styles. People with less flexibility often become stuck in one or two styles of responding. Strong-willed people tend to become polarity responders. Highly competitive and combative people (aggressors) tend to become competitive responders.

Figure 10.1: The Meta-Programs Sorting Grid

Temperamental Factors and Identity Factors:

1. EMOTIONAL COPING:

____________	____________	____________	____________
Avoidance Flight Passive	Avoidance with some Approach	Approach with some Avoidance Aggressive	Approach Fight

2. TEMPERAMENT:

____________________	____________________
Compliant (Open/Easy)	Strong-Will (Can t be told)

*Aptitude: Gifts (Strengths, Drives):

____

____

3. SELF MODALITY FACTORS:
Self-Esteem:

__ Unconditional

__ Conditional Upon: ______________________

* Self-Confidence:

____________	____________	____________
Low	Medium	High

* Self-Experience:

__ Thoughts __ Will

__ Emotions __ Body

__ Roles/Positions

Mental Processing Factors:

4. CHUNK SIZE:

__ General: Gestalt; Deductive Thinker

__ Specific: Detail; Inductive Thinker

5. MATCH/MISMATCH SORT:

__ Sameness

__ Difference

6. REPRESENTATION SYSTEM:

__ Visual

__ Auditory

__ Kinesthetic

__ Auditory Digital

7. DATA SOURCE:

__ Uptime

__ Downtime

8. VALUE DIRECTION:

__ Toward: Future Possibilities

__ Away From: Past Assurance

9. OPERATIONAL STYLE:

__ Options: Free to Move and Alter Things.

__ Procedures: Rules/Steps.

10. INFORMATION GATHERING STYLE:

__ Sensor: In Uptime (Empiricists, Pragmatists)

__ Intuitors: In Downtime (Visionaries, Rationalists)

11. PERCEPTION:

__ Black-and-White: Extremes

__ Continuum: Grays, Middles

12. ADAPTATION STYLE:

__ Judgers: Adapt the World to Them

__ Perceivers: Adapt to the World

13. REACTIVE STYLE:

______________	______________	______________
Inactive	Reflective	Active

* Scenarios:

__ Best Possible: Optimist

__ Worst Possible: Pessimist

Referent Factors—Emotional Sorting Factors:

14. REFERENCE FRAME: (Authority Sort)
    __ Self-Referent (Internal)
    __ Other-Referent (External)
    __ Circumstance Referent
    __ Data Referent

15. MODAL OPERATORS: (Linguistic Regulators of Operation)
    __ Necessity (must, should, have to)
    __ Possibility (could, might, may, can)
    __ Desire (want, desire)
    __ Impossibility (can t, shouldn t must not)
    __ Choice (want, will, choose)

16. EXPERIENCE OF EMOTION:
    __ Associated: (Emotionally Sensitive)
    __ Dissociated: (Objective/Computer Mode)

17. CONVINCER SORT (Believability)
    __ Visual: Looks Right (Observer)
    __ Auditory: Sounds Right (Auditor)
    __ Kinesthetic: Feels Right (Feeler)
    __ Auditory Digital: Makes Sense (Thinker)
    __ Experiential: Experiencer (Doer)

18. PREFERENCE FILTER: (Primary Interest)
    __ People (who)
    __ Place (where)
    __ Object (what)
    __ Activity (how)
    __ Time (when)

19. VALUES MOTIVES: (What are the Central Criteria of this person?)
    __ Power (Control)
    __ Affiliation (People)
    __ Safety
    __ Self-Esteem
    __ Love/ Affection
    __ Self-Actualization
    __ Superiority/Supremacy
    __ Independence
    __ Achievement/Mastery
    __ Sex/Romance
    __ Peace
    __ Pleasing
    __ Good Feelings
    __ Comfort
    __ Competition
    __ Optimism
    __ Success

* Buttons:
Trauma Buttons (Sensitivities): ______________________________

20. GOAL SORT/VALUE STYLE:

___	___	___
Disengaged (Reject Goals	Optimization	Perfection

21. VALUE BUYING SORT:

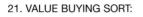

* EMOTIONAL DIRECTION SORT:

__ Unidirectional
__ Multidirectional

Time Factors:

22. TIME-TENSES

__ Past
__ Present
__ Future

23. TIME EXPERIENCE:

__ In Time, Random
__ Through Time, Sequential

Relational Factors:

24. PEOPLE PREFERENCE:

__ Extrovert
__ Introvert
__ Ambivert

25. AFFILIATION FILTER:

__ Independent
__ Dependent
__ Team Player
__ Manager

* Demonstrative Style:

___	___	___
Low	Medium	High

Communication Factors:

26. SATIR STANCES (Communication Mode)

__ Blamer (Accusatory)
__ Placator (Pleasing)
__ Computer (Dissociating)
__ Distracter (Crazymaking)
__ Leveler (Assertive)
__ Telling
__ Disclosing (at what level)
__ Problem Solving
__ Problem Reporting:

27. RESPONSE STYLE:

__ Congruent
__ Incongruent
__ Polarity
__ Competitive
__ Meta

* RESPONSIBILITY STYLE:

__ Over-Responsible (Caretaking Role)
__ Balanced/Skilled in Negotiating
__ Under-Responsible (Receiver Role)

Summary: MODEL OF THE WORLD

VALUES:

1. ______________________________
2. ______________________________
3. ______________________________
4. ______________________________
5. ______________________________

PROCESSING STYLE:

1. ______________________________
2. ______________________________
3. ______________________________

EMOTIVE KEYS:

1. ______________________________
2. ______________________________
3. ______________________________

TEMPERAMENTAL KEYS:

1. ______________________________
2. ______________________________
3. ______________________________

REFERENT KEYS:

1. ______________________________
2. ______________________________
3. ______________________________

COMMUNICATION/RESPONSE STYLE:

1. ______________________________
2. ______________________________
3. ______________________________

SELF-MODALITY ELEMENTS:

1. ______________________________
2. ______________________________

Exercises for Skill Development with Meta-Programs

Exercise #1

In a group of three or four, A talks about a positive experience—a time when s/he felt enthused, successful, brilliant, creative, decisive, a winner. B, C and D then ask questions and make comments to elicit more of the content of A's experience. After 5 minutes, B, C, and D present A with a 'reading' of his or her Meta-Programs and check with A to determine the accuracy.

Exercise #2

The Sales Encounter. In a group of four, A identifies something that s/he would never, but never, buy. B then attempts to sell that very item to A. As B gives this sales pitch A essentially remains silent for the rest of the exercise apart from saying, "No. Not interested." B now forges ahead regardless of A's verbal and non-verbal resistance. During this process C and D write down all the Meta-Programs they can detect in both A and B by paying special attention to the linguistic markers that each person uses in their language patterns.

Exercise #3

The Dating Game. In a group of four, A asks B open-ended questions:

> "What would you want to know about a person before you asked him or her out?"

"What would you need to know to have an evening out with a good friend?"
"What would be a delightful evening out with someone?"

C and D make a list of all the Meta-Programs that they can detect.

Exercise #4

Asking for a Favor. In this exercise B persuades A to do him or her a favor. First, B asks A ten questions to identify their basic Meta-Programs. After gathering this information, B frames the request for the desired outcome in words that reflect A's most compelling Meta-Programs. B invites A to gauge the effectiveness of the request and to offer feedback about how it could be made even more compelling.

Exercise #5

The Experience of Liking. In a group of four, B elicits from A a time when s/he liked someone upon their first meeting. B asks,"How did you decide that you liked that person?" Using the Meta-Program sorting list, B elicits as much information as possible about A's decision. B repeats this for a time when A disliked a someone upon their first meeting. "How did you decide that you disliked that person?" C now feeds back to A information about how s/he saw and heard A respond in terms of his/her Meta-Programs. D then feeds back to B information about how s/he displayed his/her own Meta-Programs during the elicitation.

Exercise #6

Identifying Agreement/Disagreement Signs. In a group of three or four, begin a discussion on a subject that interests person A. B, C and D watch for A's autonomic nervous system signals of indicating Yes/No and Agree/Disagree. Calibrate and elicit Yes/No responses while calibrating to the subtle cues that indicate them even when there is no verbalization. When B, C and D feel that they have calibrated, they should ask A not to respond verbally or demonstrate his or her thoughts-feelings in any obvious way. They now speak for 2 minutes that maintain rapport; 2 minutes that totally break rapport and get disagreement; and a further 2 minutes building rapport again.

Exercise #7

Create a context in which B persuades A to do a favor. "I want you to go to the store for me to buy some milk." "I want you to come over and watch my kids." "I need $10." As B tries to persuade A, A remains unpersuaded and just says "No". A and C detect B's Meta-Programs, and then, using those Meta-Programs, identify B's sorting style Meta-Program. Once they have gathered the information, A and C might practice offering a suggestion or recommendation to B, framing it in words that reflect B's sorting style.

Conclusion

Although we all deal with the same external reality, we also all live in different worlds experiencing different internal realities. We each experience the world very differently, and create very different models of it. The ways we pay attention to sensory data, process our thoughts, and code information all determine our map of reality. Meta-Programs offer an invaluable tool for identifying and using these patterned ways of communicating and relating to others.

Once you have a way of sorting and paying attention to these patterns, you will have a key for understanding and predicting how someone else will experience you and your communication.

Chapter Eleven

Kinesthetic Time-Lines

Cleaning Up the Past to Become Free in the Present

[The following is derived primarily from Will McDonald]

Some NLP trainers, it seems, tend to teach practitioners to work almost exclusively with internalized time-lines, using the visual modality. Classic NLP change technologies using time-lines such as The Decision Destroyer and running the Phobia Cure above the time-line essentially involves taking a resource (such as confidence, assertiveness, forgiveness, firmness) into the past. Taking such resources into the past, and facilitating a trance state to amplify such transformation, primarily presupposes the ability to visualize. Yet many people do not make internal pictures with much clarity, or at least not enough to feel compelling.

Therefore the following three patterns use the same techniques. They differ only in that they use the kinesthetic modality. These patterns still use much of the same time-line elicitation and construction, but the difference lies in that we are using our muscle movements and memory, physical locations and directions, and other kinesthetic codings to shift our representations of time and the things we have carried (a kinesthetic predicate) with us over time.

De-Fluffing Nominalization 'Time'

Because we exist as a species who sort, process and make distinctions about time we therefore have a very powerful resource for making life either a heaven or a hell on earth. This will depend entirely on how we use our powers of abstraction. (Korzybski defined human beings as a 'time-binding species' to suggest the unique factor separating us from the 'space-binding' animals and the 'chemical-binding' plants. Prior to his classic *Science & Sanity*, he wrote *The Manhood of Humanity* (1921), in which he described how we 'bind' the learnings and understandings of previous generations over time into our nervous systems using symbolism. Then he began questioning how we use this ability to use symbols as a map-making mechanism. Korzybski, alluding to Einstein's *Theory of Relativity*, argued that we should hyphenate the words 'time-space' since time cannot exist apart from space, nor space apart from time.)

How could we use the NLP Meta-Model to describe the word 'time'? What kind of a word is 'time'? It functions as a noun in such sayings as:

> "I've run out of time."
> "She never has enough time."
> "I like him; he respects my time."

It seems as though we are referring to some kind of tangible thing. Further, we usually respond to the word 'time' as though it represents what Korzybski called a 'true noun'—a person, place or thing with physical existence in the world. But 'time' does not work like that. We cannot see, hear, or feel time directly. We cannot 'put it in a wheelbarrow'—the test for a true noun in NLP.

The word 'time' describes a kind of mental construct, which refers to some process or relationship between separate events that we have turned into a 'pseudo-noun' or nominalization. Therefore it pays to unpack this nominalization in order to recover a verb pointing to some underlying process.

How do we recover the verb hidden within the word 'time'? By the term, we are referring to our perception of 'separation' between events, using the metaphor of distance to map onto the way we measure the (analog) amount of experience, or the (digital) number of intervening events which come between the two events we are considering. We may do this by using the common experience of a regular, ongoing process such as the daily movement of the sun across the sky, or the yearly seasonal changes as our planet moves around the sun. This then acts as a common referent with which to measure (quantify) this abstraction (mental construct) that we call time. We can measure off and mark time-space intervals using other abstract concepts: years, months, days, hours, minutes, seconds, nano-seconds, and so on.

As with other mental constructs, this concept of 'time' only exists in our minds. We conceptualize the understanding that one event occurs before or after another—using spatial prepositions. 'Time' also refers to our awareness of the relationship of events occurring sequentially. Then we conceptualize the concept of causation between events—that because event B follows event A, it means that B was caused by A. We also create a correlation between the number of other events between Event C and Event D, and say that the greater number of other events, then the greater the amount of time between them. In this way we create and use our concept of time. (For a fuller treatment, see Bodenhamer and Hall, *Time-Lining: Adventures in Time*, 1997).

Given this nature of time, how do we represent and mentally map out this distinction in terms of our modalities? We might imaginatively see a time-line such as those presented in history textbooks in school. Such linear time-lines usually stretch from left to right in a continuum, as they measure and mark significant events in the 'distant past' up to the 'present' and on into the 'future.' For most people in Western civilizations, a time-line typically represents using this kind of visual continuum. But now let us shift gears and start playing around with kinesthetic time-lines. So how would you actually represent a time-line kinesthetically?

Experiencing Time Kinesthetically

Developing a Kinesthetic Time-line

The following pattern provides a technology for externalizing our time-line. The value in doing this occurs mostly for those people who do not use the visual system as a primary representation system. This gives a way to use many of the NLP time-line processes. This would be especially useful for those who do not make internal pictures easily or who lack awareness of his or her internal pictures; using a kinesthetic time-line will enable him or her to use NLP techniques that over-rely upon the visual remembered and construct systems.

As we work through these processes, remember that a 'time-line' is not objectively 'real,' but a mental construct or metaphor than enables us to make sense of the relationship between events.

Our memories contain representations of events that we have somehow coded as being in our 'past.' Although they are now 'over' and 'out' of time, we nevertheless represent these memories as if they continue to influence things in an ongoing manner. Even though those events have already occurred, we code them in such a way as to cue our brains that those events continue with us as part of our ever present reality. If we experienced those events as traumatic in the first place, this way of coding can create continual and/or even cumulative hurt in an ongoing fashion. In order to deal with such representations of previous experiences we can take them out of our time-line and recode or reframe them in more neutral and less compelling ways, and then reinsert them into our time-line. We can also use this process to amplify our existing helpful resources, and even to put new resources into our personal history, so that we can feel as though we have had them with us for a long time. →●

The following process explores using a kinesthetic time-line:

1) Have the person lay his or her time-line out on the floor. Invite them to stand up, and say something similar to the following:

   "As you stand here in this spot, allow yourself to turn appropriately and to point in the direction of your past.... In which direction does it feel or seem to you that the past lies? Point to it. Now point to your future.... Now let's mark this out by walking back to last month... last year... five years ago."

   Then walk the person into his or her past by walking along the time-line in the direction s/he indicated, until s/he has a kinesthetic sense of being at those times in the past.

2) Identify the configuration of the person's time-line. You can identify this kinesthetically by having them walk through their past, present, and future, and then inviting them to step aside from the time-line on the floor and to simply notice its configuration, size, and so on. Taking this meta-position will

give him or her experience in associating and dissociating from his or her time-line as well as working with his or her sense of it.

3) Invite the person to identify a behavior which s/he wants to change. Ask him or her to notice the kinesthetics associated with that undesired behavior. Let him or her get a feeling for that problematic behavior. "Just noticing it...." Then, when s/he feels ready, ask the person to amplify it. Say, "And I want you to recognize this feeling (K^-) and allow yourself to go back in time to when you first had this feeling." Here you want to get a good anchor for the old problematic behavior that the person now finds limiting and un-useful.

4) Invite the person to step back in small steps to where s/he previously had that same kinesthetic sensation. As you use the anchor for the undesired behavior to move him or her backward in time, notice and anchor it again each time it arises. Now gradually go back even further, asking, "How old do you now feel or sense yourself?" "Do the kinesthetic sensations diminish or intensify as you take this step backward?" Have the person back all the way up to the point where the kinesthetics first began. At each of the kinesthetic spots have the person identify his/her age, before taking another step backward.

5) When you have moved the person all the way back to the earliest experience of those kinesthetics, ask him/her to take meta-position by stepping off his/her time-line. This assists in inquiring about the origin and structure of the experience: "Where did you first experience those sensations? When did that occur? What do you need to go through life and time and to feel different about yourself? What do you need so that you do not need to re-experience life as you did?"

At this point, index the where, when, how, and other people involved, etc., in relation to the old trauma feelings. This helps the person bring into consciousness aspects that his or her may not have previously indexed. Asking such questions also assists the person to identify the resources they need. Continue by asking, "Do you have these resources now?" If they do not, help them find reference experiences for those resources—from others (modeling); by imagination (construction); or by putting together bits and pieces of history. Access as many resources as the person needs until you get a Yes to, "Does this supply all that you need to effectively handle those events?"

6) Anchor each resource as it comes up, and begin to stack these resources on the person's elbow. Do this from the meta-position or even by bringing the person up to the 'present.' Here, also, you can reframe any limiting meanings that emerge for the person. If the person says that some event 'made him or her a failure,' validate and reframe it as an experience of learning—of trial and error learning. Feel free to assist the person in using various NLP techniques for updating the meanings that s/he had previously attributed to the events and to the life that s/he was living which had become troublesome and disempowering.

7) Use various conversational reframes to give new meaning to experiences. Assist the person in redefining the meanings which s/he has attributed to some painful experience. "While you have found this very painful and upsetting (pacing), you can begin to realize that this has also taught you something very important in life."

8) From the meta-position, invite the person to walk around his or her younger self. This step will assist the person in gaining new and different information from different perspectives. It typically shakes a person out of limiting tunnel-vision while simultaneously building up a broader perspective.

9) Have the person step back onto the time-line. Once s/he has gathered all the resources needed and has some new reframes to use, invite him/her to step back onto the time-line at the place of the first instance of the unwanted behavior. Now give the following process instructions: "Now I want you to quickly walk up through time on your time-line, taking all your resources with you. Do this quickly!" As you say this, and s/he begins to move, fire the resource anchors on his/her elbow as you walk with him/her, taking him/her all the way up the line to the present.

10) Stop when you arrive at the present. Depending upon the emotional experience of the person at this point, you may want to give him or her a moment to process things before adding the following instructions: "And now let all of these learnings and experiences integrate fully into a new sense of yourself, into feeling so much more resourceful." Give the person a little while to do this integration.

11) Have the person turn around. When they feel ready, have him or her turn around to face the past. "Now as you look back at your past, you can allow yourself to notice how this has become different and continues to become different, now, and into the future, providing you new ways of thinking and feeling about it." Allow them some time to let that perspective become integrated.

12) Have the person face his or her future. When you have finished with facing the past, invite him/her to turn around to face his/her future. "And now as you look at your future, you can notice how the future has also become different, how it has become brighter and more hopeful, and you can wonder just how much brighter it will become.... What changes do you now notice in your time-line itself? How will this assist you as you move into your future?"

13) Take another meta-position. Have the person step aside from the time-line, or from the end of it, and have him/her look at his/her present and their future from an 'out of time' perspective. Then repeat this from one or two other perspectives. "What effect does this have on you?" "What else does this allow you to learn that you can use in a positive way?"

From the end of the future time-line, offer the following perspective, "As you look back over your lifetime, and as you notice the things you could do after the present, which you did in that exercise, what would have enabled you to have developed even more fully so that you would have become even more resourceful in your future, now?"

14) Reorient back to the present. End this process by bringing the person back to the present and add one more general process instruction: "And now you can take one step forward."

Some trainers refer to this exercise as building and utilizing an externalized time-line, a process utilizing the time-line as a structure for changing personal history.

Practicing the Externalized Time-Line

1) A visualizes, imagines, or feels a line representing his or her past, present and future and lays this down on the floor. B invites A to identify a spot for the present. B asks A to step onto the line in the present. Then B invites A turn toward the past with the instruction to 'notice whatever comes into your awareness.' Do the same thing for the future. A, while standing in the present facing the future, gets in touch with and amplifies the feeling associated with the behavior s/he wishes to change.

2) B then instructs A to move backwards along the line, moving back in time, until s/he finds a place where s/he has the same feeling of the unwanted behavior. Each time A identifies an experience that generates the same feeling, B asks A's age and suggests that s/he takes another step backwards in time to discover if the feeling diminishes or disappears entirely. Continue until the feeling goes completely.

3) B invites A to step off the line to look at that younger self in that first experience. B then has A walk around the younger self, seeing him or herself in that experience from different perspectives. A steps off the line (dissociated). A identifies all of the useful resources for that younger self. B anchors and stacks resources in A.

4) B then assists A in swishing kinesthetically forward to the present, bringing resources forward to recode and reorganize A's experience for optimal learning. Do this as quickly as possible. A stays at the present point for five minutes or for as long as it takes to integrate. B should observe the 4-tuples that

occur. A now steps in front of the time line and checks that s/he has all the pieces there. A steps on the present line again, and closes eyes. When ready, B should have him or her 'put the best foot forward.'

Debriefing

This exercise provides a physical metaphor to work with. Actually, you could create a physical metaphor such as a line and put any mental construct on it. For instance, you could create a kinesthetic line on the floor and allow it to represent the Introvert/Extrovert continuum, with Introvert on one end and Extrovert on the other. Ask the person, "Where do you now stand? Where would you like to move to that would represent your goal or ideal?" Now invite them to move backward and forward until they feel comfortable. "Now, take another step in that direction.... What happens?" Anchor that state. Take them off the line. "Where (how) would that become useful in your life?" By making distinctions and putting the behavior in context, it can become a resource. Fire the anchor, "How does this feel, sound, look different? See yourself in that context" (anchor).

By creating a kinesthetic continuum in this way you can use this process to depolarize any behavior that has become extreme in someone's life. Think of this pattern as a Kinesthetic Behavior Generator.

You can use this following list to explore this continuum:

- Shy/Bold
- Poverty/Wealth
  (To shift someone's Comfort Zone: "Is this outside your comfort zone?")
- Unconscious/Super-conscious
- Weak/Strong
- Passive/Aggressive
- Incapable of learning/Super learner
- Insecure/Confident

Submodality Change

The Fast-Forwarding Generative Behavior

The following pattern provides a way for you to program your future. We call this a Kinesthetic Chain.

1) Create a time-line on the floor, and then stand on it facing the future. Mentally zoom in on a one-to-two week period of time that lies out in front of you. If you are coaching another person, ask him or her, "Where do you have one week from today represented in terms of the space that stretches out from you on this line?" Then have him or her go forward to that spot (whether a foot away, 10 feet away or whatever) and mark that spot for that person. Do the same thing with and mark where the person has his or her fifth day from now, third day from now, and tomorrow.

2) With that preparation, ask, "Imagine that you develop a skill from this moment and out into next week—a skill that you would really like to have in seven days from now—just notice the submodalities that you use to code that developed skill.... And you can notice fully what those submodalities look, hear, and feel. And as you do this, allow yourself to create a dissociated picture of that future you with that skill. And now deeply register that picture of that you with that skill in your mind and body. Now, as you release the picture, clear your mental screen."

3) Then say, "Now of course, as with any skill, if you can imagine the skill as having come into existence at that place after a period of seven days, then that would also have had to exist, in a lesser form, on the fifth day, would it not? Therefore, allow yourself to imagine what that you would look like with those skills at that stage of development as you create another dissociated picture of that future you. As you do, again identify the submodalities that make up that image.... After you have done that, you can let it go."

4) Whether by yourself or coaching another person, repeat the same process by imagining the skill at the stage of development

that it would have on the third day; and then on one day hence. After each time that you (or another) imagine the form of the developing skill, release those pictures and images, those sounds, and those sensations.

5) Next, give the person the following instructions."In a moment, we will quickly go into the future, and walk right into the pictures of that developing skill, and, as we do, I want you to gather up all the resources that you would find there as you step into and through each of the pictures you have imagined. And we will do this very quickly. Very quickly. In just a moment, when I say, 'Now!' I want you to move very quickly forward into next week from this moment through all those pictures."

"Okay, 'Now!' ... Come all the way up to next week and stop there so that you can fully allow all of the submodalities of those pictures to become fully sensed and integrated into the current you. Because as you went through each picture you associated with it and now you can simply allow your unconscious to gather all of those developing resources into yourself with the growing sense that you have stepped through all the stages of the developing skill...."

De-briefing The Pattern

In case you didn't notice, this pattern has been designed (as we do with many NLP patterns) to trick the unconscious mind in a very nice way. Because as you gather your resources into yourself (from your unconscious mind), you begin to have available to you more of those resources that existed in your unconscious mind in the first place. You then accessed a chain of K+ anchors which you walked through and associated with.

To practice this progressive development of a resource state through time, stepping into more and more fully developed expressions of the skill as coded in ever increasing submodality representations, do the following.

1) Let A identify something s/he does well and wants to do better.

2) Ask A to establish a one week time-line on the floor and spatially mark it out for the days starting with Now, extending to Tomorrow, and then Days 3, 5 and 7.

3) Person B invites A to see him or herself a week from the present engaged in an activity using the skill while performing at an optimum level.

4) B invites A to notice the resulting submodalities at the Day 7 experience.

5) Now, backing up, B has A notice the images at the fifth day from now, when one would expect the skills to be at a lesser stage of development.

6) Repeat as A sees him or herself at Day 5 with the skill development of that day, and do the same for Day 3 and then for Tomorrow.

7) B now sets the frame for moving (somatically swishing) through all of those frames in just a few seconds, then, when fully ready, physically guides A in moving rapidly along the kinesthetic time-line from the Now to Day 7.

8) Test and future pace.

Stepping Back for Resourcefulness

If you liked that pattern, then *Stepping Back for Resourcefulness* provides yet another variation. You may find that one works as well as, or better than, the other. After you have tried both, pick your pattern of choice.

1) Identify a stressful state, one where you feel bad, tense, and stressed, and one where you want to develop more choice and power. Once you have done this, go ahead and amplify the state.

2) Now, simply step back… literally. Physically take a step back from where you were standing when you accessed the

stressful state. Stepping back will help you to take a meta-position to yourself. Now, look at that you who stood there a moment ago who had those problems and felt those stressful feelings. From this position (#2), engage in some meta-exploration: "What resources does that person need?" "Just imagine that where you are now standing at this very moment, you actually have those resources, and imagine what it would feel like to have them right now."

3) Repeat step 2. Take a meta-position to your first meta-position. Do this by taking another step backward. Now you spatially stand at a meta-meta-position to where you began in step 1(#1). You are now able to see yourself seeing your original stressed-out self (#3). Once you access this state, then explore: "What does the previous 'you' (#2) need in order to become even more resourceful?" Imagine and feel your answers vividly and associatedly so that you see them, hear them, and feel them fully.

4) Make yet another step back (of step 2) again, becoming aware of the previous person (#3, #4, and so on…) until you develop a floating sense (the feeling of floating above yourself… and you will). In fact, these floating feelings will let you know that you have attained a dissociated state from that original problem state.

5) If you're coaching someone through this, take his or her arm and quickly walk him or her back into the previous step (all those representations of self just four, three, two, one steps away from the original stressful state). And as you step through these resourceful states you can gather up the resources that you have accessed and developed in him or her and feel more empowered than you have ever felt before. Otherwise just step quickly back to the previous position yourself, bringing the resources back with you. Do this with each step until you arrive back to the time-line.

6) Stop at the original problem state (#1). As you do, say, "And you can let all of these resources that you have accessed and amplified, when you stepped back and went meta to this state, integrate fully into yourself, so that you can feel this

empowerment whenever you find yourself in this kind of a situation." Use any language patterns you know that will enable the person to fully access the resources.

7) Allow the person some time to integrate the learnings from this, and end the process by saying, "Take one step forward." Check: How does that person (or yourself if working alone) now feel?

Conclusion

In these patterns, by utilizing your kinesthetic representational system for coding time you will have discovered and experienced some new and different structures for working with problems. As a Master Practitioner, you can also feel completely free to experiment with these patterns, to invent others as you play and experiment, and to mix and combine them with other patterns. By so doing you will not only find new and creative ways to 'put the past behind you,' but also to future pace a passionately exciting future for yourself.

And now, after all you have mastered here, just *Go for it!*

Appendix A

Why I Used E-Prime in Writing this Book

One of the key ways I altered the text of the Bandler Master Practitioner Training involves how I *E-Primed* the text. As a general semanticist, I learned from my studies of Alfred Korzybski and General Semantics that the word 'is' creates all kinds of problems. The two 'ises' play an especially toxic role in human map-making: the 'is' of identity and the 'is' of prediction. As a language distinction, these two 'ises' provide as much, if not more, ill-formedness in mapping the territory as any distinction in the Meta-Model.

The 'is' of Identity sets up identities between different things and thereby generates a false-to-fact representation of reality. It usually confuses things that exist on different logical levels. "He *is* stupid" "She *is* lazy..." confuses a multi-dimensional person with a mental evaluation or label.

The 'is' of prediction asserts ('predicts') things of, and in, the human nervous system as if existing 'out there' beyond our skin. "It *is* good" "That rose *is* red." These 'ises' create a language structure which implies that something out there contains these qualities of 'goodness' or 'redness'; that 'goodness' and 'redness' exist out there independent of, and apart from an abstracting human nervous system. The little 'is' suggests that such things exist independent of the speaker's experience. Not so!

Actually, these descriptions speak primarily about our internal experience and indicate judgments and values, not the structure of the world. To more accurately map things, we would say, "I evaluate it as good..." "I believe she behaves in a lazy way..." "That statement strikes me as stupid...."

David Bourland, Jr. invented the extensional device in General Semantics that he dubbed E-Prime. By this term he refers to writing and producing English (the E) primed of or minus the 'to be' verb family (is, am, are, was, were, be, being, been). Numerous values accrue from practising primed English. Not the least of these involves reducing the 'is' of identity and the 'is' of prediction. Subsequently, I decided to write in E-prime, except where quoting from others.

Neuro-linguistically, the previous 'is' statements distract us from the true structure of things, confuse logical levels of abstracting, and subtly communicate that such value judgments exist in the world of 'objective' reality as real 'facts.' Not so. The evaluations (i.e., good, red, lazy, stupid) function as definitions and interpretations in the 'mind' of the speaker. To say, "The rose is red" falsely allocates the 'redness' to a position outside of the person experiencing the redness via their interacting neurology.

The 'to be' verbs pose another danger. They presuppose that 'things' (actually, events and processes) stay the same. Another false-to-fact conclusion! Using the 'to be' verb subtly creates the impression of fixedness. Though very 'natural' to the ear, they map our world as one set in concrete. Numerous writers in General Semantics have noted that they create 'a frozen universe.' In using them, the dynamic nature of processes become coded statically. "Life *is* tough." "I *am* no good at math." "She *is* just a big know-it-all!" A long time ago, Ernest Fenollosa (1908) said, "'Is' suffers from 'the tyranny of medieval logic.'"

'Is' statements sound so definitive and so godlike. "That's the way it is!" They sound like a pronouncement of the last word about reality. Bourland and Kellog have called this use of 'is,' "the deity mode" of speaking. No wonder some people so over-use 'is', 'am' and 'are' etc.! It conveys a sense of power. "And that *is* the truth!"

'To be' also carries with it a sense of completeness, finality, and time-independence. Yet if we can discern the difference between the map and the territory, then we recognize that these phenomena exist on different logical levels. Using E-Prime helps us to reduce the chances of slipping in groundless authoritarian statements.

If we use a language expression in describing reality that causes us to confuse description of facts with evaluation (our inferences, judgments, valuations, etc.), then we begin 'identifying.' "He is a Republican." "I am a teacher." "She is just a housewife." Such identifications make for *unsanity*. Actually, there 'is' (the 'is' of existence) no absolute, final, non-changing 'is' to which we can point. 'Is' functions as a non-referencing word. To use it leads us into semantic mis-evaluations. Conversely, writing, thinking, and speaking in E-Prime generates more consciousness of abstracting. Korzybski's cure for unsanity.

Personally, I like E-Prime because it facilitates speaking and thinking with more clarity and precision. It automatically induces one, whether as a speaker or writer, to go back to a level of presenting a first-person account of things, and that recovers the Lost Performative. Priming English of the 'ises' further reduces the passive verb tense. "It was done." "Mistakes were made." And it restores statements to the speaker who made them, thereby contextualizing statements.

E-Prime helps to foster in us a worldview whereby we perceive the world more holistically as an interdependent whole of connecting parts. It enables us to see the world as dynamic and changeable rather than frozen and static. For these, and other, reasons, I wrote this book (and others) in E-Prime. For more on this fascinating linguistic device that contributes to well-formedness, see Bourland's writings on E-Prime.

Appendix B

The New NLP Domain of Meta-States

Self-Reflexivity in Human States of Consciousness

Korzybski explored the relationship between what he called 'first order' effects and the effects of 'second order,' 'third order,' etc., in his 1933 classic, *Science & Sanity*. Later the NLP model described these logical levels of abstractions as states, as in states of consciousness, or mind-body states of thoughts-feelings. As NLP incorporated ideas from Information Theory, Gestalt Therapy, Computer Science, Family Systems Therapy, Transformational Grammar, and so on, it developed its own model for tracking the structure of subjective experience which creates these semantic or neuro-linguistic states.

In 1994 I happened upon this newest development in NLP which combines the best of NLP's states and strategy models and General Semantics. The model quickly became called the Meta-States Model. This new meta-level model utilizes the insights of Korzybski and Bateson on logical levels of abstraction to provide a tracking language for *states about states*, or meta-states.

When a person becomes afraid of fear (paranoid), or angry for feeling afraid (a self-conflicting state), or guilty about feeling angry about feeling afraid (higher level self-torturing pattern), he or she has moved to a second or third order (level) of abstracting. The person has experienced a negative meta-state. More positively, we experience a state-*about*-a-state when we *enjoy* learning, *embrace* confusion as the gateway to new learnings, *accept* grief, etc.

The Meta-States model not only addresses such 'dragon-like' semantic states, but also those 'princely' states of self-esteem, resilience, proactivity, magnanimity, forgiveness, etc. In such meta-states a person abstracts (thinks-feels) about other abstractions (such as *self, time, purpose, destiny*, and so on) and develops gestalt configurations of states-about-states. Experiencing meta-states takes us into the realm of semantic reality where we generate meta-level experiences, believing, valuing, and so on. Some time after discovering and articulating this model, the International Association of Trainers in NLP (IATNLP) awarded it their prize for the most significant contribution to the model of NLP in 1994/5. With this arose the third Meta-Domain in NLP after the Meta-model and the Meta-Programs.

States About States

Beginning with a 'regular' or primary state of consciousness, the NLP Model provides a description of the study of this piece of subjectivity by identifying its components in terms of mind and body. Two key components create and drive a neuro-linguistic state. First we have 'mind'—which takes the form of internal representations, beliefs, values, meanings, and second, we have body as expressed in physiology, neurology, and health habits. Using the NLP strategy model, we even have a specific way for tracking down the movements of mind-and-body in the generation of a state. Every day (including this very minute) we all use our mind-body system to induce various states in ourselves. Thereafter, our neuro-linguistic states govern our effectiveness, happiness, and resourcefulness.

In NLP we use this two-fold avenue into the subjective experience of states of consciousness (mind-and-body) as two 'royal roads.' This model empowers us to 'run our own brain'—to use the Bandler/Grinder description. Learning to run our own brain gives us the choice and the skills for becoming as resourceful, confident, optimistic, resilient, playful, and productive as we desire.

When you want to put yourself into a highly focused and effective learning state, what instructions do you have to give yourself? What pictures, sounds, sensations, and so on (VAK) assist you in getting into that state? What memories and/or imagining do you use? What words facilitate the process? What breathing, posture, gesture, etc?

Mind—
(I.R. VAK)

Body—
(I.S. Physiology)

Figure B1: A neuro-linguistic state of consciousness

These two royal roads—mind and body—inform our understanding and skill as we work with our own states or the states of others. Here mind includes all of the content of how we internally represent things (what we see, hear, smell, feel) in the theater of our *mind*, and also all of the words we use as we talk to ourselves about those sights, sounds, and sensations. Here *body/physiology* refers to the multitude of aspects that comprise our state of health, body, neurology, and all the other factors that make up and affect our somatic experience.

This gives us two primary ways of accessing a desired state. We can *remember* a state and we can *create* a state. In remembering, we use our mental-kinesthetic memory to 'recall a time when…' we experienced the desired state. "Think of a time when you felt confident, relaxed, angry, etc." In creating a state, we use our imagination to wonder about 'what would it look, sound, and feel like if…' we experienced this or that state (curiosity, playfulness, generosity, and so on). Our primary states are driven by information coded in various modalities and submodalities.

Further, in a primary state (e.g. fear, anger, joy, calmness, sadness) *the object* of our state refers to something outside our nervous system. We are referring to some object: "I fear speaking before a group." "I feel tense and uptight about my new job." "I enjoy playing with the baby." "I get a kick out of roller-blading." "I relax in a hot tub."

Now mental-emotional states do not (and cannot) stay the same. Every day we go into multiple states which are forever shifting, changing, altering. As we increase our awareness of our states, we can learn to take charge of them and alter or transform them deliberately. Over time our states can become habitual because if we run the same programs and get the same neuro-linguistic results, we end up creating a neuro-linguistic predisposition to 'fly' into certain states. When this happens, how we do that drops out of conscious awareness, and we just do it. This describes the power of habit. Therefore, effective state management often begins by bringing our processes back into conscious awareness.

In NLP we speak about 'state amplification' as our way of using the internal representations in our sense and language modalities to increase the emotional feeling of the state. This works because the same mechanisms that create a state also amplify a state. However, not all states have the same level of intensity. Discover this for yourself by simply gauging the intensity of your states. This will enable you to recognize the drivers of your states. State management becomes possible because we always have a choice about *what* to represent and *how* to code that representation. We call this 'representational power.'

As we gain more depth in understanding our states and the unique processes by which we put ourselves into various states, we can contrast our resourceful and unresourceful states, by asking "What is the difference?" We call this 'running a contrastive analysis' on our states.

'State-dependency' refers to how our states govern our entire experience: our learning, memory, perception, behavior, communication, and so on. From our mental-emotional states come emotions, talk, behavior, actions, etc. State dependency leads to emotional expectation sets and conceptual expectation sets which in turn determine what we see and hear. Two people with entirely different emotional or conceptual expectation sets will experience the same event in radically different ways.

For any state, we can set up a trigger (e.g. sight, sound, sensation, movement, gesture, word) and link it to that state. In NLP terms, this we call an anchor for the state. It provides us with a 'user-friendly Pavlovian conditioning tool' for state management.

In NLP we speak about state utilization as the process of putting our ability to induce, elicit, and design neuro-linguistic states to good use. After all, if a state offers a resourceful way to think, feel, perceive, communicate, behave, remember, etc, then we only need to inquire about where and how to use this power. Where would I like to use this state? What would it look, sound, feel like to have this state in this or that situation?

Finally, we devise the sequential steps that constitute a strategy for entering the state by examining the information (VAK), neurology, responses, and so on, by which we put ourselves into the state. NLP tracks down such sequences and models the pieces of the strategy in order to replicate excellence and design engineer even better ways to function in the world.

Advancing to a Meta-Level: Meta-States

When we access one state and relate it to other states, we create a 'Meta-State.' These complex states arise because our self-reflexive consciousness relates not to the world, but to ourselves or to some conceptual mental state, such as a Kantian category. Here we access a state of thoughts-feelings (T–F) that we apply and bring to bear upon another state of thoughts-and-feelings (T–F). We feel upset about our anger; joyful about freedom; anger at our fear.

Korzybski (1933/1994) describes levels of abstraction based on how we abstract from the world all of the energy manifestations 'out there' beyond our nervous system. This information comes in via our sense receptors, from which we then abstract again and process in specialized parts of our cortex as sensory representations (VAK), about that lead of abstraction we then abstract again as we say sensory-based words (Ad), about which we then abstract and use evaluative-based words—about which we can abstract again and say more evaluative-based words, and so on.

Abstracting at higher levels, or 'going meta,' refers to moving to a higher logical level and there abstracting about the lower level. Doing this creates an 'about-ness' at the meta-level. So while primary states refer to some external content ("I'm afraid *of* John's anger"), Meta-States refer to another state. "I'm afraid *of* my fear." "I feel disgusted *with* my anger." In a Meta-State (as a layered state-about-a-state) we shift logical levels and move to a higher state which recursively refers back to a previous state.

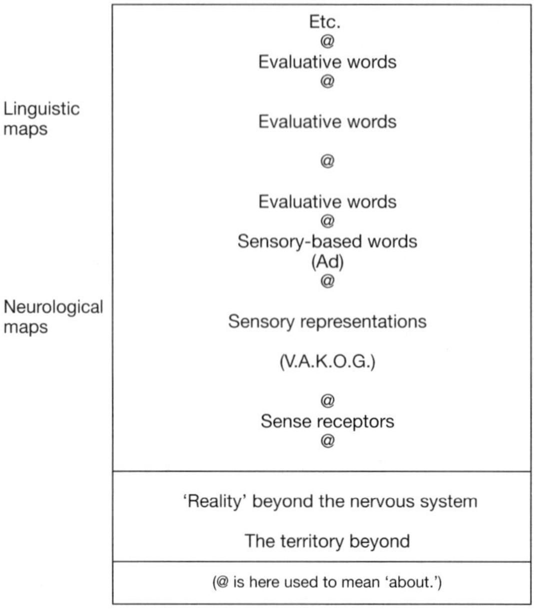

Figure B2: Neurological and linguistic maps of reality

As an operational definition, a Meta-State designates a state of consciousness *above, beyond,* and/or *about* (meta) any other primary state of consciousness. To get a feel for this, access a state of appreciation *about* your joy *about* your learning.

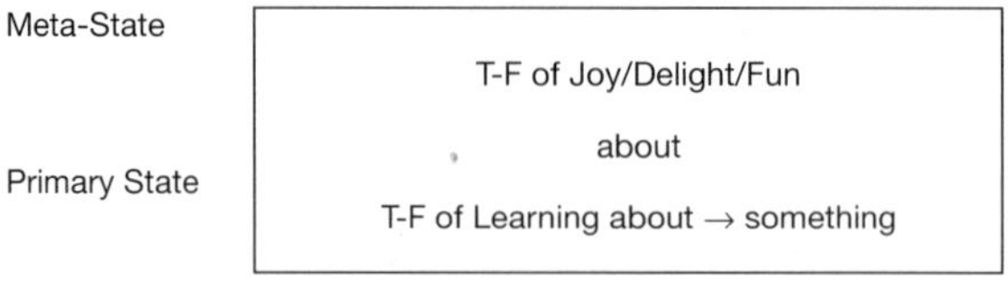

Figure B3: Primary states and meta-states

We describe the mechanism that drives our ability to go meta and to take a meta-position to ourselves (our thoughts, feelings, states, understandings, concepts) as self-reflexive consciousness. This gives rise to:

- meta-cognition, meta-awareness, meta-communication, meta-feelings, and so on.

- our ability to create, learn, and use the Meta-Model (as we think and talk about thinking and talking).

- the ability to perceive, recognize, and work with our perceptions (the Meta-Programs) by which we sort for information and pay attention to things.

- the ability to create and experience higher level neuro-linguistic states namely, beliefs, values, understandings, intelligences, identity, etc.

This power of consciousness (self-reflexivity) relates to how we can use our thinking and emoting to reflect on our thinking and emoting. It works recursively like a system. It begets systemic consciousness, and hence systemic states. Consciousness and experience now become recursive and take on many of the qualities of a system.

Consider how you experience 'anger at your fear.' Here a primary emotion targets another primary emotional state, hence 'self-anger.' A hundred years ago Sigmund Freud commented that anger turned inward will often show up as depression, self-contempt, or self-judgment. In other words, the state of anger can reflexively turn upon itself, and when it does, it takes on new complications (gestalts, holistic configurations). When a state recursively feeds back onto another state it often creates a closed-loop system, which in turn creates a self-reinforcing, self-validating and self-fulfilling prophecy. Here the Meta-states Model takes the NLP model of mind, neurology, personality, etc. further by adding systemic qualities and processes—primarily the feedback loop. (See Hall (1997) *Advanced NLP Modeling: NLP Going Meta*).

The Meta-States Model provides a new synthesis of the strategy and the state models and also integrates the three meta-domains (the Meta-model, the Meta-Programs, and Meta-States) into modeling. The NLP strategy and state models already cover a tremendous range of human experience and subjectivity, but not all.

Some experiences call for another kind of analysis, one that goes beyond strategies and states. Complex, layered, and systemic processes call for a model that can handle experiences sequentially and holistically, deal with feedback loops, meta-levels, reflexive consciousness, and so on. In the Meta-States model, thoughts-and-emotions (a neuro-linguistic state) feed back onto a previous state. Thus, in 'self-contempt' we have thoughts-feelings of 'contempt' about our 'self' (itself a concept inasmuch as we judge our 'self' with relation to some primary state such as anger, fear, or timidity.

"Now Let's Play" (NLP)

In the spirit of playfulness, imagine all of the wild and weird, helpful, and hurtful, and empowering and dis-empowering Meta-States that we can generate as we observe how states interact (interface) at different logical levels to create new gestalts. The following list comes from Korzybski (1933, p. 440) as he played with these ideas back in the first part of the twentieth century.

curiosity of curiosity—intense curiosity!
attention of attention—attending attention
analysis of analysis—study of analysis
reasoning about reasoning—science
choice of choice—freedom, lack of blockages
consideration of consider—cultured thought
knowing of knowing—consciousness of abstracting
evaluation of evaluation—a theory of sanity
worry about worry—morbid worrisomeness
fear of fear—paranoia, agoraphobia
pity of pity—self-pity, pitifulness
belief in belief—fanaticism, dogmatism, intolerance
conviction of conviction—dogmatism
ignorance of ignorance—innocence
choice of choice—empowering choice
anger at fear—self-anger
joyful about anger—celebrative use of anger
sad about anger—awareness of misusing anger
angry about sadness—inappropriate sadness
fearful about sadness—self-paranoia
guilt about anger—self-judgment for anger
inhibition of an inhibition—positive excitation
hate of hate—love or nullification of emotion
doubt of doubt—scientific criticism

procrastination of procrastination—taking action
interruption of interruption—confusion
prohibition of... anger, fear, joy, etc.—stuck

Distinguishing Primary and Meta-States

I have noted that primary states differ radically and significantly from Meta-States. Table B1 offers some of the differences.

Table B1: Distinguishing primary and meta-states

Simple/direct First-level	**Complete/indirect** Second/third levels, etc.
No layers of consciousness	Several or many layers of consciousness
Immediate, automatic	Layer levels of consciousness/mediated by symbols
Synesthesia (V—K)	Meta-level synesthesias—the Collapsing of Levels
Primary kinesthetics	Meta-kinesthetics or 'emotions'/ Evaluative Emotions
Primary emotions	Judgments coded in the soma (body)
Modality (VAK)	Affected by submodalities, but not driven
Submodality-driven	Linguistically-drien, linguistically located
Kinesthetically experienced +/–	Less immediate or localized kinesthetics
Associated	Dissociated from primary emotions
Easily anchored	Chains of anchors—glued together by words Chains connected by multiple anchors

(continued)

Table B1: Distinguishing primary and meta-states (continued)

Simple/direct Intense to very intense	**Complete/indirect** Less intense: more thoughtful, 'mindful'
Strong, primitive, deep	Weaker, less primitive, more modified by cognition
Quicker, shorter	Lasts longer, more enduring, stable
Animal	Human: dependent upon symbol-using capacities
More focused	Multiple-focuses simultaneously
One time learning	One time learning less frequent
	Repetition needed to drive in and install
1st position	2nd, 3rd, 4th and other positions
	Consciousness expanded & transcendental
Thought@world	Thoughtfulness/mindfulness
Object: external—in world	Object: internal—in mind-emotions
Sensory-based linguistics	Evaluative based linguistics
Empirical qualities	Emergent qualities/properties: having no lower order counterparts
Somewhat projective	Highly projective
	Once coalesced the state begins to operate as a Primary State with a seamless logical level synesthesia

Dragon Slaying

On the Slaying, Taming, and Transforming of Dragons (i.e.'Dragon States')

Not all neuro-linguistic states serve us well. Some make life a living hell. Some operate and feel like fire-breathing dragon states; some turn us into dragons! This brings to light the importance of effective state-management skills, does it not? In dealing with dragons, we need first to identify them. List some of your typical states. Which states could you do very well without? Which states empower you to experience more of your personal resources?

Unresourceful states	**Resourceful states**
'Dragon' states	*'Princely' 'Royal' States*
Stress, tense, uptight	Relaxed, calm, reflective
Anger, sarcastic, raging	Accepting, managing anger well
Fearful, apprehensive	Managing fears well, courageous
Timid, dreadful	Courageous, optimistic
Pessimistic, negative	Optimistic, positive
Worried	Calmly reflective
Self-contempt, rejection	Self-accepting, esteeming
Sullen, hateful	Connecting, loving
Bitter, resentful	Forgiving, releasing
Over-serious	Joyous, playful

Here we have an infinite ability to go meta. Korzybski noted that we can always abstract about the abstraction we just created. He noted this as an example of the 'infinite regress' that springs from our self-reflexive consciousness. We can always think about our thinking (meta-thinking), talk about our talk (meta-communication), feel about our feelings (meta-emotion), model our model (meta-model), etc., meta-cognitions and meta-feelings, in fact, make possible the multi-layering of our states, namely, our Meta-States.

From this emerges our ability to access complex negative Meta-States such as fear of fear, guilt about anger, upsetness about worry, judgment about self as inadequate, unlovable and unworthy, etc. Our glory and excellence arises from the very mechanism (reflexivity) that also create our deepest hells of emotional pain, namely, our dragon states.

Learning how we have meta-stated ourselves into such painful states allows us to learn how we can to stop. We can learn how to slay our inner dragons. We can pull apart those morbid and sick meta-states of negativity and pessimism that perpetuate misery for ourselves and others.

From Dragons To Princes

We can also use our self-reflexive power to become more resourceful and to build positive Meta-States that make us integrated, centered, and congruent. This, in turn, helps us in interacting with others in business and personal relationships. With self-reflexiveness we can build, create, and install all kinds of empowering meta-states such as self-esteeming, resilience, proactivity, forgiveness, un-insult-ability, inner serenity, magnanimity, etc.

This process enables us to more effectively manage our meta-states. We can work methodically with our consciousness to become calm about our anger, insightful about our impatience, happy about our frustrations, etc. The possibilities stretch out endlessly in terms of all of the princely states we can generate!

Building Powerful Meta-States

The following process describes how to access and build positive and empowering meta-states. Such meta-stating offers a way to design engineer state-upon-state structures that will set resourceful frames for our lives. You can now custom-make those most appropriate for yourself, a kind of human design engineering.

1. *Identify a desired Meta-State that you find positive and empowering.* Move to a meta-position by stepping back and considering what resourceful meta-states you would like to have as part of your model of the world as you live your everyday life. These states differ from primary states (joy, contentment, courage,

boldness, sensory awareness, confidence, etc), inasmuch as they refer to states-about-states (self-esteem, proactivity, courage, resilience, and so on).

2. *Design the Meta-State with well-formedness conditions*. Use everything you know about well-formedness conditions in designing desired outcomes (goals) to customize a meta-state structure that will serve you well. State positively what you want in this meta-state structure in vivid VAK detail, in process terms, small chunk size bits, which inform you as to what you can do and which identify the steps and stages, and which provide you with evidence that you have achieved your outcome.

Inasmuch as every thought does not and will not put us automatically into state, we can apparently think in ways that prevent state induction. We can think in un-energized ways, dissociatedly, analytically, doubtfully, etc. and thereby deprive our thoughts of the necessary juice to induce the neuro-linguistic state.

This raises an important question. "What kind of thoughts will induce, access, and/or create a state?" The kind of thoughts that we energize and empower with compelling vividness and meaning and with a semantically well-formed desired outcome. So, to energize thoughts, start with the content of your thought, and then:

- Make it vivid! Rich in detail, graphic.
- Give it completeness so that it compels you.
- Value it. Give it meaning and significance.
- Repeat it until your mind quickly goes to it.
- Desire it. Turn up your want and passion for it.
- Language it. State it in compelling, congruent words.
- Act on it. Connect it to your physiology and neurology through action.

3. *Sequence the state and the Meta-State with compelling linguistics*. Because meta-states arise as functions of our linguistic representations (rather than visual, auditory, or kinesthetic codings), create some empowering and compelling linguistics that will glue the meta-state together for you. Utilize your

knowledge of the Meta-Model about how language works to build the kind of cause-effect statements, complex equivalency statements, nominalizations, and so on, that you find as 'just the right words' for you. These will have a powerful effect on your neurology and induce you into the desired state. Use also the Milton Model languaging patterns. These patterns offer a great resource in building empowering linguistic constructions.

4. *Eliminate all incongruence in the Meta-State.* Check for internal objections to the meta-state by noticing your internal acceptance or rejection of the state. Check also the experiences ecology. Make sure that you have eliminated any incongruence you find. If you get an objection from a 'part,' use the Six-Step Reframing process. Then use the internal objections in building the necessary reframes, representations, and meanings. Such objections actually provide wonderful feedback information about other internal programs. Use and answer the objections as you build the answers into the meta-state.

5. *Sequence the Meta-State and rehearse the process.* Sequence the set of primary states that build up the strategy format that gives birth to the meta-state. Then rehearse the pieces of the meta-state individually and together in an effective sequence. This rehearsal process highlights another difference between primary states and meta-states. The layeredness of consciousness, complexity of linguistics, and sequencing necessitates abundant rehearsal in order for the meta-state to cohere as a self-organizing frame.

6. *Step into and fully experience the Meta-State.* As you do, allow your awareness to expand as you notice how the meta-state drives your lower primary states in new and different ways, and how this gives rise to other new emergent features.

7. *Future pace the Meta-State into your time-line.* Future pace to the specific environment you desire and imagine the state vividly, associatedly, in that context. This has the effect of beginning to install the meta-state.

8. *Let your unconscious mind pick an icon or other symbol for the Meta-State*. What metaphor, story, icon, proverb, image, sound, emerges which you can use as a symbol of the meta-state and use to anchor this neuro-linguistic state?

Meta-Stating Results

The impact of state-upon-state, one layer of thoughts and feelings about a previous layer, a higher frame about other products of consciousness can generate numerous emergent properties. What do you specifically create or accomplish by meta-stating yourself (or another)? Actually, all kinds of things. Meta-States can create a large number of wild and sometimes strange effects. After all, NLP grandfather, Gregory Bateson (1972) noted that meta-messages always modify lower-level messages. Among those modifications we find many of the following:

1. *Reduce painfully intense states*. Some meta-states will reduce the primary state: calm about anger; doubt about doubt.

2. *Intensify states*. Some meta-states will amplify and turn up the primary state: worry about worry; anxious about anxiety (hyper-anxiety), calm about calm, appreciate appreciation, passionate about learning.

3. *Exaggerate and distort states*. The intensity factor will cause some primary states to become so exaggerated, that it creates a demon: anger about anger; fearing fear; sadness about sadness (depression). Hesitating to hesitate (talk non-fluently) creates stuttering (Wendell Johnson, *People in Quandaries*, 1989: p. 453).

4. *Negate a state*. Some meta-states actually negate the content emotions and thoughts at the lower level as the higher state completely blows away the lower state. In doubt about my doubt, I usually feel more sure. In procrastinating my procrastination, I take action and put off the putting off.

5. *Create paradox*. Some meta-states create a paradox by shifting the experience to a higher and different level. This offers many

possibilities for transformation. It explains powerful techniques as paradoxical intention as in the 'Be spontaneous now!' paradox (Watzlawick et al, 1972):

"Never say 'never'."

"Never and always are two words one should always remember never to use."

"I'm absolutely certain that nothing is absolutely certain."

6. *Interrupt states*. Sometimes the state (thoughts-feelings-neurology) we bring to bear on another state so jars and shifts the first state, it totally interrupts it: humorous about serious; anxious about calmness; calmness about anxiety.

7. *Create confusion*. Some will create the interruption or reduction by generating confusion as various thoughts-feelings collide and fuse with each other in ways that we do not comprehend.

8. *Create dissociation*. Sometimes the meta-state will cause one to become dissociated from the primary state.

Canopies of Consciousness

We build our original metastates via our self-reflexive consciousness as our thinking-and-emoting reflect onto other products of awareness. Then as those meta-states habituate, they begin to operate as a 'canopy of consciousness.' I am using this metaphor to mean that they begin to engulf our primary states by surrounding them completely. As they do, the canopy or umbrella then filters all incoming information and outgoing perception and understanding. As these canopies of consciousness increasingly surround us, they generate more and more state-dependency. We begin to live in a world whose reality operates as a function of our habituated neuro-linguistic states.

Eventually they become what we might call a mega-state that engulfs and embeds all of our other states within it. We live in that *canopy of consciousness* as our mental-and-emotional universe and lose awareness of our role in creating it. The primary state becomes embedded within the larger context (or frame) of the first meta-state. And perhaps a first order meta-state also becomes embedded in a larger order meta-state. As meta-states grow up to become mega-states (canopies of consciousness) that function as a pervasive psychic force pervading all facets of life. From them emerge our sense of reality.

Given this pervasiveness of habituated meta-states, and how they become canopies of consciousness, now imagine embedding all of your states with a mega-state like acceptance. As your largest canopy (your outframe) acceptance would then apply to your self, negative emotions, positive emotions, fallibility, etc. Appreciation would then operate as one of your primary perceptual filters. It would then become one of your very character traits. It would function as an ultimate belief system. It would become your key dispositional style for how you orient yourself in the world.

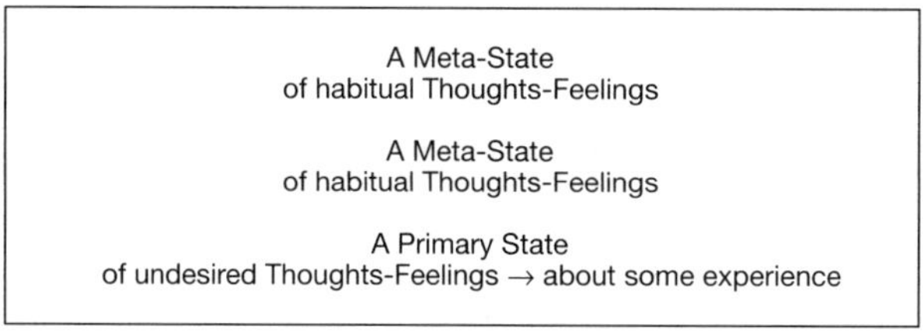

Figure B4: Habitual Thoughts-Feelings

If we were to build canopies of meta-states into the very structure of our consciousness, then we would not have to access the state, say, of appreciation or acceptance, or whatever. Appreciation would rather operate as so much a part of our structure of awareness (our Reality Strategy) that it would simply function as how we perceive the world. We would experience it as 'just the way things are.' Nor would we have to access the state of acceptance. After all, we live in that world. As our canopy of consciousness, that universe of thinking, feeling, believing, understanding (as our model of the world) would simply govern all our thinking-and-emoting. It would then operate as our mega-state, the neuro-linguistic state out of which we operate.

As a symbol-using species who make maps to operate in the world, we already develop meta-states and canopies of consciousness. Our neurology already works this way. We typically do not learn to meta-state ourselves with appreciation, acceptance, respect, dignity, or other resources. Rather, we tend to meta-state ourselves (and others) with contempt, blame, fear, anger, dread, skepticism, pessimism, etc. As self-reflexive people who have already generated thoughts about our thoughts and who inevitably experience the habituation of our thoughts-feelings, we already operate out of mega-states and canopies of consciousness. With the Meta-States Model, we can now find them, slay, tame or transform the dragons, and build up royal states.

This description of states, meta-states, and the mega-states of consciousness canopies explains much of our difficulty in helping someone who operates out of a primary state, or meta-state, embedded in a canopy of pessimism. Consider this:

> How would you help someone when everything you say and do gets filtered through his or her filter of pessimism?

Any and all optimistic, hopeful, encouraging, and helpful suggestions that you would give the person at the primary level would inevitably get filtered out and re-interpreted. S/he has a higher frame that governs things; pessimism. S/he lives in that universe.

When we deal with someone in a primary state of pessimism, we typically have enough difficulty interrupting that state and shaking the person out of it. His or her state dependent learning, memory, perception, etc, will slow down our communication. If this applies to a basic and primary state, how much more will it apply to the person who operates from a meta-state of pessimism? When a meta-state becomes a canopy of consciousness, it structures the person's reality strategy. From the outside, we will find the pessimism pervasive and as thick as a set of filters. The person will experience the concept of pessimism as 'the way things really are.' Accordingly, we will experience that person as 'thick-headed,' 'hard to get through to,' and so on.

The Meta-States Model opens up a Whole New Domain

This third Meta-Domain of NLP has led to a reformatting of much of NLP itself inasmuch as going meta, taking a meta-position, and working with and designing logical levels has played a major role in a meta-discipline such as NLP in the first place. More recently, trainers and writers have found that Meta-States provides a new flexible way to operate as a NLPer.

For more on this domain, see *Meta-States* (1995), *Dragon Slaying: Dragons to Princes* (1996), *Mind-Lines: Lines for Changing Minds* (1997, Meta-States applied to the Sleight of Mouth patterns), *Figuring out People: Design Engineering Using Meta-Programs* (1997, Meta-States applied to Meta-Programs), *Time-Lining: Advanced Patterns of Adventures in Time* (1997, Meta-States applied to Time-Lines), *The Three Meta-Domains Model* (1998). *Secrets of Personal Mastery* (2000), *Frame Game* (2000).

Other Works By Michael Hall

Meta-States: *Self-Reflexiveness in Human States of Consciousness* (1995). First presentation of Meta-States. Second edition (2000).

Dragon Slaying: *Dragons to Princes* (1996). A popularization of Meta-States, transcribed from a workshop.

Becoming a More Ferocious Presenter (1996). A book addressing the subject of applying the spirit of NLP to managing your state as a presenter or trainer. Written originally as Trainers Training notes, and greatly expanded over the years, the work applies the NLP Model to designing trainings using NLP criteria for well-formedness, handling audiences, communicating using Meta-Programs and Meta-States, hypnotic languaging, nested loops, advanced platform skills, etc.

Languaging: *The Linguistics of Psychotherapy* (1996). Exploration into the art and science of therapeutic language found in four psychotherapies using the formulations of general-semantics: NLP, REBT (Rational-Emotive Behavior Therapy), Reality Therapy/

Control Theory, and Logotherapy). The emphasis: therapy operates as a languaging phenomenon. Using qualitative research methodology, two models are proposed: a structural languaging model that extends the Meta-Model with six new distinctions; and a content languaging model that offers a list of ideas that heal. The work also presents a model of mind about human consciousness as a languaged phenomenon itself.

Advanced NLP Modeling: *NLP Going Meta* (1997). An advanced treatment of modeling, strategies, and meta-level states.

Figuring Out People: *Design Engineering With Meta-Programs* (2000). L. Michael Hall, Ph.D. and Bob G. Bodenhamer, D.Min. The most extensive book on NLP Meta-Programs and how they govern information sorting. It identifies 51 Meta-Programs using a logical level format.

Time-Lining: *Advanced Patterns for Adventuring in 'Time'* (1997). Bob G. Bodenhamer, D.Min. and L. Michael Hall, Ph.D. The newest book since 1988 on Time-Line Therapy. Introduces multiple new Time-Lining patterns and processes, integrates General Semantics, and explores time as a nominalization, multiordinal term and the many meta-levels of time itself. A must for all those wishing to stay current in the field.

Patterns For Renewing the Mind: *Christian Communicating & Counseling Using NLP*. Bob G. Bodenhamer, D.Min. and L. Michael Hall, Ph.D. Application of NLP to the field of Christian Counseling, designed primarily for those who wish to understand NLP from a Judeo-Christian perspective.

The Sourcebook of Magic: *A Comprehensive Guide to The Technology of NLP* (1999). L. Michael Hall, Ph.D. and Barbara P. Belnap, M.S.W. Covers 78 NLP patterns for transforming habits, emotions, personality, etc. For the first time, one volume that contains all the central NLP patterns and a great many others.

Mind-Lines: *Lines For Changing Minds* (1997). L. Michael Hall, Ph.D. and Bob G. Bodenhamer, D.Min. An exploration of the patterns of conversational reframing in NLP known as the Sleight of Mouth patterns. The model reworked in terms of its logical levels and presented in terms of the seven directions of consciousness with 20 Mind-Line patterns. Third edition (2000).

Communication Magic: *Exploring the Structure and Meaning of Language* (2001). A revised and substantially expanded edition of the classic *The Secrets of Magic, Communication Magic* takes the Meta-Model to new levels of significance. In his development of the Meta-Model, which lies at the heart of Neuro-Linguistic Programming, Dr. Hall demonstrates how your life can be dramatically enriched by having complete control over how you communicate using language. Essential reading for anyone who wants to stay current about the Meta-Model.

Instant Relaxation *How to Reduce Stress at Work, at Home and in your Daily Life* (1999). Debra Lederer with L. Michael Hall, Ph.D. Quick and effective NLP and yoga-based exercises and techniques for reducing stress in all areas of your life.

Secrets of Personal Mastery: *Advanced Techniques for Accessing Your Higher Levels of Consciousness* (2000). *Secrets of Personal Mastery* enables you to *access your executive levels* and *take charge of your mental-emotional programming*. Treating mind as an emergent process of our entire mind-body-emotion system, this book teaches you that it is not so much what you are thinking that controls your destiny and experiences, but how you're thinking—*your frames of reference determine your experience of life.*

The Structure of Personality: *Modeling "Personality" Using NLP and Neuro-Semantics* (2001). L. Michael Hall, Ph.D., Bob G. Bodenhamer, D.Min., Dr. Richard Bolstad and Margot Hamblett. Another excellent book from these accomplished authors addressing general behavior problems and specific personality disorders such as schizophrenia, paranoia and addiction. It is an essential reference for counsellors, therapists and NLP practitioners, presenting effective solutions to personality disorders.

The Structure of Excellence: *Unmasking the Meta-Levels of Submodalities* (2000). L. Michael Hall, Ph.D. and Bob G. Bodenhamer, D.Min.

Accelerated Motivation: *Human Propulsion Systems.*

Games Business Experts Play: *Winning at the Games of Business* (2002). Presenting insights into how business experts become successful, this revelatory book applies NLP techniques that target behaviour, transforming you into an effective business player.

The User's Manual for the Brain Volume I: *The Complete Manual for Neuro-Linguistic Programming Practitioner Certification* (1999). Bob G. Bodenhamer, D.Min. and L. Michael Hall, Ph.D. The most comprehensive NLP Practitioner course manual ever written. A fully revised and updated edition, it contains the very latest in Neuro-Linguistic Programming, particularly with regard to the Meta-states model and the Meta-model of language.

The User's Manual For The Brain Volume II: *Mastering Systemic NLP* (2003). L. Michael Hall, Ph.D. and Bob G. Bodenhamer, D.Min. This much anticipated volume continues in the tradition of Volume I as the most comprehensive manual published to date covering the NLP Practitioner course. The authors now introduce the latest advances in the field and invite you to reach beyond Practitioner level to Master level where you will develop the very spirit of NLP.

Bibliography

Aristotle, 1998, *Nicomachean Ethics*, Dover Publications, New York.

Bandler, Richard & Grinder, John, 1975, *The Structure of Magic, Volume I: A Book about Language and Therapy*, Science & Behavior Books, Palo Alto, CA.

Bandler, Richard & Grinder, John, 1976, *The Structure of Magic, Volume II*, Science & Behavior Books, Palo Alto, CA.

Bandler, Richard & Grinder, John, 1979, *Frogs into Princes: Neuro-Linguistic Programming*, Real People Press, Moab, UT.

Bandler, Richard & Grinder, John, 1982, *Reframing: Neuro-Linguistic Programming and the Transformation of Meaning*, Real People Press, Moab, UT.

Bandler, Richard, 1985, *Magic in Action*, Real People Press, Moab, UT.

Bandler, Richard, 1985, *Using your Brain for a Change: Neuro-Linguistic Programming*, Real People Press, Moab, UT.

Bandler, Richard & MacDonald, Will, 1988, *An Insider's Guide to Submodalities*, Meta Publications, Cupertino, CA.

Bateson, Gregory, 1972, *Steps to an Ecology of Mind*, Ballantine, New York. Reprinted (2000). University of Chicago Press, Chicago.

Bateson, Gregory, 1979, *Mind and Nature: A Necessary Unity*, Bantam Doubleday Dell Publishing Group, New York.

Bodenhamer, Bob G. & Hall, L. Michael, 1997, *Figuring Out People: Design Engineering with Meta-Programs*, Crown House Publishing, Wales.

Bodenhamer, Bob G. & Hall, L. Michael, 1997, *Time-Lining: Adventures in Time*, Crown House Publishing, Wales.

Dilts, Robert; Grinder, John; Bandler, Richard; DeLozier, Judith, 1980, *Neuro-Linguistic Programming, Volume I: The Study of the Structure of Subjective Experience*, Meta Publications, Cupertino, CA.

Dilts, Robert, 1983, *Applications of Neuro-Linguistic Programming*, Meta Publications, Cupertino, CA.

Dilts, Robert, 1983, *Roots of Neuro-Linguistic Programming,* Meta Publications, Cupertino, CA.

Dilts, Robert, 1990, *Changing Belief Systems with NLP,* Meta Publications, Cupertino, CA.

Dilts, Robert & Hallbom, Tim, 1990, *Beliefs: Pathways to Health & Well-Being,* Metamorphous Press.

Ellis, Albert, 1962, *Reason and Emotion in Psychotherapy,* Lyle Stuart, New York.

Ellis, Albert, 1973, *Humanistic Psychotherapy: The Rational-Emotive Approach,* Julian Press, New York.

Ellis, Albert and Harper, Robert A., 1976, *A New Guide to Rational Living,* Prentice-Hall, Inc., Englewood Cliffs, NJ.

Frankl, V.E., 1957/1984, *Mans Search for Meaning: An Introduction to Logotherapy,* (3rd ed.), Simon & Schuster, New York.

Gilliland, Burl E., James, Richard K., & Bowman, James T., 1989, *Theories and Strategies in Counseling and Psychology,* (2nd ed.), Prentice Hall, NJ.

Glasser, William, 1965, *Reality Therapy: A New Approach to Psychiatry,* Harper & Row, New York.

Glasser, William, 1976, *Positive Addiction,* Harper & Row, New York.

Glasser, William, 1984, *Control Theory: A New Explanation of How We Control our Lives,* Harper & Row, New York.

Glasser, W., 1986, *Control Theory in the Classroom,* Harper & Row, New York.

Glasser, Naomi, (Ed.) 1989, *Control Theory in the Practice of Reality Therapy: Case Studies,* Perennial Library, New York.

Hall, Michael, 1994, *Linguistic-Semantic Resourcefulness,* Metamorphosis Journal, 14, Empowerment Technologies, Grand Junction, CO.

Hall, L. Michael, 1995, *Meta-States: A New Domain of Logical Levels, Self-Reflexiveness in Human States of Consciousness,* Empowerment Technologies, Grand Junction, CO.

Hall, L. Michael, 1996, *Languaging: The Linguistics of Psychotherapy*, Empowerment Technologies, Grand Junction, CO.

Hall, L. Michael, 1998, *The Secrets of Magic: Communicational Excellence For The 21st Century*, Crown House Publishing, Wales.

Hall, L. Michael & Belnap, Barbara, 1999, *The Sourcebook of Magic: A Comprehensive Guide To The Technology of NLP*, Crown House Publications, Wales.

Jacobson, Sid, 1986, *Meta-Cation, Volume II: New Improved Formulas for Thinking about Thinking*, Meta Publications, Cupertino, CA.

James, Tad & Woodsmall Wyatt, 1988, *Time Line Therapy & the Basis of Personality*, Meta Publications, Cupertino, CA.

Johnson, Wendell, 1946/1989, *People in Quandaries: The Semantics of Personal Adjustment*, International Society for General Semantics, San Francisco.

Korzybski, Alfred, 1921, *The Manhood of Humanity*, International Non-Aristotelian Library Publishing Co., Lakeville, CN.

Korzybski, Alfred, 1933/1941, *Science & Sanity: An Introduction to Non-Aristotelian Systems and General Semantics*, (4th ed.), International Non-Aristotelian Library Publishing Co., Lakeville, CN.

Korzybski, Alfred, 1949, *Fate and Freedom*, in Lee, Irving, J. (Ed.), *The Language of Wisdom and Folly*, Harper & Brothers, New York.

Korzybski, A., 1990, *Collected Writings: 1920–1950*, Kendig, M. and Read, C.S. (Eds.), Institute of General Semantics, Englewood, NJ.

Kuhn, Thomas S., 1962, *The Structure of Scientific Revolutions*, University of Chicago Press.

May, Rollo, 1969, *Love and Will*, W. W. Norton & Co., NY.

McClendon, Terrence L., 1989, *The Wild Days: NLP 1972–1981*, Meta Publications, Cupertino, CA.

Robbie, Eric, 1987, Sub-Modality Eye Accessing Cues, *The Journal of NLP International*, Vol. I, No I.

Robbins, Anthony, 1986, *Unlimited Power: The New Science of Personal Achievement*, Simon and Schuster, NY.

Robbins, Anthony, 1991, *Awaken the Giant Within: How to Take Immediate Control of your Mental, Emotional, Physical, & Financial destiny!* Simon & Schuster, NY.

Robbins, Anthony, 1996, *Live with Passion* (tape).

Russell, A.N. & Whitehead, A., 1910, *Principia Mathematica*, University Press, Cambridge.

Turnbull, C.M., 1961, *What You See is What You've Learned: Observations regarding the experiences and behavior of the BaMbuti Pygmies*, in Hock, Roger R. (1992).

Forty Studies that Changed Psychology: Explorations into the History of Psychological Research, Prentice Hall, Englewood Cliffs, NJ.

Turnbull, C. M., 1961, *The Forest People*, Chatto & Windus, London, pp. 226–228.

Watzlawick Paul, Weakland John H., & Fisch, R., 1974, *Change: Principles of Problem Formation and Problem Resolution*, W.W. Norton & Co., NY.

USA & Canada *orders to:*
Crown House Publishing
P.O. Box 2223, Williston, VT 05495-2223, USA
Tel: 877-925-1213, Fax: 802-864-7626
www.CHPUS.com

UK & Rest of World *orders to:*
The Anglo American Book Company Ltd.
Crown Buildings, Bancyfelin, Carmarthen, Wales SA33 5ND
Tel: +44 (0)1267 211880/211886, Fax: +44 (0)1267 211882
E-mail: books@anglo-american.co.uk
www.anglo-american.co.uk

Australasia *orders to:*
Footprint Books Pty Ltd.
Unit 4/92A Mona Vale Road, Mona Vale NSW 2103, Australia
Tel: +61 (0) 2 9997 3973, Fax: +61 (0) 2 9997 3185
E-mail: info@footprint.com.au
www.footprint.com.au

Singapore *orders to:*
Publishers Marketing Services Pte Ltd.
10-C Jalan Ampas #07-01
Ho Seng Lee Flatted Warehouse, Singapore 329513
Tel: +65 6256 5166, Fax: +65 6253 0008
E-mail: info@pms.com.sg
www.pms.com.sg

Malaysia *orders to:*
Publishers Marketing Services Pte Ltd
Unit 509, Block E, Phileo Damansara 1, Jalan 16/11
46350 Petaling Jaya, Selangor, Malaysia
Tel : 03 7955 3588, Fax : 03 7955 3017
E-mail: pmsmal@po.jaring.my

South Africa *orders to:*
Everybody's Books
Box 201321 Durban North 401, 1 Highdale Road,
25 Glen Park, Glen Anil 4051, KwaZulu NATAL, South Africa
Tel: +27 (0) 31 569 2229, Fax: +27 (0) 31 569 2234
E-mail: ebbooks@iafrica.com